Double Crossed

Double Crossed

The Failure of Organized Crime Control

Michael Woodiwiss

PlutoPress
www.plutobooks.com

First published 2017 by Pluto Press
345 Archway Road, London N6 5AA

www.plutobooks.com

Copyright © Michael Woodiwiss 2017

The right of Michael Woodiwiss to be identified as the author of this work has been
asserted by him in accordance with the Copyright, Designs and Patents Act 1988.

British Library Cataloguing in Publication Data
A catalogue record for this book is available from the British Library

ISBN   978 0 7453 3202 4   Hardback
ISBN   978 0 7453 3201 7   Paperback
ISBN   978 1 7868 0093 0   PDF eBook
ISBN   978 1 7868 0095 4   Kindle eBook
ISBN   978 1 7868 0094 7   EPUB eBook

Typeset by Stanford DTP Services, Northampton, England

Simultaneously printed in the United Kingdom and United States of America

To Laurie and Sophia – always

Contents

PART III
COVERING UP FAILURE: CONSTRUCTING AN
ACCEPTABLE RESPONSE TO "ORGANIZED CRIME"

PART IV
SELLING FAILURE: SETTING THE GLOBAL AGENDA ON
DRUGS, ORGANIZED CRIME AND MONEY LAUNDERING

Acknowledgements

Researching and writing this book builds on the work I have already done for three earlier books and many people have helped me bring them all to completion. As a historian, my main debts are to Patrick Renshaw of Sheffield University and Hugh Brogan of Essex University. I must also thank my brother, Anthony Woodiwiss, Distinguished Visiting Professor of Seoul National University, not least for the original idea that led to all these books.

A few years ago Klaus von Lampe, editor of *Trends in Organized Crime*, encouraged me to conduct email interviews for a special issue of the journal with seven people whose careers gave them unique insights into the workings of organized criminality in America, Europe and at international levels, as well as the implementation of these efforts. I owe a debt to those I interviewed – Dwight C. Smith, Frederick Martens, Selwyn Raab, James Jacobs, Cyrille Fijnaut, Petrus van Duyne, Alan Wright and the other contributors including Francesco Calderoni, Ernesto Savona, Matthew Yaeger and Cameron Telford. Jeff McIllwain of San Diego State University also contributed a fine historiographical tribute to "criminology's revisionist Godfather" Joe Albini. Albini was one of the first to reveal the absence of evidence and logic behind mainstream thinking on organized crime.

In 2000 I was fortunate enough to be invited to a seminar series on transnational organized crime organized by Adam Edwards of Cardiff University and Peter Gill of Leicester University. Adam and Peter put together several of the best researchers from Europe and North America in the area of organized crime, with a roughly equal number of practitioners representing various British and international policing and revenue agencies. My interest in transnational organized crime and, in particular, British perspectives on the problem stem from this series. I would like to mention the work of the following as particularly inspirational: Dick Hobbs, Nicholas Dorn, Nigel South, Michael Levi, Sean Patrick Griffin, Gary Potter, Nikos Passas, William Howard Moore, Steve Tombs, Laureen Snider, R.T. Naylor,

Margaret Beare, David Bewley-Taylor, Letizia Paoli, Alan Block, James Shepticki, Paddy Rawlinson, Martin Elvins, David Critchley, Kris Allerfeldt, Bill Tupman and the late William Chambliss. Frank Pearce, author of *Crimes of the Powerful* (Pluto, 1976), has been a friend and guide from the outset of my interest in the subject and I am contributing to a conference and edited collection, *Revisiting the Crimes of the Powerful*, which will pay tribute to Frank's pioneering work. There are of course many others including my research partner Mary Alice Young and her work on financial crime and its control which makes her "the real deal."

As the book will show I am "ambivalent" about the work of mainstream journalists who write about organized crime, but I have nothing but admiration for those who follow the tradition of Murray Kempton of the *New York Review of Books* and question the conventional wisdom. I hope most of my other debts are acknowledged in the notes and, needless to say, any mistakes and misinterpretations in *Double Crossed* are my own responsibility.

Thanks also to Anne Beech, Robert Webb, Dan Harding, Neda Tehrani and others at Pluto Press for editing and publishing support.

Finally, I would like to thank the following for their help and support: Bob and Sue Morgan, Anna Brewer, Graham Barbrooke, Dan Hind, Paul Hoyles, Gerry and Alyson Dermody, Solomon Hughes, Kathy Jones, Phil Vinall, Mary Bennett, the "Brownie Dad Support Group," my colleagues in History at UWE, Roger Woodiwiss, Laura, Althea and Edmund Woodiwiss, Dee Dee Woodiwiss, Margaret Farrow, Simon, Shona, Hettie and Jake Kitson, Danny Kushlick of Transform, Rachel Cooper, Helen Cooper, Franco Farrell, Hugo Harding, Ellie Formby and, as always, my mother Audrey Lady Lawrence, my brothers and sisters – Anthony, Simon, Min, Mary and Jo – my children, Laurie and Sophia, and someone new in my life, Barbara Kenton.

Preface

"Organized crime" and its more recent extension, "transnational organized crime," are social and political constructs that were made in the United States of America. These constructs have aided a large number of individuals in terms of career advancement in media, politics, business and bureaucracies, but have not aided the understanding or control of systematic criminal activity. Many fundamental and virtually unchallenged assumptions about the past of "organized crime" derive from these individuals and continue to underlie a global consensus about transnational organized crime that helps to perpetuate almost unlimited levels of criminal opportunity. *Double Crossed* will challenge these assumptions about the past.

Most writers begin their "histories" of organized crime in America at the end of the nineteenth century when hundreds of thousands of Italians immigrated, bringing with them secret societies, notably the Mafia. During the Prohibition era, so the story goes, the Mafia – and therefore, it was thought, organized crime – became more centralized, and took over those activities that from the Cold War era onwards were most associated with the construct: illegal gambling, drug trafficking and labor racketeering. The storytellers began to convey the idea that organized crime was a national security threat that required a national security response, involving draconian laws and decisive law enforcement and criminal justice action. From the 1970s, so the accounts continue, the government, mainly in the shape of the Federal Bureau of Investigation (FBI) and the Drug Enforcement Administration used new organized crime control powers effectively and broke the alleged hold of the Mafia. But they added caveats to this success. Success was offset by the emergence of what the government referred to as "emerging crime groups," mainly of foreign origin but including home-grown, white outlaw bikers gangs, such as the Hells Angels. From the end of the Cold War, "true crime" writers echoed a new narrative, derived primarily from sources inside the American government. Globalization, it was now thought, had been a game-changer that let a number of super-criminal, centralized hierarchical organizations join the Mafia and assume control of drug trafficking and other transnational illegal activities. This perspective remained dominant until supplanted by one that emphasized the multitude of criminal networks. Misha Glenny's 2007 book *McMafia* reflects the current dominant perspective. It has also been spelt out by US government officials, such as William F. Wechsler, Deputy Assistant Secretary of Defense for Counternarcotics and Global Threats. The structure of criminal groups has changed, he claimed:

> Hierarchical, centralized organizations have, in many cases, yielded to loose, amorphous, highly adaptable networks that are decentralized and flat. There are still leaders, to be sure, but these are leaders of networks, not leaders of hierarchies. These structural characteristics have rendered transnational criminal organizations ... more flexible and agile than the government agencies chartered with degrading or defeating them. ... these realities demand new policy approaches that are networked, whole-of-government, and adaptable.[1]

There has been little focus on America's continuing internal "organized crime" problem since the end of the 1980s. This has coincided with an intense drive to export American organized crime control strategies through diplomatic and bureaucratic pressures. Many nations now have their own FBI-like academies for training in organized crime control techniques, and just as many now have their own versions of the FBI itself. The United Kingdom, for example, unveiled its third "British FBI" in 15 years in 2013. The supremacy of American organized crime control techniques is rarely challenged.

The argument to be made in the following pages would agree with Wechsler that criminal groups are flexible and agile but would disagree with Wechsler's confident claim that hierarchical, centralized groups "yielded" to the new "network" versions. Successful criminal groups in illegal markets have always been flexible and agile, and therefore off the radar of honest police agencies. Successful criminal groups in legal markets have, for reasons detailed in *Double Crossed*, been rendered barely visible.

Versions of the storyteller history, in fictional or non-fictional form, have been endlessly recycled and updated in every form of media communication, including Wikipedia and television shows such as the popular *Boardwalk Empire* series. Accounts are enlivened by often invented anecdotes about career criminals such as Al Capone, Lucky Luciano, Meyer Lansky, John Gotti, Pablo Escobar and Joaquín "El Chapo" Guzmán. The anecdotes are also often enlivened by the use of recycled descriptive words and phrases: "Godfather," "cartel," "capo di tutti capi," "hydra-headed," "tentacles" and "octopus" being the most popular. Most of the popular accounts of organized crime, however, are based on hearsay stories that slide seamlessly from the undeniable to the unbelievable, and as a result conceal far more than they reveal.[2]

On the foundation of fictionalized history, it is usually implied or stated by commentators that gangster organizations have gained an unacceptable level of power through violence and the ability to corrupt weak, greedy and therefore passive public officials and otherwise respectable business people and professionals. Organized crime in this sense is a threat to, rather than a part of, society. Therefore, storytellers argue, the only answer to the problem of organized crime involves increasing the law enforcement power of every individual nation state on the American model and, since many of these organizations are known to operate globally, increasing the collective power of the international community. A complex issue that should involve a thorough re-examination of each nation's laws and institutions and the constraints put upon the making of policy by commercial interests and misguided international commitments has therefore been reduced to an easy-to-swallow package. The issue has become a simple good versus evil equation that admits only one solution – give governments more power to get gangsters or those associated with gangsters. Historically not many governments have deserved this trust.

By providing both an explanation for the past and a justification for the present, the conventional history of organized crime summarized above is an interpretation that fits in well with the United States' own view of its past – one that is based on a narrative of problems faced and overcome by a united and free people, and presented as a moral and pragmatic example for the rest of the world to follow. *Double Crossed* tells a different story that helps explain the institutionalization of authoritarian and xenophobic crime control tendencies long before Donald Trump became US president in 2016.

He who controls the past controls the future. He who controls the present controls the past.

George Orwell, *1984*

PART I

Dumbing Down: Constructing an Acceptable Understanding of "Organized Crime"

Introduction

Before the Cold War there was no fixed understanding of the phrase "organized crime," but the trend towards a reduced understanding of organized crime had already begun. Whole areas of American organized crime history were unknown or unrecognized by early twentieth-century Americans. Systematic crimes of fraud and violence against native and African Americans were either excused as the result of a "higher" racial law, or forgotten by the beginning of the twentieth century. The commentators and academics who did most to develop the literature on organized crime, did not, for example, consider the systematic criminal activity directed against native Americans and African Americans as crime let alone organized crime; "the Indian problem" and "the Negro problem" were not for them part of the "organized crime" problem.[1]

* * *

By the end of the nineteenth century, businessmen were the people of power in America and they were developing new ideas about the role of government. Their predecessors usually held that governments should do little more than maintain order, conduct public services at minimum cost, and subsidize business development when appropriate but otherwise do nothing to disrupt the laws of free competition. Twentieth-century businessmen, however, expected much more government involvement in the economy and society, and many became active participants in the era that would later be labeled "Progressive." Business interests could not initiate or control all economic and social reform during these years but, as several historians have demonstrated, they could set outer limits on what would succeed.[2] By the time of the First World War, although mainstream American thinking had become pro-state, businessmen succeeded in ensuring that it also remained just as pro-business and dedicated to private profit as before. In the new regulated business environment, capitalism was to be checked but not in ways that constituted any effective deterrent to organized crime activity within legal markets.

The systematic criminal activity of businessmen, as we shall see, was considered to be a serious problem until around the time of the First World War. After that, corporations successfully disassociated themselves from the taint of any kind of organized criminality.

1
The Rise and Fall of Muckraking Business Criminality

Americans at the beginning of the twentieth century would have been as likely to associate organized criminality with the schemes and practices of the rich rather than the poor. They would as likely look for coordinated criminal activity among native-born businessmen or politicians rather than groups of foreigners finding their way in a strange new land.

The sense that the real problem of crime and corruption stemmed from the top of the economic and social order grew with rising working class and farmer militancy towards the end of the nineteenth century. Henry Demarest Lloyd crystallized these feelings in 1894 in *Wealth Against Commonwealth*, when he wrote a scathing exposé of the Standard Oil Company. His conclusions were that,

> If our civilization is destroyed, it will not be by ... barbarians from below. Our barbarians come from above. Our great money-makers ... are gluttons of luxury and power, rough, unsocialized, believing that mankind must be kept terrorized. Powers of pity die out of them, because they work through agents.[3]

The new American order came under increased scrutiny and criticism at the turn of the nineteenth and twentieth centuries. Many more writers denounced the systematic criminal activity of the powerful. These writers, who included Ida Tarbell, Lincoln Steffens, Upton Sinclair, Ray Stannard Baker and Samuel Hopkins Adams, showed in graphic detail how the practices of big business and their allies in politics were corrupt, destructive and often illegal. Ida Tarbell, in particular, made a devastating case against John D. Rockefeller and Standard Oil, finding that they had normalized business criminality from "bankers down to street vendors." "In commerce," she wrote, "the interest of the business" justifies breaking the law, bribing legislators and defrauding a competitor of his rights. This business creed, she concluded, is "charged with poison."[4]

Various forms of organized business fraud and theft were common. One notable example involved the combining of various New York street railways into the Metropolitan Street Railway Company by William C. Whitney and Thomas F. Ryan in the early twentieth century. This merger, according to the historian Gustavus Myers, was "accompanied by a monstrous infusion of watered stock." Worthless stock was sold to the public while Whitney and Ryan became multimillionaires. A contemporary noted that the "Metropolitan managers have engaged in a deliberate scheme of stealing trust funds, their own stockholders' money. Their crimes comprise conspiracy, intimidation, bribery, corrupt court practices, subordination of perjury, false reporting, the payment of unearned dividends year after year, the persistent theft of stockholders' money, carried on over a long period by a system constituting the basest kind of robbery."[5] Although this scandal attracted press attention, other forms of intimidation, bribery and destruction of evidence went largely unremarked, and Whitney and Ryan kept their looted millions and even enhanced their reputations. The world they operated in worshiped money whatever its origins.

Fraud, larceny, bribery and exploitation on an immense scale were revealed in many businesses including oil, meat, sugar, railroads and life insurance. The case against big business criminality was made in popular magazines like *McClure's*, *Hampton's*, *Harper's Weekly*, *Collier's* and *Success*, novels such as Upton Sinclair's *The Jungle* (1906), and to a lesser extent in the popular newspapers of the day.

Muckrakers were able to use the government statistics to expose malpractice in many business practices and to call for these practices to be criminalized. Safety at work was an afterthought for the bosses. United States Bureau of Labor experts estimated that at the turn of the century industrial accidents killed 35,000 workers each year and maimed 500,000 others. The United States Geological Survey reported in 1908 alone that 3,125 coal miners in the previous year had been killed and 5,316 injured. The survey explained, however, that the figures did not give "the full extent of the disasters, as reports were not received from certain States having no mine inspectors."[6] As

David Rosner and Gerald Markowitz concluded in *Dying for Work: Workers' Safety and Health in Twentieth Century America*, "Speed-ups, monotonous tasks, and exposure to chemical toxins, metallic, and organic dusts, and unprotected machinery made the American workplace among the most dangerous in the world."[7]

Informed American opinion was never more conscious of the cost and the consequences of organized business crime than at the beginning of the twentieth century. Following in the tradition of Henry Demarest Lloyd, many writers found that America's barbarians came from above.

Lincoln Steffens, in *The Shame of the Cities* (1904), revealed corrupt alliances between business and politics at a local level. He detailed different types of corrupt activity in six major cities beginning with St. Louis. St. Louis exemplified "boodle" where public franchises and privileges "were sought, not only for legitimate profit and common convenience, but for loot." The results were "poorly-paved and refuse-burdened streets," and public buildings such as the City Hospital that were firetraps in a city that boasted of its wealth. Steffens found that "the big businessman" was the chief source of corruption in every city he visited: "I found him buying boodlers in St. Louis, defending grafters in Minneapolis, originating corruption in Pittsburgh, ... and beating good government with corruption funds in New York. He is a self-righteous fraud, this big businessman ... it were a boon if he would neglect politics." "The spirit of graft and lawlessness," he concluded famously, "is the American spirit."[8]

Few informed Americans would have disagreed with Steffens' verdict.

The academic who came closest to articulating a new understanding of modern crime based on the avalanche of evidence of business wrongdoing was Edward A. Ross in *Sin and Society* (1907). Ross argued that lawless and destructive business practices had created a need for a redefinition of ideas about crime. Ross summarized the organized criminality of men of power as follows: "The director who speculates in the securities of his corporation, the banker who lends his depositors' money to himself under divers corporate aliases, the railroad official who grants a secret rebate for his private graft, ... the labor leader who instigates a strike in order to be paid for calling it off, the publisher who bribes his text books into the schools." The "criminaloid," as Ross termed the criminally powerful, was

> [too] squeamish and too prudent to practice treachery, brutality, and violence himself, he takes care to work through middlemen. Conscious of the ... difference between doing wrong and getting it done, he places out his dirty work. With a string of intermediaries between himself and the toughs who slug voters at the polls, or the gang of navvies who break other navvies' heads with shovels on behalf of the electric line, he is able to keep his hands sweet and his boots clean.

"Thus," Ross concluded, the man of power "becomes a consumer of custom-made crime, a client of criminals, oftener a maker of criminals by persuading or requiring his subordinates to break law." He informs agents what he wants, provides the money, insists on "results," but "vehemently declines to know the foul methods by which alone his understrappers can get these – results." Not to bribe but to employ and finance the briber; not to shed innocent blood, but to bribe inspectors to overlook your neglect to install safety appliances: such are the ways of the criminaloid. He is a buyer rather than a practitioner of sin, and his middlemen spare him "unpleasant details." Ross' book was prefaced by a letter from President Theodore Roosevelt. Roosevelt was "in full and hearty sympathy" with Ross' views: "You war against the vast iniquities in modern business, finance, politics, journalism." "As you well say," Roosevelt continued, "if a ring is to be put in the snout of the greedy strong, only organized society can do it." Although Ross and Roosevelt shared many of the race and class assumptions of their elite contemporaries, they also understood that the new type of criminal was far more dangerous than "his low-browed cousins" or the "plain criminal."

By pointing out that the sins of modern industrialists were more destructive than more familiar, older forms of crime, Ross was thus attempting to broaden the definition of crime. Big business "criminaloids" robbed and killed on a much grander scale than before but, "so long as morality stands stock-still in the old tracks, they escape both punishment and ignominy. The man who picks pockets with a railway rebate, murders with an adulterant instead of a bludgeon, burglarizes with a 'rake-off' instead of a jimmy ... does not feel on his brow the brand of a malefactor." "Like a stupid, flushed giant at bay, the public heeds the little overt offender more than the big covert offender."[9]

Ross and Roosevelt had found, like many other Americans, that business crime was also organized crime. Millions of Americans, informed by national "muckraking" magazines, newspaper reports and legislative assemblies, would have placed the most dangerous organized criminals among the political and corporate elite. From the end of the Civil War to the First World War, scandal after scandal, revelation after revelation, would have confirmed this assessment.

Ross' recommendations on addressing organized business crime involved making directors individually accountable for "every case of misconduct of which the company receives the benefit, for every preventable deficiency or abuse that regularly goes on in the course of business." "Strict accountability," he continued, would send flying the figurehead directors who, when the misdeeds of their protégés come to light, protest they "didn't know." It would bar buccaneering insiders from using a group of eminent dummies as unwitting decoys for the confiding investor or policyholder. It would break up the game of operating a brigand public service company (owned by some distant "syndicate") from behind a board of respectable local "directors" without a shred of power. And accountability would be enforced by the reality of prison rather than the "flea bite" deterrent of fines. "Never will the brake of the law grip these slippery wheels until prison doors yawn for the convicted officers of lawless corporations."[10]

Through a manipulative process, as we shall see, only a few remaining American dissenters felt that organized criminals came from above by the 1940s; the majority had been convinced that the serious organized criminals came first from foreign and immigrant stock. Organized business crime was, by then, not considered to be organized crime. This process involved smoke, mirrors and a large amount of brutal financial power.

In the following decades there were far fewer indictments of what is now known as corporate crime and violence. Lawyers and other business representatives colluded with government legislators and regulators and continued to help many corporations circumvent or ignore much of the legislation passed to protect workers and consumers. On health and safety at work, for example, a new class of industrial psychologist tended to find the causes of workplace injuries and deaths in the defects or carelessness of individual workers rather than factors which affected profitability, such as rate of production or adequate safety devices and adequate lighting. Corporate violators were occasionally discovered but rarely faced more than the minor deterrent of fines. Organized business crime, therefore, continued to cheat large numbers of American workers, consumers and taxpayers, and cause the death and injury of thousands of Americans.

* * *

For all the revulsion at the criminal and destructive practices of big business, the period of Progressive reform did not lead to a diminution of corporate power and influence in American society. By the time Woodrow Wilson, the president most associated with progressivism, took office in 1912, the age of muckraking was over. Many of the magazines which had publicized the crimes of big business found themselves faced with damaging libel costs or forced out of business in other ways.

In 1910, *Hampton's*, for example, had run a series of articles on the rise and illegal practices of the giant New York, New Haven and Hartford railroad, despite receiving threats of reprisals. From that time on, as the historian Louis Filler narrates, the magazine's owner, Benjamin Hampton, was marked:

> Spies ferreted their way into his offices, and one in the accounting department found the opportunity to copy out the entire list of stockholders. Each stockholder was separately visited and regaled with stories of how Hampton was misusing company funds. Wall Street agents of the railroad made extraordinary bids for the stock in order to indicate it was losing value.[11]

Hampton, recognizing the threat, convened a committee of stockholders and received endorsements for $30,000. These were then taken to the bank and accepted. Hampton was able to draw money on them until, the following day, he was ordered to return the money and take back the notes from the bank. "Such banking practice was illegal," Filler continued, "but the manager of the bank told Hampton that he was powerless to do anything else; 'downtown' people were giving the orders, and he had to take them." The downtown people he was referring to were associated with J.P. Morgan, the most powerful investment banker in the United States:

> Hampton now tried and failed to float a loan. One banker who declared that he would stand by Hampton in his crisis, whether the "Morgan Crowd" willed it or not, was forced to stop his transactions and was himself forced out of business within several months.
>
> Within ten days Hampton had to turn his affairs over to his lawyers. Facing receiverships, he chose what seemed the lesser of two evils; he relinquished the magazine to a group of promoters who offered impressive introductions and gave promises that the magazine would be fully supported. In a few months Hampton became convinced that the new owners had no intention but to loot the magazine. He was later told by the bookkeeper that they abstracted $175,000 from the property, and then took the books down to the East River and threw them from a bridge.[12]

Other muckraking outlets were also destroyed or their editors expediently turned away from exposing the corporations towards safer subjects. The muckrakers themselves either had to go along with the pro-business tide or look for careers outside mainstream journalism. Criticizing the powerful was not a good career move.

* * *

By the end of the First World War, crime commissions had been set up to put pressure on the police and the courts to enforce laws against any crimes that adversely affected business interests. They collected facts and expert opinion on aspects of the crime problem and issued reports and statements to the media to win support for specific recommendations to improve the efficiency and honesty of criminal justice and law enforcement.[13]

The most influential of these, in terms of capturing the organized crime concept, was the Chicago Crime Commission (CCC). This was set up by local businessmen in 1917. It was described by its first director as:

> An organization of bankers, business and professional men who are applying modern business methods to correct a system which has, through inertia, been allowed to grow up in the departments of state and municipal government having to do with the prevention, apprehension, prosecution, and punishment of crime and criminals ... The Chicago Crime Commission is purely and simply an organization of business men determined to do its duty, without fear or favor, to the end that organized crime in Chicago is destroyed.[14]

Because the CCC, like other commissions, was funded by business it did not see organized business crime as organized crime. As we shall see, the commission and other representatives of the business community began to focus on the sons of immigrants as representative of something they claimed was new – crime organized as a business. Crime commissions in general tended to ignore organized criminality within legal markets and focus public attention on organized criminality in illegal markets such as alcohol during Prohibition and gambling during and after the repeal of the Eighteenth Amendment.

* * *

From the second decade of the twentieth century to the late 1960s, "investigative" reporting meant for the most part exposing soft targets and inventing threats in ways that would often benefit and rarely challenge the interests of corporate America. Academics tended to shun the topic of organized crime unless it was to be located firmly at the bottom of American society, as in the case of the two early classics of organized crime literature, Frederic Thrasher's *The Gang* (1927) and John Landesco's *Organized Crime in Chicago* (1929). Ways were found to excuse or ignore business criminality or explain it as a deviation from normal practice. Even when big business criminality was too blatant to ignore, the business class and their allies in the press found ways to ensure that the status quo was not unduly disturbed.

2
America's Moral Crusade and the Making of Illegal Markets

American business leaders, as we have seen, were contemptuous or evasive about laws that attempted to restrain their activities. However, they did care about order. Order in the workplace, order in the streets and order in the home. In particular, they cared about moral order, and many added their weight to the campaigns to make America a more moral and abstinent society.

The United States experienced its most significant moral crusade in the first two decades of the twentieth century. As millions of immigrants struggled to make new lives for themselves in the cities, many native-born Americans saw a threat to the dominance of Protestant values and reacted by joining anti-vice, anti-intemperance societies, and lobbying intensely in state capitals and city halls for laws to eradicate gambling, prostitution and drug-taking. Tens of thousands of new laws attempted to prohibit these activities. The intention was to end all behavior that a Protestant and business-oriented culture defined as sinful and non-productive; the paradoxical result was a vast area of American business opportunity that those prepared to break the law could exploit.

Business interests provided the crucial financial backing and political pull in the campaigns to put morality on the statute books. Laws intended to make workers more moral and abstinent made dollar-sense. Businessmen thought that drinking, gambling, prostitution and drug-taking diverted wages from the purchase of manufactured goods and alcohol, in particular, decreased work efficiency at a time when most managers were searching for ways to get more productivity out of their workers. Business interests also used their alliance with prohibitionists and America's preoccupation with vice and crime to divert the reform element from attacks on corporate corruption.

In the cities, the boss or political machine system was thought to be the primary obstacle to moral reform and good government. Reformers concentrated on the connections between politicians, police and illegal enterprise to highlight the corruption of boss rule in their campaigns to clean up city government. During these campaigns, variations on the phrase "organized crime" began to be used more frequently. In 1895, for example, the Reverend Charles Parkhurst described a police captain in New York who tolerated illegal gambling operations as one factor in "a colossal organization of crime." He contended that the police represented "organized municipal criminality," the machine, "the organization of crime." Parkhurst was by then President of the New York Society for the Prevention of Crime, which described itself in its 1896 annual report as: "A small, compact body, completely organized for offensive operations and thoroughly committed to a policy of exposing and breaking down official misconduct and organized crime."[15]

This was perhaps the first time reformers had used the phrase "organized crime" in a way that gave it a distinct meaning – gambling and prostitution operations that were protected by public officials. The public officials he most had in mind were those appointed by the Democratic Party, organized in Manhattan by the political machine known as Tammany Hall.

Parkhurst had become president of the Society in 1891 and he boosted its prospects, largely by getting the support of wealthy business interests and directing attention away from business criminality. Other commentators began to take the lead of Parkhurst's organization and use the phrase "organized crime" as almost synonymous with the municipal corruption that protected vice and intemperance.

Throughout Parkhurst's work and other contemporary writings was the assumption that the "foreign element" was much more likely than native-born Americans to succumb to the bribery and corrupt promises of machine politicians. Those wishing to reform criminal justice, such as Roscoe Pound, one of the most influential jurists of the early twentieth century, shared this assumption. Reform was necessary, he argued in 1912, because the current system was outdated "in a heterogeneous community, divided into classes with divergent interests, which understand each other none too well, containing elements ignorant of our institutions." Referring to the immigrant ghettoes he continued that this was especially true of a community "where the defective, the degenerate of decadent stocks, and the ignorant or enfeebled victim of severe economic pressure are exposed to temptations and afforded opportunities beyond anything our fathers could have conceived."[16]

In 1921, Pound crystallized the reform argument when he concluded that the administration of justice had nearly collapsed and was not able to perform its basic task of punishing criminals and preventing crime. The problem, he wrote, was threefold: "men, machinery, and environment." And, most importantly, he suggested the way forward for the next generation of law enforcement and criminal justice professionals. According to Pound, the administration of justice demanded better-qualified personnel, changes in the structure of agencies to remove obstacles to speedy justice, and eliminating the corrupting influence of the political environment.[17] The implication was that administrative changes could ensure that all laws, including the laws that prohibited "sin," could be enforced.

There was undoubtedly substance to the charges of Parkhurst and Pound – politicians and police had been protecting different forms of organized criminality since the beginning of the Republic. But they misrepresented the degree of centralized control in vice operations. The historian Timothy Gilfoyle has noted, for example, that "Tammany Hall's relationship with the underground economy rested upon the actions of individual members. No directives came from the general committee of the hall ... Relations between Tammany and the prostitution business were informal and fluid, varying according to the neighborhood and the individual leader."[18] When reforms eventually replaced direct political rule in local government with more bureaucratic systems, and old-style political machines like Tammany disappeared from the American political scene, other informal and fluid relationships ensured that prostitution, gambling and other protected criminal activity did not. American consumers continued to gamble and pay prostitutes whether or not it was against the law.

*   *   *

Moralists who were contemporaries of Parkhurst and Pound also ensured the success of the campaigns to prohibit alcohol and drugs.

This success can only partly be explained by the undoubted harm that these substances can do to individuals. Although the campaigns did detail many of the sad and often tragic consequences of alcoholism and drug addiction, they would not have succeeded without the mobilization of a virulent racism across the country. Mass immigration and migration of non-white groups from the late nineteenth century onwards led to a bigoted backlash from America's white majority, stirred by moralistic politicians and organizations. Chinese, African Americans and Mexicans, in particular, were vilified and perceived as having habits that threatened the American mainstream.

Racism lay behind the alcohol prohibition campaigns, and the Southern states' vanguard of the anti-saloon movement did not attempt to hide this. Some southerners argued that white and black mixing in the saloon would weaken the "stronger" race and promote all kinds of vices. "The saloon," according to one concerned southerner, "is a place of rendezvous for all classes of the low and vulgar, a resort for degraded whites and their more degraded Negro associates, the lounging place for adulterers, lewd women, the favorite haunt of gamblers, drunkards and criminals. Both blacks and whites mix and mingle together as a mass of degraded humanity in this cesspool of iniquity."[19] Others concentrated on the need to protect white women from "drink-crazed" black men.

Every Southern state had prohibited alcohol by the First World War. Once passed, however, enforcement of the Southern Prohibition laws was minimal and largely directed against African Americans. The South was already by reputation the hardest-drinking section of the American nation and it continued to be able to make this claim after the dry laws were passed.

A southerner introduced the first national prohibition resolution in the House of Representatives. In 1914, Richmond Pearson Hobson, a congressman from Alabama, used the following theory of race to make his case:

Liquor will actually make a brute out of a Negro, causing him to commit unnatural crimes ...

The effect is the same on the white man, though the white man being further evolved it takes longer time to reduce him to the same level. Starting young, however, it does not take a very long time to speedily cause a man in the forefront of civilization to pass through the successive stages and become semicivilized, semisavage, savage, and, at last, below the brute.[20]

Hobson's resolution helped to bring the Eighteenth Amendment to the Constitution a step nearer.

Opium consumption was associated with Chinese immigrants, cocaine with blacks, and from the 1920s, marijuana with Mexicans. In 1910, for example, the *Report on the International Opium Commission* claimed that cocaine made rapists of black males and that blacks acquired immense strength and cunning under its influence. Dr. Hamilton Wright, the man most responsible for this report and for much of the national and international anti-drug effort that followed, came to the conclusion that "this new vice, the cocaine vice, the most serious to be dealt with, has proved to be the creator of criminals and unusual forms of violence, and it has been a potent incentive in driving the humbler negroes all over the country to abnormal crimes."[21]

The development of American drug control policies was also shaped by a persistent and dogmatic moralism that survives to the present day. Drugs were thought of as products of the Devil, breaking down a person's self-control and leading to unimaginable consequences for the rest of society. The moralists who campaigned for anti-drug laws in the late nineteenth century felt that promising damnation for the users of certain kinds of drugs was inadequate, given the perceived severity of the problem. For them, drug use, not to mention drug production and trafficking, were scourges or cancers that had to be extirpated from society.[22] As with gambling, commercialized sex and liquor, the thought of regulating drug use was as unthinkable as regulating violence or robbery. By the early twentieth century, America's moral leaders could smell legislative victory and got the laws they wanted to prohibit drugs and make the personal behavior of millions of Americans a problem that the police were then supposed to control.

The anti-drug laws failed to prevent large numbers of Americans from consuming the newly illegal drugs. Addicts were forced to pay more for their habits and many were prepared to commit crimes to get the needed funds. Their suppliers capitalized on the fact that the laws inflated the value of cocaine and heroin substantially. The main impact of these laws gave a similar boost to criminal activity internationally.

The laws made crops that were easy and cheap to grow and substances that were easy and cheap to produce far more profitable. In the New York of the 1920s, as the historian Alan Block narrates, the demand from users and addicts fed a fragmented and sprawling industry in cocaine. "Cocaine was imported, wholesaled, franchised, and retailed ... It was traded in movies, theaters, restaurants, cafes, cabarets, pool parlors, saloons, parks, and on innumerable street corners."[23] From the beginning, trading in drugs was horizontally organized with deals between separate actors characterizing the drug business.

From a law enforcement perspective, moralists were wrong to equate drugs with murder or robbery. Drug deals involved cash transactions between willing parties; no one complained to the police and served as a witness as a result of a drug deal. The police therefore had to learn to develop cases through informers and covert methods, before making arrests, seizing evidence and carrying out interrogations. Until a case reached the courts, the police controlled the situation totally since they alone decided whether an offense had been committed and whether they had a legal case against the suspect. This situation increased the possibility of corruption and decreased the possibility of ever controlling this corruption. In 1917 the first American police officer was convicted for taking a large bribe to protect a drug trafficking operation.[24] Police officers abroad were just as unlikely to resist temptation. The anti-drug crusade has been fatally compromised by corruption ever since.

American leaders were never able to accept the reality of drug prohibition, that anti-drug laws turned the undesirable problem of dangerous drug use into a tragedy of immense proportions. Instead of changing their approach to drugs, they looked abroad for scapegoat explanations. This allowed them to continue to believe that drug prohibition at home could be achieved by establishing a global drug prohibition regime. In the 1920s, for example, the prohibitionist Hobson, who set up the World Narcotics Defense Association to influence press and political opinion, claimed that North America was surrounded by other dangerous continents. According to Hobson, "South America sent in cocaine; Europe contributed drugs like heroin and morphine; Asia was the source of crude opium and Africa produced hashish." These poisoned the US by supplying the demonic substances. Asia, in particular, he claimed, was just as responsible for "the scourge of narcotic drug addiction" as it had been for "the invasions and plagues of history."[25] Hobson's xenophobia was not exceptional in the America of the 1920s. The fact that the demand for drugs came from the richest nation on earth was passed over.

Global drug prohibition, Hobson argued, was the only answer to this "malignant racial cancer" which threatened the whole of white civilization. In 1930, Hobson applied unsuccessfully to be the US government's chief anti-drug enforcement officer as Commissioner of the Federal Bureau of Narcotics (FBN). Harry J. Anslinger, the man who got the job, however, shared many of his opinions, racist assumptions, and ambitions for a toughened-up national and global response to drugs. The international response of recent decades has been to build on the prohibitionist framework designed and implemented by the likes of Wright, Hobson and Anslinger.

Paradoxically, therefore, there was one area of American business life, where laissez-faire was not thought to be appropriate: the business in "sin." Local, state and federal governments were expected to eliminate, not just control, the supply of alcohol and certain kinds of drugs, the selling of sex, and the provision of opportunities to gamble.

The basic problem with the criminalization of "sin" or aspects of undesirable personal behavior was noted by several of the early serious commentators on the problem of organized crime. In 1936, for example, the economists E.R. Hawkins and Willard Waller argued that much organized crime is economically productive:

> The prostitute, the pimp, the peddler of dope, the operator of the gambling hall, the vendor of obscene pictures, the bootlegger, ... all are productive, all produce goods and services which people desire and for which they are willing to pay. It happens that society has put these goods and services under the ban, but people go on producing them and people go on consuming them, and an act of the legislature does not make them any less a part of the economic system.

Bootleggers, by that time, were becoming rarer, confined to the few Southern states that maintained prohibition. Illegal gambling operators and drug traders, however, remained productive, offering goods and services that people desired. In time most forms of gambling became legal, accessible and controlled by tax-paying corporations.

The "peddlers" of many and varied types of "dope," however, remained a very lucrative part of the American economic system and then, as other nations followed America's lead on drug prohibition, a very lucrative part of the international economic system.

The US, Hawkins and Waller argued, needed to study the economic effects of crime:

> We need to know the nature and immediate results of a crime crusade. We need to be more cognizant of the permanent consequences of crime as an organic part of our society ... What is the effect of crime in redistributing the national income? What unintended consequences for the larger social order have such crimes as bank robbery, embezzlement, counterfeiting, and racketeering? ... What are the roots of crime in legitimate business? [26]

Unfortunately for America, and other nations that have followed their lead on organized crime control, questions of this type were not ones that American opinion-makers wished to see addressed. Meanwhile, as the representatives of the business community ensured that organized business crime was not described as "organized crime," organized criminality permeated the American business system.

Inset 1: The Origins of Mafia Mythology in America

Scapegoating immigrants for the problems of the United States has a long history. In 1857, for example, a New York State committee voiced fears about the impact of different cultures and religions: "we must as a people, act upon this foreign element, or it will act upon us. Like the vast Atlantic, we must decompose and cleanse the impurities which rush into our midst, or like the inland lake, we will receive the poison into our whole nation system."[27]

The idea of organized crime as a specifically Italian import began to take root more successfully after a series of incidents in New Orleans in the last decade of the nineteenth century. From the 1880s, Italians were the largest ethnic group to arrive in America and they received the most violent and abusive welcome of any of the European newcomers. Reports of beatings, shootings and lynchings came in from all parts of the country. Instead of condemning these acts of violence committed by US citizens, some politicians and commentators looked for ways to excuse them.

They achieved this most effectively by shifting attention to Italian criminality. Ordinary crimes committed in Italian neighborhoods became more significant when the perpetrators were said to use "stiletto knives" and "muskets with the barrels shortened," and to belong to a "secret, malignant, treacherous organization of assassins." Italians became stereotyped as particularly prone to violence, vengeance and conspiracy.[28]

The word "Mafia" itself was first commonly used when anti-Italian feeling was at its peak following the killing of New Orleans Police Chief David Hennessy on October 15, 1890. There had been several other unsolved assassinations of public figures in the city's recent past and no one will ever know for sure who shot Hennessy. But two pieces of circumstantial evidence suggested that Italians might have been responsible. First, Hennessy had been investigating a commercial dispute over parts of the South American fruit trade between rival groups of southern Italians and Sicilians at the time of the shooting. Second, on his deathbed, Hennessy was reported to have said that "dagoes" shot him. Reported last words are not necessarily accurate.

The city's mayor, Joseph Shakspeare, reacted to the murder by sending large numbers of police into the Italian sector. These arrested more than a hundred Sicilians and Italians, and on October 18 the mayor announced that:

> Heretofore these scoundrels have confined their murderings among themselves. None of them have ever been convicted because of the secrecy with which the crimes have been committed and the impossibility of getting evidence from the people of their own race to convict. Bold, indeed, was the stroke, aimed at their first American victim. A shining mark have they selected on which to write with the assassin's hand their contempt for the civilization of the new world.
>
> We owe it to ourselves and to everything that we hold sacred in this life to see to it that this blow is the last. We must teach these people a lesson they will not forget for all time.[29]

The city's police department released a list of "assassinations, murders, and affrays committed by Sicilians and Italians" over the previous 25 years to add some credibility to Shakspeare's charge. When a historian, Humbert Nelli, researched these murders he found no substance in the charge that they were somehow connected as Mafia executions. By comparing the list with coroners' reports, Nelli found that the list "contained errors in almost every case outlined and each error served to blacken the reputation of New Orleans Italians."[30]

Nine Italians were placed on trial for the murder of Hennessy on February 16, 1891. After three weeks of inconsistent and contradictory testimony the jury found six of the accused not guilty and could not agree on a verdict for the remainder. Many of the city's most prominent citizens refused to accept this leniency and called for a public meeting "to remedy the failure of justice in the Hennessy case."[31] On March 14, speakers at this meeting urged a crowd of several thousand citizens to storm the parish prison. Prison officers decided not to resist and the shout went up, "Kill the Dagoes!"[32] Eleven Italians were shot or clubbed to death, before being lynched purely for spectacle. Four of the victims had never been implicated in the Hennessy case; they happened to be Italian and unfortunate to be in the wrong place at the wrong time. None of the lynchers was brought to trial.

In reality, the contemporary accounts grossly exaggerated the importance of Sicilian and southern Italian crime in New Orleans. Without doubt some Mafiosi did accompany the millions of law-abiding Italian immigrants to America and some newcomers did join Mafia-type groups with initiation rituals involving finger-prickings and secrecy oaths. Organized violence, trickery and intimidation existed in Italian American communities, just as it did in other communities. However, it is fanciful to describe New Orleans-based, small-time criminals as members of highly structured organizations. Even banded together they were a small minority of parasitic individuals, gaining a limited degree of power and profit by preying on their neighbors. The lynchings are better understood as examples of southern lawlessness in a city and a region with a long-established reputation for corrupt, selective and often non-existent law enforcement where much crime was, of course, organized.

3
Charles G. Dawes and the Molding of Public Opinion on Organized Crime

From the end of the nineteenth century onwards, influential Americans made exaggerated charges about the extent and importance of Italian American crime, and began to raise the alarm about the importation of the Mafia and other Italian secret societies.

Vigilante lawlessness was generally ignored or excused in the contemporary press. The assassination of Hennessey, according to *Harper's Weekly* in 1890, was committed by "an oath-bound, murderous society, long formidable in Sicily, and transplanted to this country by Sicilian immigrants." Senator Henry Cabot Lodge, writing in the *North American Review* the following year in a call for restricting immigration from southern and eastern Europe, noted that the Mafia was "a secret society bound by the most rigid oaths and using murder as a means of maintaining its discipline and carrying out its decrees ... It is anything but self-limited, and in a political soil like that of New Orleans it was pretty sure to extend."[33]

Early American commentary on the Mafia was similarly motivated by the well-supported and ultimately successful effort to restrict immigration. From the 1921 Immigration Law onwards, immigration from southern Italy and Sicily was drastically cut. From then on, however, unsourced tales about Mafiosi, "Black Handers"[34] and other Italian criminals were refashioned to fit new political agendas. Charles G. Dawes, a Republican party colleague of Lodge, was the first to see the potential here for determining what should be classed as "organized crime."

Born in August 1865, Charles G. Dawes trained as a lawyer but laid the foundations of a large personal fortune in 1894, when he began to take control of a number of gas and electric plants in the Midwest. Operating from a suburb in Chicago, he began a banking career in 1902, when he founded and became president of the Central Trust

Company of Illinois, commonly called the Dawes Bank. Parallel with his business career, he also had a career in government, beginning with the comptrollership of the currency in 1898. According to the painstaking research of Raymond B. Vickers in *Panic in the Loop: Chicago's Banking Crisis of 1932*, in this and other high-ranking positions in government, Dawes abused his power to advance his political career and increase the fortunes of his family and political allies.

Dawes is usually described as a "great American patriot" and is often credited as an early crusader against organized crime. In *Scarface Al and the Crime Crusaders: Chicago's Private War against Capone*, Dennis E. Hoffman, for example, claimed that "While Al Capone is Chicago's 'best known citizen,' Charles G. Dawes was arguably Chicago's 'best citizen'. ... His urge to create a better Chicago led him to find a way to get the federal government involved in his city's battle against Prohibition-era gangsters."[35]

In reality Dawes was a "criminaloid," to use the terminology of Edward Ross. His political power protected corrupt practices in his banking, transportation and mining interests. Dawes resisted all efforts to check his unaccountable power and bring him to justice. He claimed, as did all other criminaloids according to Ross, that it was "un-American" to wrench patronage from the hands of spoilsmen, "un-American" to deal federal justice to rascals of state eminence, "un-American" to pry into "private arrangements" between shipper and carrier. Criminaloids know "full well," Ross had argued, "that the giving of a fountain or a park, the establishing of a college chair on the Neolithic drama ... will more than outweigh the dodging of taxes, the grabbing of streets, and the corrupting of city councils." Even the evolving business lexicon protected the criminaloid, as a bribe became a "retainer," investigative probing became "scandal-mongering," critics became "foul harpies of slander," and "regulation" became "meddling."[36]

When the US entered the First World War, Dawes was able to put a number of scandals behind him and establish a national reputation for efficiency by integrating the system of supply procurement and distribution for the entire American Expeditionary Force in the European theater of war. In the process he was promoted to brigadier general. After the war he maintained this reputation as director of the budget under President Warren Harding and, in 1923, he chaired a League of Nations committee that dealt with the problem of

German war reparations.[37] In sum, he was nationally and internationally known as efficient and tough-minded and, in his own mind at least, a candidate to be America's savior at a time of labor unrest and increasing fears about a breakdown in law and order. It helped that he was a classic insider; few could match his political, military and business connections.

In May 1923, he established the Minute Men of the Constitution which was set up to emulate Mussolini's contemporary Fascist Party in Italy. Dawes' group was named after famed Revolutionary war fighters. Before the end of the summer it had 47 chapters and 20,000 members, many of whom were war veterans associated with the American Legion. It was a short-lived and vaguely defined movement, being committed to "Americanism" and intended "to uphold Good Government and Law" thought to be under threat from trade unionists, bootleggers and Italian immigrants involved in "black hand warfare" in the north-west section of Chicago.[38] The St. Louis *Post Dispatch* editorialized that "General Charles G. Dawes is on the warpath again" and then made a comparison with Mussolini's black-shirts, claiming that if the Republican National Convention "says a word about minimum wage laws the Dawes brigade will invade the hall, break up the convention and shoo the delegates back home."[39]

The Minute Men movement fizzled out by the end of the summer. It seems to have been mainly a vehicle for Dawes to keep his name in the limelight. "In fact," as his political opponents charged, the movement was "typical of Dawes ... It was high-sounding claptrap in which he is a past master." It was an "organization formed under the guise of '100 per cent patriotism' to fight and crush the labor movement." They noted that Dawes was the type of man who won arguments by shouting and aggression. He "thumps his desk until it makes a loud noise," "booms his voice like an empty bass drum" and "cusses like a real he-man." In fact they claimed that he "cussed" his way into the vice-presidential nomination for the presidential election of 1924, sharing the ticket with the incumbent Calvin Coolidge.[40]

Opposing politicians cited Dawes' role in the pre-war corruption scandals during the campaign. Senator Burton K. Wheeler, for example, attacked "the crooked bank deal of banker Dawes" that robbed "4,000 Chicago citizens of their savings," while Senator Smith W. Brookhart accused him of being "unfit for public service." Dawes' attorney, John

Barton Payne, claimed in response that "no possible basis exists for criticism of General Dawes," although Payne failed to acknowledge that he had a conflict of interest, being a major shareholder in Dawes' bank. He added that "what was done by the Central Trust Company and General Dawes in providing the case, and by the auditor of the State of Illinois in counting it, knowing that it had been provided for that purpose, had been the practice in Illinois for generations."[41] His argument was, therefore, that fraud was acceptable because it was common practice by members of the business elite. The revelations made no difference to the election result, which the Coolidge/Dawes ticket won by a landslide.

As vice president, Dawes' reputation as a plain-speaking advocate of law and order persisted, and on February 27, 1926 he was the man that introduced the US government to an interpretation of organized crime that would eventually become dominant. He had been given a petition by representatives of the Chicago and Cook County business community that put the blame for organized crime squarely on foreigners and appealed to the "Federal Government to rescue Chicago from a reign of lawlessness under alien domination." The petition's language paraphrased Dawes' own Minute Men pronouncements on the topic and read in part:

> There has been growing up in this community a reign of lawlessness and terror, openly defying not only the Constitution and laws of the State of Illinois, but the Constitution and laws of the United States.
>
> There has been for a long time in this city of Chicago a colony of unnaturalized persons, hostile to our institutions and laws, who have formed a supergovernment of their own – feudists, blackhanders, members of the Mafia – who levy tribute upon citizens and enforce collection by terrorizing, kidnapping and assassinations. ...
>
> Many of these aliens have become fabulously rich as rumrunners and bootleggers, working in collusion with police and other officials, building up a monopoly in this unlawful business and dividing the territory of the county among themselves under penalty of death to all intruding competitors.

Dawes had thus introduced the idea that there was a foreign "super-government" of crime which, as we shall see, would be relentlessly repeated until the mass of the population believed it.

The syndicated Trenton *Evening Times* reported that the petition asked for the Senate's Immigration Committee to make a complete investigation "with a view to having deported those aliens who are alleged to form the backbone of outlawry in the nation's second largest city."[42]

For the next four years, Dawes remained the best hope for the business community for the "honest and fearless" leadership thought necessary to wage war on organized crime. An Associated Press piece, for example, on July 28, 1928 reported that the vice president was being urged by the CCC to lead "an organized array of all the various forces that are now attempting to fight crime in Chicago." Two years later, the Cleveland *Plain Dealer* described him as the "Red Meat" that could give "new vigor to the long-overdue offensive against gangland."[43] Dawes declined, but the offer buttressed his claim to be an anti-crime leader.

Dawes completed his term as vice president in 1928. In 1931, two years into the Great Depression, caused in part by the type of insider abuse associated with Dawes, he was invited by President Herbert Hoover to head the newly created Reconstruction Finance Corporation (RFC). After a few months he resigned, implying in his resignation statement that the Depression (which lasted through to the end of the 1930s) was almost over, "Now that the balancing of the national budget by Congress is assured, the turning point towards eventual prosperity in this country seems to have been reached."[44] In the meantime panicked depositors in his bank who had already been taking out millions of dollars a month, took out more than $4 million on a single day – Saturday, June 25. The day before, Dawes applied to his former agency – the RFC – for a $16 million loan, an amount worth about $251 million today. The RFC did not even require Dawes to fill out a loan application. The loan was approved and made available straight away despite the bank's obvious inability to pay it back.

On the Sunday, as Vickers narrates:

> Instead of drawing on the $16 million loan commitment he had just received, Dawes threatened instead to liquidate his bank unless the

RFC bailed him out of *all* of his deposits. He told his colleagues at the RFC that this would require a sum of $95 million, an amount worth nearly $1.6 billion today; nothing less was acceptable ... His audacity and the magnitude of his demands were remarkable.[45]

Despite this, the RFC board agreed to the bailout, perhaps not surprisingly because several of the agency's board of directors were close allies of Dawes. The Chicago banker still had to guarantee that the loan was for ongoing operations and not for liquidation purposes. Vickers quotes from the minutes of the relevant board meeting: "General Dawes assured the members of the Board by telephone last night that the loan applied for is for current requirements including the payment of deposits, in order to keep the bank open and not in contemplation of liquidation." By this time he was intending to liquidate the bank and so the statement was false. Also federal law clearly prohibited Dawes from using the loan for the purpose of financing a new bank, which Dawes ignored. Vickers then details not only Dawes' illegalities but the illegalities of the RFC in letting him get away with them: "When the RFC directors approved the bailout package, they violated federal law and their fiduciary obligations because they failed to complete the due diligence examination of the bank's assets."[46]

Dawes' old bank was liquidated and his new one – the City National – opened with much fanfare on October 6, 1932. Its low-cost deposits and absence of liability for the RFC loans allowed it to make millions of dollars from then until May 24, 1946 when Dawes' old bank was finally dissolved, leaving the RFC with millions of dollars of losses. Vickers makes the point that the RFC should have forced the new bank to comply with the terms and conditions of the original loan agreements, including the payment of principal and interest. Instead "the new Dawes bank was allowed to generate windfall profits that were distributed to Dawes and his family in the form of salaries and benefits and dividends."[47]

To put Dawes' organized corporate criminality in context, while he was using bluff, bluster, deceit and influence to preserve his fortune illegally, the hardships of the Great Depression had become more visible. President Hoover, while bailing out millionaires like Dawes, was determined to do nothing to help the mass of the American people directly.

After his death in 1951, a biography by Bascom N. Timmons was published, entitled *Portrait of an America: Charles G. Dawes*. A syndicated review of the book summed up the conventional view of his career: "Besides being an astute businessman and a sound financier, he was a brilliant lawyer." He was also a "liberal" with a "strong sympathy for the underdog."[48] More accurately, to adapt a phrase now associated with the bailout of banks during the 2008 global "meltdown," Dawes was found to be "too big to charge."

* * *

While Dawes was concealing his criminality, better American minds had been concentrated by America's economic plight. Every thoughtful commentator knew that the Depression had shown that something was fundamentally wrong with American capitalism and that the cure would involve much more than the orthodox dependence on the market righting itself.

Some wrote scathingly of the problems of capitalism exacerbated by laissez-faire, including the many opportunities to organize and profit from crime that the lack of effective regulation made possible. Commentators such as Charles Beard, Walter Lippmann and Murray Gurfein argued that organized crime was one of the unfortunate products of unfettered capitalism. It followed from their analyses that more rigorous business regulation was necessary to lessen the opportunities for successful organized crime in legal markets. In 1931 for example, Beard, a leading historian of the time, wrote an article on the widely disseminated myth that America's greatness was based on "rugged individualism." "The cold truth is that the individualist creed of everybody for himself and the devil take the hindmost is principally responsible for the distress in which Western civilization finds itself – with investment racketeering at one end and labor racketeering at the other. ... It has become a danger to society."[49] The same year, Lippmann, an influential newspaper columnist, recommended that Americans should at least inquire "whether certain forms of racketeering are not the result under adverse conditions of the devotion of legislatures, courts, and public opinion to the philosophy of laissez faire."[50] Again in 1931, Gurfein, a legal expert, wrote a definitional essay on "racketeering," – a term synonymous with "organized crime" – that can now be seen as remarkably prescient given the wave of corporate and banking scandals that have characterized the twenty-first century to date. He listed the following characteristics of the American business system as key to the problem of organized crime: "the pegged market in stocks, the manipulation of subsidiary companies, the reckless puffing of securities, the taking by corporate management of inordinately large bonuses, the rather widespread evasion of taxes, the easy connivance of politicians in grabs." These "illustrated the temper of the times" and furnished "a key to the parasitical racketeer," he continued. "The racketeer as a type," he summed up, "is a natural evolutionary product of strict laissez faire."⁵¹

The cures chosen for organized business crime were radical and successfully sustained America through the Great Depression – the greatest crisis in its history – helping the country to prosper until the 1980s. Particularly important were the Glass–Steagall Banking Act of 1933 and the Securities Exchange Act of 1934. The first established a clear division between deposit-taking institutions and investment banks – so that banks were unable to use government-guaranteed deposits for high-risk speculation.

The second set up a new agency – the Securities and Exchange Commission – charged with enforcing basic marketplace rules. In other words, these reforms and others put the business world under basic restraints and policed them. These reforms did not end organized business crimes but they ensured that business crimes were checked to the extent that they could not pose a risk to the stability of the capitalist system. As we shall see in Part III, these Roosevelt-era checks were removed in the last decades of the twentieth century.

In the meantime, organized crime was defined and combated in ways that de-emphasized organized business crime and corruption. Dawes' main importance in the context of organized crime control is that he was the man who introduced the US government to an understanding of organized crime that associated the problem almost exclusively with gangsters of foreign origin. A seed had been sown that got America's laws, systems and "respectable" criminals off the hook.

Dawes had put into circulation the idea that crime was organized by a foreign "super-government." However, the idea would have faded away without someone the press and the business community could call the head of this crime super-government. In October of 1926 they found one in Al Capone. A flurry of articles reported that he was "king of the underworld."[52] It was nonsense but repetition made it universally believed.

4

Al Capone as Public Enemy Number One

On October 18, 1928, after two years' pressure from Dawes, President Calvin Coolidge authorized the special intelligence unit of the US Bureau of Internal Revenue to begin an investigation into the income tax affairs of Al Capone.[53] The effort intensified after St. Valentine's Day 1929 when the killing of seven men associated with the bootlegger Bugs Moran was thought to be Capone's work. Soon afterwards, a deputation of Chicago business interests, led by Frank Loesch of the CCC, went to Washington to ask President Herbert Hoover to intervene. Hoover then pressured Andrew Mellon, Secretary of the Treasury, to go after Capone. There was irony here given that Mellon later testified before Congress that he used thugs like Capone to break workers' unions while building up his family's empire in aluminum. Mellon was also found to have been evading taxes on a scale that made Capone's tax infractions seem minimal.[54]

Loesch and the CCC are usually described, like Dawes, in fulsome terms in the Capone literature, as brave, upright "crusaders" against crime. Loesch, the CCC's most prominent publicist during the 1920s, was a corporate lawyer who, like many of his white Anglo-Saxon colleagues, believed strongly that only his class, race and faction possessed honesty and integrity.[55] Loesch also followed Dawes in articulating the crudely xenophobic interpretation of organized crime that came to dominate popular and professional perceptions of the problem. In a speech to students at Princeton University in 1930, Loesch proclaimed: "It's the foreigners and the first generation of Americans who are loaded on us ... The real Americans are not gangsters ... the Jews [are] furnishing the brains and the Italians the brawn."[56] He would have been thinking, in particular, of the Jew, Arnold Rothstein, in New York, and the Italian, Capone, in Chicago.

Shortly after his speech, according to Loesch's account, he had a colleague from the CCC bring him a list of "the outstanding hoodlums, known murderers, murderers which you and I know but can't prove." He selected 28 mainly Irish, Italian and Jewish men from the original list and, as he related, "put Al Capone at the head and his brother [Ralph] next ... I called them Public Enemies, and so designated them in my letter to the Chief of Police, the Sheriff, every law enforcing officer."[57] Calling ordinary criminals "Public Enemies" was another early step in the process of making organized crime a national security issue.

After Loesch and his allies' trip to Washington, a coordinated attack was launched on Capone. Eliot Ness of the Treasury Department's Prohibition Bureau made sudden, unexpected wrecking expeditions on Capone's operations and destroyed valuable equipment and merchandize but otherwise achieved very little despite the adulation that was heaped on him. The media presented Ness as Capone's nemesis, the representative of good, professional, efficient and modern policing in a triumph against omnipotent evil. The headline story on Capone's tax indictment, for example, was "Tapped Wires Closed Net on Scarface Al – Eliot Ness, Graduate of Chicago University, Wins Credit for Long Effort." It began: "The assault by the Federal Government on the ramparts of the king of the underworld reached a climax today when Al Capone and sixty-eight of his vassals were indicted in what investigators from Washington termed the greatest prohibition case ever developed."[58] Ness in fact played only a supporting role in this case.

Capone's ultimate arrest and imprisonment for tax evasion in October 1931 was orchestrated by the Intelligence Unit of Elmer Irey, chief of the United States Treasury Enforcement Branch, aided in significant ways by a group of businessmen that became known as the "Secret Six" owing to a desire to operate anonymously. "Secret Six" money, for example, enabled one of Irey's chief investigators, Pat O'Rourke, to buy gaudy clothes in gangster styles: a white hat with a snap brim, several purple shirts, and checked suits. He also used "Secret Six" money to rent a room at the Lexington Hotel, which Capone was known to frequent, reading newspapers or playing dice games with bodyguards.[59] The money also helped Treasury agents to produce informants and collect documentary evidence.

Crime writer Gus Russo's verdict on Dawes, Loesch and the "Secret Six" is accurate and damning:

> the Chicagoans "crusade" was in large part a self-serving exercise in hypocrisy ... [It] was another xenophobic lynch mob that had no qualms about establishing its fortunes on the backs of musclemen provided by Capone's syndicate. Their civic activism was a barely concealed attempt to improve their own business fortunes by getting the gangs off the streets in time for the upcoming World's Fair.[60]

Capone was indeed, as an Internal Revenue Service (IRS) agent put it at the time, a "fathead, just a front for respectable businessmen who pulled the strings behind the scenes."[61]

At the trial, the only defense his lawyers could offer was that Capone had not known that money from illegal businesses was taxable. He was sentenced to eleven years in a federal penitentiary.[62]

The representatives of big business, mainly in the guise of the CCC, the "Secret Six" and the press, led the way in creating a Capone of mythical demonic proportions. Loesch of the CCC, in his efforts to exaggerate Capone's importance, often revealed an anti-union agenda. Testifying before a judiciary committee in 1932, for example, he made the often-repeated and rarely challenged claim that "fully two thirds of the unions in Chicago are controlled by, or pay tribute to, Al Capone's terroristic organization." No substance was offered to support the claim beyond Loesch's assertion that "those who know the situation" believed it.[63] Many authors in the years that followed chose to repeat the claim without taking the trouble to substantiate it. In reality, most unions were as honestly or dishonestly run as the business organizations that backed the CCC. By the 1920s some unions did begin to ape the tactics of businesses during strikes and enrolled gangsters to break the heads of strikebreakers. Both sides in these cases used violence and deceit and in every way possible fought dirty to win.

5
Al Capone and the Business of Crime

With Capone's conviction, big government, pushed by big business, had got its man. Few took notice when the gangster made a rather pathetic attempt to reach an accommodation with the authorities, including big business interests. He told the Washington *Herald*: "I don't interfere with big business. None of those big business guys can say that I ever took a single dollar from them. I don't interfere with their racket. Why can't they leave my racket alone?"[64]

Capone never bossed Chicago or even his many gangster partners. On the contrary, as the historian Mark Haller has demonstrated, "The group known to history as the Capone gang is best understood not as a hierarchy directed by Al Capone but as a complex set of partnerships." Capone, his brother Ralph, Frank Nitti and Jack Guzik formed partnerships with others to launch numerous bootlegging, gambling and vice activities in the Chicago Loop, South Side and several suburbs, including their base of operations, Cicero. These various enterprises, Haller continues, "were not controlled bureaucratically. Each, instead, was a separate enterprise of small or relatively small scale. Most had managers who were also partners. Coordination was possible because the senior partners, with an interest in each of the enterprises, exerted influence across a range of activities." Like other criminal entrepreneurs, Capone did not have the skills or the personality for the detailed bureaucratic oversight of a large organization. Criminal entrepreneurs are, as Haller demonstrated, "instead, hustlers and dealers, for whom partnership arrangements are ideally suited. They enjoy the give and take of personal negotiations, risk-taking, and moving from deal to deal."[65]

Capone's business dealings resembled those of Rothstein, his contemporary in New York, and most other gangster businessmen. Neither of them set up any formal criminal organizational structures – which would have increased the chances of prosecution. "The strength of all these separate partnerships and deals," according to one astute writer, "lay in their separateness. The failure of one did not jeopardize the others."[66] Rothstein was murdered in 1928. Donald Henderson Clarke, Rothstein's first biographer, took issue with the many reporters who called him "a criminal mastermind." "Rothstein was a great money lender," Henderson wrote, "Those closest to him admit that the money he handled was 'dirty,' but they don't believe that Rothstein himself ever arranged the details of any criminal racket. He would finance persons, of whose ability to repay he was certain, and his power and prestige went with the backing."[67] Popular fiction writers, notably F. Scott Fitzgerald and Damon Runyon, influenced a later generation of "true crime" writers who constructed Rothstein, "The Brain," as a kind of Jewish mentor to the Sicilian Charles "Lucky" Luciano, therefore adding minimal substance to claims that he was a "founding father" of "modern organized crime." Loesch had sown the seed for these claims with his xenophobic claim that with organized crime, "the Jews [are] furnishing the brains and the Italians the brawn."[68]

Capone was finished as a criminal power even before the Valentine's Day massacre. His temporary, ballyhooed success, however, showed the way for many more discreet operators to make deals or set up and run the many thousands of ventures that provided Americans with illegal goods and services, effectively nullifying all prohibitions.

Some of these operators went further and set up enterprises that made a mark in industries and areas that were not yet fully dominated by corporations such as in entertainments, sports and leisure. Unless they were fools they would "go with what's working" – an old show business maxim – and fade away, taking their profits, when things started to unravel.

Inset 2: The Legends and Lives of Al Capone and Eliot Ness

In 1931, Capone's first biographer, Fred D. Pasley, called him the "John D. Rockefeller of bootlegging," "supreme and unchallenged as Chicago's bootleg boss," "commissioner of lawlessness."[69] "To enforce his will," according to another biographer in 1971, Capone, "had an army of sluggers, bombers and machine gunners, 700 to 1,000 strong."[70] Martin Short, author of a 1984 book and a television documentary series, *Crime Inc.*, wrote that he was "The most powerful man in the city [of Chicago]".[71] In 2010, a more recent biographer, Jonathan Eig, called him "the undisputed boss of the Chicago crime scene."[72] Thousands more books, magazine articles, documentaries and films reflect his imaginary supremacy over Chicago. The version that most writers of the Capone story present to Americans and the rest of the world is that he was "King" of Chicago. This was the description that Tin Tin's creator, Hergé, used to describe Capone to generations of children and the mothers and fathers who read *Tin Tin in America*, first published in 1931 and still selling well more than eight decades later.[73] The only substance for these claims about Capone's supremacy is repetition.

* * *

Born in 1899, as a young man Capone contracted syphilis at a time during or soon after the First World War when the disease was common. He was one of the 20 percent of syphilis victims of the time to die from the disease.[74]

For a few years during the 1920s, Capone and his partners made a great deal of money in scores of businesses that illegally provided Chicagoans opportunities to drink alcohol, gamble and visit prostitutes. When Capone was convicted of tax evasion in 1931, his career was over. He served most of his sentence at Alcatraz, a small island in San Francisco Bay. In 1936 Capone was reported as "dodging death" as fellow prisoners were threatening to kill him, allegedly for not buying a boat in which to escape.[75]

On November 16, 1939 Capone was released after having served seven years and having paid all fines and back taxes. By then he was suffering from paresis derived from the untreated syphilis. He spent some time in hospital before retiring to his Florida home where his doctor described him as having the mentality of a twelve-year-old. He died due to a stroke and pneumonia on January 25, 1947. He was said to have died penniless; certainly his children did not lead affluent lives.[76] His departure from Chicago's criminal world made no impact on the organization of bootlegging, gambling and prostitution – Chicagoans continued to pay for these goods and services and corrupt networks continued to supply them.

Although Capone and his partners did make big profits they had to share it with large numbers of professionals and officials who allowed their enterprises to function. Professionals such as doctors, accountants, bondsmen and defense lawyers, and professionals within the law enforcement and criminal justice systems, were essential to the success of any illegal enterprise. Capone and his partners took most of the risks, mainstream professionals took much of the money with minimal risk.

The most obvious risk for gangsters was that of being shot at by rival gangsters. This happened most spectacularly on September 19, 1926 while Capone was having lunch at the Hawthorne Hotel in Cicero. "Seven or eight large automobiles," according to the *Rockford Morning Star*, "swept down the street in front of the inn and poured their bullets towards the building." Capone survived this machine gun assault flat on the floor of the hotel's restaurant.[77] Not surprisingly Capone was a nervous man. After this attempt on his life he traveled around in an armored sedan, appropriately described as a "portable fort."[78]

Capone's political weakness was amply demonstrated by the treatment he received during the autumn of 1927 when Bill Thompson, the mayor of Chicago, made an attempt to gain the Republican nomination for the presidential campaign of the following year. Realizing that Capone's notoriety was a liability for his ambitions, he ordered his chief of police, Michael Hughes, to begin a campaign of harassment against Capone – arresting those working with Capone on tenuous charges, repeatedly raiding brothels, gambling houses and breweries associated with Capone, and keeping the man himself under constant and intrusive surveillance.

On December 5, Capone announced that he was going to leave Chicago for St. Petersburg in Florida but, in the event, went to the west coast instead. In Los Angeles he registered at the Hotel Biltmore under the name Al Brown but lasted less than two days before he was recognized. On being told to leave the city by the police, he was quoted as making the complaint, "Whoever heard of anybody being run out of Los Angeles that had money?" As he traveled eastwards by train there were police waiting at every stop to make sure he didn't get off. When he got to Joliet, Illinois, 40 miles south-west of Chicago, he was arrested and charged with carrying a concealed weapon. He spent a night in jail and then a few days later paid a fine to get free. When he finally got to Chicago he was a virtual prisoner in his mother's home. William O'Connor, Chicago's Chief of Detectives, ordered ten policemen to prevent him from leaving. They were told to "arrest the gangster as a suspicious character if he ventures out and to arrest any of his followers who try to visit him." He would only be let out to catch a train out of the city.[79]

Early in 1928 Capone found somewhere in Florida that would accept him and his money. He bought a mansion on Palm Island in Biscayne Bay. The property was a testament to the profits to be made from illegal enterprise. It had 14 rooms, a 100-foot frontage with a three-room gatehouse, and ran 300 feet back to the bay. Capone then spent around $100,000 on improvements, including possibly the largest private swimming pool in Florida.[80] After a brief respite from his troubles with the law and the lawless, the federal authorities ended his criminal career completely.

He never "ran" Chicago nor its rackets. As corporations were showing by the 1920s, and as governments had shown for millennia, you need bureaucracies to run things, and Capone and his partners did not work within bureaucratic structures. They paid for the services of accountants, lawyers and other professionals but their enterprises were not large-scale hierarchical organizations. Some failed, many did very well.

Although Capone died in pathetic circumstances in 1947, his fame continued to grow and spread mainly through print and film media. Thanks to Hergé, and countless other writers, film directors, newspaper editors and documentary makers, Capone remains the world's most famous gangster by a distance. His face has become a brand worthy of being placed on trainers and underpants. Millions throughout the world are able to bring to mind at least some of the iconic moments and images associated with "Scarface Al's" career: jazz-era bootlegging and speakeasies, the bulletproof Cadillac, the Atlantic City "conference" (see Part II, Chapter 1), the St. Valentine's Day massacre, the naming of Capone as "Public Enemy Number One," the pursuit of him by "Untouchable" federal police officers, led by Eliot Ness, his conviction on tax charges and finally imprisonment on Alcatraz Island, an iconic federal prison intended to isolate "criminals of the vicious and irredeemable type" from the rest of society. Capone's association with these moments and images is not enough, however, to explain his continuing status as history's most famous gangster, and an explanation for this will be offered in Part II.

Eliot Ness, who had played a minor if exaggerated role in the pursuit and conviction of Capone, had as sad an end as Capone himself. After his time in Prohibition-era Chicago, he became public safety director for the city of Cleveland, and attempted without success to build on his crime-busting reputation. His tenure was marred by a failure to solve or even to contribute to solving a case known as the "Torso Murders." A serial killer had murdered and dismembered at least six victims in the Cleveland area over a period of two years while Ness showed little interest in the case or any other that promised little by way of favorable publicity. One of his most self-delusional stunts has been described by Capone biographer, Laurence Bergreen:

> Ness cultivated his image as a gangbuster by addressing impressionable audiences, for whom he inflated his deeds in Chicago to heroic proportions. "Thousand Young Dick Tracys Thrill and Cheer As Ness Tells How G-Men Got Capone Gang," ran a representative headline in the *Cleveland News*. The audience consisted of children, who, before receiving their Dick Tracy badges, had to submit to a lecture by Ness about his exploits on the trail of Al Capone. When Ness finished and they received their souvenirs at last, Ness told the cheering throng, "You have a badge just like mine, only maybe yours is a little smaller. When you grow up to be a man with long pants perhaps your badge will grow up with you, and when that time comes I'd like to have you all working with me as real detectives."[81]

However, Ness' stock, already falling because of the "Torso Murders," fell even further when, ironically as public safety director, he drunkenly drove into another car, injuring its driver, before leaving the scene of the accident too quickly but not before the driver had noticed that the license plate of the car that had injured him was the very distinctive EN-3.[82]

After failed efforts to join the Federal Bureau of Investigation (FBI) and win elections for political office, Ness moved from job to job, bar to bar, and became in Bergreen's words "a sad, sweet-natured drunk," or in the description of his colleagues at work, "Elegant Mess." He eventually found in Oscar Farley, a sportswriter with United Press International, someone to listen to his embellished gangbusting stories, with "Eliot Ness cast into the starring role reality had denied him."[83] Ness died in 1957 before his "as-told-to" book was published as *The Untouchables* and before the Colombia Broadcasting System televised the book, as a two-part film that would turn into a series. Subsequent films that featured Ness drew more from the TV series than the historical record.

6

Americanizing Mussolini's Phony War against the Mafia

Prompted by the killing of Mafiosi, Tony Lombardo, on September 7, 1928, Frank Loesch of the CCC chose to announce that the Italian dictator Benito Mussolini's recent "annihilation" of the Mafia should be replicated in America. Like many claims made by and about "Il Duce," the claim that he had annihilated the Mafia was false. Although Mussolini's campaign was more fraud and repression than substance, its mythical success played a significant part in the construction of organized crime control in the United States and elsewhere that to date has not been acknowledged.

Loesch declared that:

law enforcement ... has broken down completely when it comes to the arrest, prosecution, and attempt to convict such gang murderers as the Mafia gunmen. Who are the gangsters seemingly tied up to this family tree? Scarface Al Capone, vice, gambling and liquor king, and the recently murdered Tony Lombardo. Lombardo is dead, but his organization – the Mafia – is still organized and ready to function uninterruptedly ... All the kidnappings, blackmail, terrorism, murders, and countless other crimes committed in the name of the dread Mafia sprang from the minds of Lombardo and the men fighting to take the place vacated by his death ... The Mafia must be suppressed here as it was by Mussolini in Italy. The upper hand which the criminals are obtaining in this city by their alliance with politicians not only gives the city a bad reputation, but it will certainly end in anarchy if permitted to go on a few years longer.[84]

Loesch was one of many who openly expressed admiration for Mussolini. In 1927, the *Literary Digest*, responding to a sense of a leadership vacuum in the world, conducted an editorial survey entitled,

"Is There a Dearth of Great Men?" The survey found that Mussolini was mentioned in newspaper editorials more frequently than any other.[85] Mussolini established good relationships with the Republican administrations of Harding, Coolidge and Hoover during the 1920s, and the Democrat Franklin Roosevelt went as far as to write in a letter to a colleague that he "was deeply impressed by what he [Mussolini] has accomplished and his evidenced honest purpose in restoring Italy" and said to another colleague, "I don't mind telling you in confidence that I am keeping in fairly close touch with that admirable Italian gentleman."[86]

Until the Second World War, Mussolini had more supporters than detractors in America, led by the publisher William Randolph Hearst. Hearst had gone to Italy in 1931 to visit "Il Duce" and was moved by the dictator's charisma and "enlightened administration." "Mussolini is a man," he had written earlier, "I have always greatly admired, not only because of his astonishing ability, but because of his public service."[87] As we shall see later in the chapter, Hearst's admiration for the Italian dictator has particular relevance for the framing of discussion about organized crime in America.

Mussolini had taken power in 1923, and after the killing of his most prominent opponent, Giacomo Matteotti, in 1924, fascist violence became more discreet. Every Italian, however, understood that the threat of violence was always there.

Every regime requires more than brute force to sustain itself and Mussolini's was no exception. His promise to impose order on post-First World War Italy gained him the support of big and small business interests, as well as landowners, north as well as south, and the Catholic Church, at least until 1931. All of these were alarmed at the prospect of a militant working class in the north and the center and the possibility of a complete societal breakdown in the south and Sicily. Soon after Mussolini's successful coup, the labor movement was no longer a threat as trade unions that fought for workers' rights were replaced by fascist unions.[88] The officials of these were more responsive to the wishes of the bosses than the workers and they would have the backing of the fascist state if they chose to use violence to eliminate dissent. Many powerful sections of Italian society may have been appalled by the extremes of Fascism, but ultimately they acquiesced in officially sanctioned plundering and murder.

Very little of this reached the world's press, and America's press in particular. For the most part both the American left and right were positive about Mussolini's regime and many looked at its policies and practices as a guide to dealing with the disorder of the post-First World War era. From the left, the muckraking journalist Ida Tarbell, for example, traveled to Italy to meet Mussolini and let the US State Department know that his regime's new labor laws "constituted an admirable social experiment."[89] A view from the right in *Collier's* represented "Il Duce's" rise to power as "the triumph of law and order over anarchy and radicalism."[90]

* * *

Mussolini's main card in gaining power was the promise to restore order – the rule of law was secondary – and, for a few years, his regime tried to bring order to that part of the nation where it was threatened by something other than socialism and trade unionism. Of the undeveloped and violent south, Sicily stood out as the most "troublesome" and "disturbed." "Attempts to implement the law," writes Christopher Duggan in *Fascism and the Mafia*, "broke down in the face of local non-cooperation; when people did agree to testify to the authorities, it was often only to bear false witness against their enemies." The state found itself isolated in this world of private justice – vendettas and day-to-day brutality settled matters more than police and courts. The state looked for an explanation that bypassed the need to address a manifestly unfair distribution of wealth and, Duggan argues, "discovered" a secret society, "led by men of violence, that tyrannized the unconsenting mass of the population."[91] Something that could be claimed to be a state within a state and therefore constituting an unacceptable threat to the fascist state. Like all conspiracy theories this one had some truth to it, but it was still a jump from the undeniable to the unbelievable. Mafias undeniably existed but they were never a centrally organized, unified secret society of crime. Local "Mafia" hierarchies existed in a region that had little transportation infrastructure to speak of, and so island-wide structures could not have existed.

Mussolini's chief response to a breakdown in order in Sicily was to appoint Cesare Mori first, in 1924, as police prefect of the province of Trapani and then, the following year, of the island's main city, Palermo.

He was a member of the northern gentry sent down to the despised south to impose a fascist order, his main task being to replace the nebulous power of various elites with the centrally organized power of the fascist state.

The Italian and foreign press chose only to report positives about the Fascists' anti-organized crime efforts, turning blind eyes to any critical reports that might have come their way. In January 1928 came the first of endlessly repeated claims that the state had crushed the Mafia. *Il Popolo d'Italia* announced that the Mafia had received "a mortal blow" and that soon "the prophylactic work of justice would be finished and the Mafia spoken of no more." Foreign newspapers followed suit. The *Times* in London, for example, stated that "Mussolini has dared to threaten the monster in its native haunts, and has throttled it with success."[92] Syndicated newspapers in the United States carried the headline: "Mussolini Gives Mafia Death Blow."[93] Mussolini's brother, Arnaldo, followed this up the following month in a leading article in *Il Popolo*, announcing that "the work of repression was over and that now the Mafia had been destroyed, Fascism should aim to improve the island's economy." The *New York Times* elaborated on the same theme with a leading article entitled: "The Mafia is dead, a new Sicily is born."[94]

Articles written by Richard Washburn Child, former US Ambassador to Italy, for the Hearst newspaper chain in April and May 1928, detailed the campaign in purple prose. They were headlined, "How Mussolini Smashed the Mafia," and serialized over several weeks. The first announced itself as the

First Thrilling Account, from the "Inside," of the Uprooting and Throttling of the World's Deadliest Secret Society, Which for Centuries Terrorized Four Million People with "the Dark, the Knife, Silence!" – Written on the Ground in Sicily by the Famous Novelist After Access to Official Files and the Orders Oaths, Rituals, and Records of Vengeance Never Before Revealed.

The second, published a week later, featured "Mussolini's plan to unmask the Mafia," described as "once a powerful sinister secret society; now a huge, fiercely writhing monster, helpless under Mussolini's heel."[95] A third, published on May 6, made a didactic point to American readers about "the lesson to American criminology in Mussolini's stamping out of the menace through his special agent, the great Mori."[96] In a fourth article, published on June 3, Child offered an early articulation of a theme that would be transmitted countless times in American popular culture over the next few decades. He told a story involving one of Mori's round-ups and concluded that one young man caught up in the arrests had learned a lesson: "the State is strong and pays – and crime is weak and loses." "This," Child stressed, "is the story Mori is telling as to the Mafia. And it is a story which will go around the world."[97] Hundreds of journalists did indeed ensure that the story of how Fascism beat the Mafia would go round the world, and few followed up on evidence that challenged the message.

Neither Mussolini, Mori nor Child had any real idea what the Mafia really was. As the historian Duggan explained, since 1860 and Italian independence the word "Mafia" had become encrusted with so many confused and sinister connotations that its most powerful aspect lay in the moral indignation that the term aroused. Separate groups of extortionists were conflated together as a single entity that was described in ways that made it into "a beast of terrifying proportions." In newspapers, for example, it was referred to as "a huge and manifold octopus with long and impalpable tentacles," "a repulsive and mastodontic sphinx" and "an insatiable she-wolf possessed of every lust." Monsters such as these were best destroyed by heroes, and Mori would often be compared to figures from Greek mythology such as Perseus and Hercules.[98]

Private violence was certainly often provided by separate Mafia brotherhoods, and these created repressive local fiefdoms within the wider regional and national structures. Mafia brotherhoods did therefore serve and sometimes dominate the more established landowning elites. However, the standard fascist interpretation of the Mussolini/Mori/Mafia story, although false, was much easier for media outlets to transmit. The Mafia, according to the fascist interpretation, was a state within the state and therefore Mussolini's regime granted Mori extraordinary powers to crush the anti-state. Among these new powers were precedents for present-day organized crime control powers, notably a 1926 law which laid down that people described by informers as bosses, partners or sympathizers of associations which have a criminal character or which are in any way dangerous to the community could be denounced, immediately arrested and put on trial.

The principle adopted, as explained by Michele Pantaleone in *The Mafia and Politics*, was that:

> no crime, even if committed several years earlier, should go unpunished, and Mori made an agreement with most of the judges by which every crime could and should provide the opportunity for liberating the countryside and the town from the greatest number of "reprobates" who were thought to be members of criminal gangs – gangs which sometimes only existed in the imagination of the police.[99]

Armed with these powers, Mori made sudden and simultaneous round-ups of hundreds of suspected Mafiosi in sweeps throughout large parts of the island. Many fugitives were brought into the dragnet by savage threats of reprisals including the public slaughtering of their livestock and the arrest of or implied violence towards their wives and children.[100] This would conclude with mass convictions of both innocent and guilty alike.[101]

As Pantaleone explained:

> Evidence was obtained with repellent cynicism, and nearly always consisted of a confession extracted after hours, often days, of medieval torture, including the so-called *cassata* torture which became famous. ... The suspected criminal was laid on his back on a wooden case about 3 feet long, 2 feet 6 inches wide and 1 foot 6 inches high. His dangling hands and feet were fastened with wires to the sides of the case. The wretched man was then drenched with brine and whipped with an ox-thong. In this way the lashes were the more painful but left no mark. Then his hair and his nails were torn out and the soles of his feet burnt. He was given electric shocks, his genitals were forcibly squeezed, and every now and then a funnel was stuck into his mouth, his nostrils were pinched, and he was made to swallow salt water till his stomach swelled.[102]

Duggan noted that Mori's police displayed some ingenuity in denying all knowledge of torture. One suspect was so badly beaten that he had to be taken to hospital. The official report of the incident noted that he had "smashed with a blow of his head the glass in the door that separates the guardroom from the security cell, and was injured!"[103]

After being tortured, suspects were then taken before the judges who would force them to confess while still in a state of shock. Judges, therefore, were knowingly instrumental in Mori's repression, furthering their careers in the process, and like the lawyers who acted as counsel in the trials, enriching themselves at the expense of justice. Only a few lawyers were brave enough to speak of the lack of firm evidence against their clients. Most concluded that it would not help their career by challenging verdicts that were foregone conclusions. Besides, they would risk being tarred as Mafiosi themselves if they did.[104]

Sometimes two different gangs were tried and sentenced for the same crime by different courts, and people were tried and sentenced for events that had never taken place. All guarantees of legality were wiped out. A great many criminals were punished but so, unfortunately, were many innocent people. There were also many victims of slanderous accusations by self-interested go-getters, for once people realized the superficiality and hastiness of legal procedure, they took advantage of it to rid themselves of enemies by giving false information to Mori's men.[105]

Between October 1927 and the summer of 1929 at least 15 major Mafia trials were held. Photos were taken for the newspapers to show Mori's men marching alleged Mafiosi from the jails to the courtroom where giant cages had been built to hold hundreds of defendants at a time. The Bagheria trial, for example, which began on October 18, 1929, had 260 defendants. Newspapers in Italy and around the world showed the photographic evidence of Italian state power, but failed to report on the slow and often inconclusive progress of the cases after the dramatic but brief caged openings. Years passed and usually, in the end, short sentences were imposed.[106]

As Duggan's account shows, Mori terrorized parts of Sicily in the manner of an invading army in ways that hit the poor hardest while protecting the interests of the local landed elites. Mussolini and his Fascists were aware that this approach condemned the island to backwardness and reaction but chose to take part in the construction of a legend to conceal the absurdities, injustices and cruelties of Mori's campaign and, in the final analysis, the crushing pointlessness of it all. He had orchestrated a massive effort that ultimately achieved very little beyond protecting the interests of the island's landed elite. Hundreds of real Mafiosi were certainly convicted but they were mostly low-level criminals who received short sentences. The state itself took over many of the functions previously performed by Mafiosi. Police state violence now controlled class tensions in Sicily just as it did throughout mainland Italy. Rural discontent in the island was then eased by the recruitment of thousands of landless peasants into the police and the army. The latter, particularly when Mussolini decided to invade Ethiopia in 1935.

The campaign against the Mafia resulted in misery for many of the Sicilian poor. Mussolini had been informed of the negative consequences of Mori's repression as early as March 1928. He was sent a report by General Antonino Di Giorgio, commander of Sicily's armed forces which informed him that The Mori campaign had been counterproductive. Its excesses and corruption had damaged the fascist regime's reputation: "The long lines of handcuffed people you see on lorries, trains and stations, the disconsolate crowds of women and children who wait in the rain outside the prisons and courts, all lend themselves perfectly to damaging remarks and the propaganda of hatred." He concluded with the understatement that "the operation against the Mafia has not had, because of the way it was conducted, a beneficial effect on society."[107]

As for organized crime control, the years of repression only amounted to a temporary disruption in the activities of the fragmented criminal groups misleadingly referred to by the Italian state and its cooperating press as a single, centralized Mafia collective. Certainly criminal networks were disrupted but they were not eradicated, and criminal violence remained a primary means of maintaining social order in the interests of the south's landowning elites. However, to support Mussolini's claim that the Mafia had been exterminated and therefore no longer existed, newspapers stopped reporting Mafia activities. Rational Mafiosi criminals became fascist criminals while "Il Duce" remained in power.

By the 1930s the word "Mafia" had almost completely disappeared from the fascist press in Italy. The international press also failed to challenge the regime's contention that the "monster" had been destroyed.

Despite Mussolini's widely reported assertions that the Mafia was dead, Mafia brotherhoods were not suppressed and his regime knew this. In response it set up the *Ispettorato Generale di Pubblica Sicurezza per la Sicilia* – a body set up in 1933 which operated through to the end of the decade. The *Ispettorato* forced confessions out of Mafioso, conducted operations discreetly and used internment processes rather than trials. The regime punished alleged criminals by requiring them to live in a specified location such as one of the islands between Sicily and Africa for months and often years. The decision was taken by a board consisting of the heads of policing authorities and the fascist militia. The difference between these campaigns and those of Mori, according to the historian Vittorio Coco, "can be seen in the press coverage: In the 1920s Mori's activities were highlighted and newspaper columns were devoted to the various trial proceedings, but in the 1930s the very word 'Mafia' almost completely disappeared."[108] The fascist press did not wish to disturb the fiction that Mussolini and Mori had destroyed the "Mafia." Since the 1980s, as we shall see in Part III, the United States has adopted similar techniques to sustain claims that policing has brought organized crime in America under control.

In 1930s Sicily, *Ispettorato* officers, working from the many insider statements by Mafia members, wrote in a report that the Mafia "is not a simple state of mind or mentality, but propagates both these from its fully organized foundations." Mafia groups were secretive groups, criminal and violent in character, and they did have initiation ceremonies, courts of justice, their own language and system of recruitment, and strict codes of honor and conduct. Since their reach was limited to small parts of Sicily they were better described as quasi-local governmental criminal groups than a united "state within a state."[109]

7

"Organized Crime" in a Fascist State

Mussolini's regime was established in the first place through violence and organized criminality, and thanks to recent historical research there is abundant evidence that, once established, rather than suppressing organized crime in its largest southern island as it claimed, it organized crime in the whole of Italy. Activities that could be described as organized crime became routine during the years of the dictatorship, as R.J.B. Bosworth and Michael R. Ebner, among other historians, have detailed. In an article that analyses "everyday Mussolinism," Bosworth concludes from a study of a number of micro-histories that:

> the practices, hopes and ambitions of Fascism were always undercut by ... a Machiavellian understanding of the human condition. The local world was by definition split into factions. A war between "ins" and "outs" never ended. In this great human contest, campaigning methods were often covert and underhand, and could be brutal and violent. Men (and to some extent women) prospered through plots and vendettas. Men needed friends and patrons. Men should be permanently on the lookout for the short cut, the secret opportunity, the chance for a special favour.[110]

Ebner's work in *Ordinary Violence in Mussolini's Italy* frames an environment that suited day-to-day corrupt practices in the context of violence, "albeit an ordinary kind of violence" that was "central to the policies and institutions of Fascist rule." The archives he consulted showed that Fascists and police regularly "killed," "beat," "clubbed," "punched," "slapped," "kicked," and "hit" citizens. This violence was illegal and so therefore criminal. The archives also detailed various forms of "legal" violence, which mainly related to the policy of "confinement" whereby suspected criminals or political dissenters were sent to islands off the mainland or to impoverished parts of the south. Confinement involved the summary removal of people from their homes in the middle of the night:

> Confinement in dirty, vermin-infested jails and prisons, without explanation or access to law courts; ... the trauma of poverty, which the police state knowingly and sometimes deliberately inflicted on wives and children of detainees: the revocation of business permits for political motives ... and the political discrimination practised by Fascists in distributing employment, welfare, and other state assistance.

The case files of Fascism's detainees, he continued,

> reveal patterns of physical attacks, threats, intimidation, and discrimination that were so mundane, banal, and similar, that they can only have occurred repeatedly ... hundreds of thousands, even millions, of times over the course of two decades. Consequently, public and private spaces – particularly the iconic spaces of public life (e.g., the bar or the piazza) – were transformed into sites of fear and intimidation.

Finally, Ebner stresses the psychological consequences of an arbitrary system of justice:

> In word and deed the Fascist regime constantly reminded Italians that although it did not engage in physical or lethal violence on a *mass* scale, it claimed the right to beat, torture and kill *select* enemies with impunity. For the intended audience, this threat meant that one truly never knew what to expect from a knock on the door. The fear of punishment unfettered by the rule of law was, for many Italians, a form of terror.[111]

People had every reason to be frightened. There were legions of spies – men and women – from all walks of life. Journalists and lawyers were prominent but there were also union officials, soldiers, academics, writers, shopkeepers and priests. There was a whole series of strategies to recruit those who had access to specific sources of information – blackmail relating to family questions such as infidelity, economic hardship or the threat of long prison sentences. At the national level the intention was to head off threats to the regime. At the local level, hotel keepers, landlords, bar owners and street traders – all those who required licenses to ply their trade – would trade information for the right to cheat their customers.[112] Taken together, of course, this was a giant system of protected racketeering.

Systems of unchecked power create countless opportunities for unchecked and unpunished organized criminality. Those who prospered during Mussolini's years in power tended to be the already rich, or a new aggressive breed who were able to exploit and cheat Italian citizens with the blessing of the Italian state. Organized crime was routine and yet, as we shall see in Part IV, Mussolini had helped set the template for national systems of organized crime control, set up in recent decades by unaccountable bureaucracies and signed off by democratic representatives who thought they were protecting their constituents from states within states. Mussolini was the first to exploit the propaganda value of portraying organized crime in all its many shapes and forms as a single entity constituting a threat to a nation. However, it was his admirers in America who carried it forward.

* * *

Mussolini, as noted earlier, had no greater American supporter than the publishing mogul William Randolph Hearst. Hearst owned not only the chain of newspapers that circulated Child's panegyrics, but also magazines such as *Cosmopolitan* and *Harper's Weekly*, and he was a powerful Hollywood movie producer. Like "Il Duce," he took care of detail in his work to the extent that anyone in his employ who wrote or made films would be careful to stay close to the politics of their boss. "We do just what the Old Man orders," a reporter was quoted as saying; "one week he orders a campaign against rats. The next week he orders a campaign against dope peddlers. Pretty soon he's going to order a campaign against college professors. It's all bunk, but orders are orders."[113] Presidents Richard Nixon, Ronald Reagan and now Donald Trump would later echo the content of Hearst's anti-crime messages.

Hearst publications remained loyal to Mussolini and his methods until America came into conflict with Italy during the Second World War. Support for the dictator turned to opposition, but Hearst writers, and many others, remained loyal to Mussolini's characterization of the problem of organized crime and the way to control it. During and after the Second World War, as we shall see in Part III, they "Americanized" the analysis, helping to embed a far-fetched conspiracy theory into the public's consciousness.

In October 1932 this process began when many American newspapers owned by Hearst prominently featured an article under the byline of Benito Mussolini that gave top American officials and opinion-shapers a way to frame discussion of organized crime. Mussolini's recipe for crime control, and organized crime control in particular, became in effect the template for American organized crime control efforts, nationally and – because of America's global influence after the Second World War – internationally. State repression was the only answer to organized crime that was seriously considered. Various historical frauds were perpetrated to sustain this claim and, as a consequence, governmental efforts to control organized crime have been as hopelessly ineffectual and just as prone to corruption as the original fascist template.

Hearst publications circulated Mussolini's article under a variety of titles, including "Insists Governments Suppress Organized Crime"[114] and "Highest-Placed Criminals Must Be Mercilessly Suppressed, Says Mussolini." The latter was subtitled, "They are responsible for organized crime declares Il Duce."[115]

Mussolini, or more accurately his ghostwriter, began his piece by stressing the need to keep states "free from influences which have disintegrating and demoralizing effects," notably the modern criminal "armed with guns and aided by telephones, cars, airplanes, chemistry and physics." States must control their criminals, he argued, and continued "Crime must be fought with a united front, methodically and mercilessly ... The power of the state must always be superior to offenders against the state. The law of the land is the state's word." He then made an early statement of a policy that would, in the late twentieth century, be relabeled "zero tolerance": "Where there is any attempt to break the authority of the state by breaking its law, the attempt must be nipped in the bud and the offenders removed from any other opportunity to challenge the law of the land. If the offenders are not removed, then the state's word is humiliated and violated and from that moment there is no longer supreme law in the nation."

The "criminal association" was a far more serious matter for him than individual offenders. "It is a threat with which no state can afford to be menaced," he wrote, and continued:

> The destructive activity of those associations is an evil to society as well as a weakening factor to the state's authority. Their organized attacks against the constituted authorities is not a thing which the state can brush aside without a decisive answer. That answer is complete annihilation of such associations ... No illegal activity can be condoned ... Condoning and permitting even the most limited extra-legal acts may well become the pretense for committing further extra-legal acts. It broadens the challenge which organized violation casts before the state.

Mussolini was putting into simple terms what many Americans, including Dawes and Loesch, were already attempting to articulate, and he had an apparent success story to tell regarding the control of organized crime. American newspapers, as we have seen, had already broadcast the idea that Mussolini had given the Mafia its "death blow." "When I came into power in Italy," he reminded his readers in 1932, "I found we had a limited amount of organized crime. We were able within a very short time to control it and later to suppress it altogether."

He then gave his account of Mori's campaign without mentioning Mori. "The Mafia," Mussolini stated, "conducted its activities for its own particular ends, even carrying this as far as to interfere with elections." Before his regime was established the police had "but timid authority ... constantly torn between two policies, namely: Being prudent without energy, or being energetic without prudence. They succeeded in neither." He decided to give the police authority and not to give them ambiguous orders which were "designed not so much to deal with the many illegal organizations as to protect officials and their higher-placed accomplices who lacked the determined will to accept responsibility for acting energetically against extra-legal, anti-state societies." "We were energetic," he wrote, "in our methods and we succeeded in suppressing all organizations which had set up themselves as a state within a state."

Immodestly he added: "It is through these circumstances and by these examples that the caliber of a real statesman is gauged ... So far as

I am concerned. I can say with a clear conscience that my government never failed in this fundamental duty toward society."[116]

This prescription for organized crime control must have reached hundreds of thousands of Americans, but thanks to Hearst's Hollywood connection another version reached millions more. Less than a year after Mussolini's piece on organized crime control, Hearst received a copy of a novel by the British writer Thomas Frederick Tweed, called *Gabriel Over the White House*, and decided to use his film company – Cosmopolitan Pictures – to turn it into a film that owed a significant debt to Mussolini's organized crime control template.

As the historian Ben Urwand has detailed, this film was one of Hearst's pet projects. Jud Hammond, the hero of the book and the film, first appears as a politician who becomes US president through charm and fraud. After a car accident he becomes possessed with an unshakeable will to solve America's Depression-era problems in ways that resemble Mussolini's efforts in Italy. Hammond acts in forceful ways to address issues as diverse as mass unemployment, war debts, arms proliferation and, most relevant here, organized crime, represented in the story by the gangster, Nick Diamond. In the film the actor C. Henry Gordon played Diamond as an oily, scarred (probably a reference to the contemporary Al Capone) and arrogant bogeyman whose main function in the film is to provide sufficient provocation to justify retributive justice. In a speech that could have been paraphrased from the Mussolini article, Hammond characterized Diamond's operations as "a malignant cancerous growth eating at the spiritual health of the American people ... evil forces that must be, shall be, eliminated, so that our citizen pursuing his peaceful way will be no longer forced to conduct his business in the shadow of extortion and debt." Diamond was then shown gunning down the president's secretary and mistress in front of the White House itself.[117] Hammond's equivalent of Cesare Mori in the film was Harvey Beekman, who summoned Diamond and his men to a court martial where they were rapidly sentenced to death. "You're the last of the racketeers," Beekman told the gangster, "and why – because we have in the White House a man who has enabled us to cut the red tape of legal procedures and get back to first principles. An eye for an eye, Nick Diamond, a tooth for a tooth, a life for a life."[118] The gangsters were then shot by a firing squad with the Statue of Liberty prominently in the background – a juxtaposition of which Mussolini would have approved.

The film's release was timed to coincide with the inauguration of the new president, Franklin Delano Roosevelt, and not surprisingly, given Hearst's reach, was reviewed ecstatically in the newspapers. Richard E. Hays, writing in the Seattle *Daily Times*, opened with: "If the solution of all our national problems is as simple, and as magnificent, as suggested in an extra-ordinary cinema opening ... the Millenium [*sic*] must be close at hand." He then described *Gabriel Over the White House* as a "great picture, gripping entertainment and with a theme that will strike a responsive patriotic chord in American hearts as no other photoplay has done in many moons." Hammond, he adds, "deals with gangsterism effectively by wiping it out with tanks." Or, as the reviewer of *Morning Olympian* summarized the story, "He demands that congress give him the powers of a dictator. He fights directly with the 'king' of the racketeers and through a federal police force wipes him out." Fred M. White in the *Oregonian* described it as "an unusually thought-provoking" film and reported that "spectators at the United Artists yesterday expressed their approval by bursts of applause, an unusual demonstration for a film audience." W.R. Wilkinson in the *Hollywood Reporter* went too far: "What will happen when this picture is first shown in any theater in America? A first performance gathering will rush out to tell all who will listen of the astounding nature of this film entertainment. If the newspapers have not heard about it up until this time, they will rush to print with laudatory comment on the entertainment, write editorials about the message it bears, and will give it more free space, more editorial space, than has ever been given a picture before."[119] Despotism had not been sold like this before.

The policing authorities in *Gabriel Over the White House* roughed up the suspects and then shot them. More generally, the important point about most gangster movies of this era is that the state's representatives won nearly every battle on screen. On screen or in comic books were the only places that the great majority of Americans and people worldwide ever saw gangsters.

8
Gangbusting and Propaganda

Roosevelt's appreciation of Mussolini and a film that was clearly in line with fascist responses to crime reflected a feeling that was shared by many contemporaries in Depression-hit America. "If this country ever needed a Mussolini," Senator David Reed of Pennsylvania said in 1932, "it needs one now." "Leave it to Congress," he continued, and "we will fiddle around here all summer trying to satisfy every lobbyist, and we will get nowhere. The country does not want that. The country wants stern action, and action taken quickly."[120]

The Depression and fears about a general breakdown of law and order were the main reasons for a shift towards an authoritarian response to crime. The kidnapping of the baby son of aviator Charles Lindberg in 1932 served to crystallize anxieties.

In 1927, Lindberg had been the first to fly the Atlantic non-stop and single-handed. News of this feat was greeted with unprecedented mass excitement, and the adulation lasted long after the 1,800 tons of ticker tape had been swept up off the streets of New York. His picture still hung in countless schoolrooms and homes when his baby was abducted. Although around 300 people had been kidnap victims that year, because of the age and innocence of the Lindberg victim and his father's place in American mythology, this was seen as more than a crime against an individual. According to the New York *Herald Tribune*, the kidnapping was "a challenge to the whole order of the nation ... The truth must be faced that the army of desperate criminals which has been recruited in the last decade is winning its battle against society."[121] It was seen as a direct attack on the home, the country's symbol of security and stability.

In response to an editorial in the *Morning Oregonian* that related the kidnapping to an "invisible government of crime," a Mr. L.M. Harris wrote a letter, published on March 15, 1932, titled "What is Mussolini's Method? Suppression of Mafia Ought to Show Us How to Suppress Gangs." It contained a summary of the history of organized crime in the US that combinations of "true crime" writers and their sources in law enforcement would later make the standard narrative.

He began by making reference to the "Mafia society in Sicily" and the "bitter experience in New Orleans" (see Inset 1), and continued:

> The Mafia were ... the original "racketeers," and their evil influence grew to a vast wave of crime and murder and intimidation in Italy. About 1890, or thereabouts, this evil organization jumped from Sicily to America via New Orleans, and went into politics, corrupting law enforcement and creating an era of crime.
>
> The police ... incurred the vengeance of the Mafia who in the end murdered the New Orleans chief of police. Eleven Sicilians were indicted on suspicion of this crime. The jury were in fear, being intimidated, and acquitted. The result caused an infuriated mob of citizens to break into the jail and lynch the 11 Italians.
>
> Later in Italy, in Mussolini's regime, Mussolini took the Mafia up and has wiped out this notorious organization.
>
> We in America have a habit of criticizing Mussolini, and displaying a certain amount of egotism. If Mussolini can clean up gangs in Italy and make a clean sweep of them, it might pay to study the secret of his procedure over there.[122]

As we shall see in Part III, the current FBI website's account of organized crime history owes a debt to the xenophobic thought processes of Harris and many others who, unlike him, wrote for a living.

The Lindberg baby was later found dead. Bruno Richard Hauptmann was electrocuted for the crime in 1936. The case was one of the most investigated in history and, needless to say, no invisible government of crime, yet alone Mafia involvement, was discovered. Doubts remain as to Hauptmann's guilt, but the authorities were able to claim a victory.

Kidnapping is a crime where the victim takes center stage. Not so bank robbery. In the early Depression years, few Americans were talked or written about more than Bonnie Parker and Clyde Barrow, "Baby Face" Nelson, "Pretty Boy" Floyd and John Dillinger; outlaws from the American South and West who robbed banks and, for a short while, got away with it. Their methods were similar. They tended to be well armed, often with submachine guns, and prepared to take part in shoot-outs with the authorities. They made their escape at speed in cars and, if necessary, crossed state lines where the jurisdiction of their pursuers usually ended.

The political use of the phrase "organized crime" first increased dramatically in 1933 and 1934 when Roosevelt's Attorney General Homer S. Cummings orchestrated a war against kidnapping and bank robbery. The country, according to Cummings and echoing Mussolini, was "confronted with real warfare which an armed underground is waging upon organized society. It is a real war which confronts us all – a war that must be successfully fought if life and property are to be secure in our country ... Organized crime is an open challenge to our civilization, and the manner in which we meet it will be a test of our capacity for self-government."[123]

Much of this war was rhetoric accompanied by symbolic action, including a prison policy that owed a debt to the Mussolini regime's penal policy. For example, on October 12, 1933 Cummings announced that the federal government now had a new type of prison. This, he continued, was "Alcatraz Prison, located on a precipitous island in San Francisco Bay, more than a mile from shore. The current is swift and escapes are practically impossible. ... Here may be isolated the criminals of the vicious and irredeemable type so that their influence may not be extended to other prisoners who are disposed to rehabilitate themselves."[124] One magazine felt it was too close to shore and called for it to be located on a remote Pacific atoll. "America," according to *Real Detective*, "needs an isolated penal colony if it is ever to shake off the tentacles of the crime octopus."[125] Nevertheless Alcatraz almost immediately became part of American folklore.

The agency chosen to represent the New Deal's commitment to enforcement was the FBI. In 1934 the FBI was given additional jurisdiction over a variety of interstate felonies, such as kidnapping and auto-theft. Its director, J. Edgar Hoover, immediately exploited the publicity value of his new powers by directing his agents against the bank robbers, who had been avoiding capture by crossing state lines. In rapid succession "Baby Face" Nelson, "Pretty Boy" Floyd and John Dillinger were shot down by Hoover's agents. Although some surrendered and were taken alive, the toughness of the federal response was encapsulated by the much-quoted advice to agents by Attorney General Cummings: "Shoot to kill and then count ten."[126] Furthermore, by 1936 the FBI could claim with some justification that every kidnapping case in the country, including that of the Lindbergh baby, had been closed.[127] The expectation of a federal presence in these cases undoubtedly encouraged a more committed and professional response by local and state police. Kidnapping and bank robbery became much riskier occupations in America from the 1930s onwards.

Also in 1934, a new censorship code put an end to the type of gangster film that had been outraging moralists by "glorifying" criminals. Films like *Little Caesar*, *Public Enemy* and *Scarface* had featured the most dynamic actors of the day – Edward G. Robinson, Jimmy Cagney and Paul Muni respectively – playing gangsters as self-made men on their way up. Instead, in 1935 there was a new Hollywood campaign to glorify G-Men – the press name for FBI agents. That year there were seven G-Man movies sold by Hollywood as its contribution to the war on crime. "See Uncle Sam Draw His Guns to Halt the March of Crime," ran the ads for one of them. In the original *G-Man* (1935), James Cagney played an FBI agent as forcefully as he had played gangster Tommy Powers in *Public Enemy*. In films, comics and radio shows, law and order were in the hands of the US government and in fact were synonymous with the US government.[128]

Hoover not only helped create a new pro-police mythology but also became a prominent part of it. Before long his publicists had created an image for the FBI agent that lasted for decades. G-Men were dedicated, clean-cut, familiar with the most up-to-date, scientific techniques of crime detection and totally incorruptible. Books, magazines, even bubblegum cards echoed the same theme as the G-Men films: "Crime Does Not Pay" so long as the elite federal policemen and J. Edgar Hoover were around.

Hoover's publicists even turned the killing of an old woman into a triumph for law enforcement. FBI agents shot Kate Barker, mother of the kidnapper and bank robber, Fred Barker. The killing of an innocent, unarmed old woman was justified by an extraordinary story circulated by Hoover's publicists.

Mother and son were shot on January 16, 1935. News stories at the time described this as another G-Man success and suggested that "Ma" Barker was the brains behind a gang of desperadoes. In

1938 Hoover made this claim himself, stating that she was "the most vicious, dangerous and resourceful criminal brain of the last decade," and that the criminal careers of her four sons were directly traceable to their mother. "This woman," he concluded, was "a monument to the evils of parental indulgence."

The idea of Kate Barker as a crime supremo is far-fetched. In fact she had never been convicted of any crime and it is very unlikely that a female hillbilly from the Blue Ridge mountain area would be allowed to interfere with what was considered to be men's business in a male-dominated society. Hoover's interpretation was not questioned at the time: few people had any doubts about the integrity of his agents. The press liked the idea of a gun-crazy old woman, and the idea that she may have been an innocent victim was unthinkable.[129]

Hoover had given the producers of popular culture an idea that could be endlessly recycled. James Hadley Chase was first with a novel called *No Orchids for Miss Blandish* in 1939. In this, "Ma Grisson" was "physically powerful and a hideous old woman; she was also the brains who determined the future of the gang ... Ma died in her office with a Thompson submachine gun in her hands, taking four cops with her." Scriptwriters began adding "Ma" Barker characters to the plots of films, most notably in *White Heat* (1949) and *Bloody Mama* (1970).

The public relations were effective. Hoover's position as the nation's chief law enforcer was as secure as his agency's ever-increasing appropriations from Congress. Every time he appeared before the House Appropriations Committee, congressmen heaped uncritical praise and taxpayers' money on the agency. Other agency heads and local officials looked on enviously and learned.[130]

9
Thomas E. Dewey and the
"Greatest Gangster in America"

The 1930s also saw the beginnings of the glorification of the prosecutor, personified in the shape of a young Midwesterner, Thomas E. Dewey.

In 1935 Dewey was sworn in as a special prosecutor to investigate racketeering in Manhattan. Dewey announced: "We can make this city too dangerous for organized crime," and for a few years he did oversee the downfall of a succession of gangsters and of Jimmy Hines, a corrupt city politician. Dewey's greatest coup, however, was the conviction of Charles "Lucky" Luciano.

Luciano, born Salvatore Lucania in Sicily in 1897, had arrived in New York in 1906. His name was Americanized to Charles Luciano, and he acquired the nickname "Lucky," some suggest, for surviving a police beating. Luciano had been involved in the buying and selling of drugs and alcohol in Prohibition New York and became wealthy through crime. In 1931, he was suspected of involvement in killing Giuseppe Masseria and Salvatore Maranzano, two gangsters in Manhattan's Little Italy, but there were no charges.

Dewey convicted him in 1936 of running prostitutes and he was sentenced to 30–50 years imprisonment. In 1946 he was deported to Italy, got involved in land deals and the hospital equipment business, and was suspected of involvement in the drugs trade. He died in 1962 after a heart attack in Naples airport. As we shall see, many fables were woven around these bare facts to claim that Luciano was a managerial mastermind. In 1998, *Time* magazine even ludicrously named him as one of the "most influential business geniuses" of the twentieth century, putting him on the same list of "builders and titans" as Henry Ford, Walt Disney, Bill Gates and the founder of McDonalds, Ray Kroc.[131]

Dewey began this process by targeting Luciano with a special squad of detectives. He directed simultaneous police raids on 41 brothels in Manhattan and Brooklyn on February 1, 1936. Over 100 women and 17 men were arrested. Some, as they later testified, were offered immunity and other inducements, and were coached by Dewey and his staff to tell convincing stories.

Dewey based his case against Luciano on building an impression of Luciano's guilt in the trial jury's minds. The main prosecution witnesses were Joe Bendix, a burglar serving a life jail term, and three prostitutes, Mildred Harris, Nancy Presser and "Cokey Flo" Brown. Bendix, hoping to have his sentence reduced, had a vested interest in supporting the prosecution's case. He testified that Luciano had offered him a job as a collector from several brothels, but that he had been arrested before he could begin. Mildred Harris said she was told "Luciano is the boss." Nancy Presser said she had been Luciano's mistress and had heard details about his prostitution racket. Under cross-examination, however, she was unable to describe Luciano's hotel suite or even remember whether the bed was twin or double. Cokey Flo merely repeated the testimony of other witnesses.

The testimony of these unreliable witnesses amounted to hearsay assertions that Luciano ran a prostitution racket. More convincingly, Dewey's cross-examination of Luciano revealed him as a liar, cheat and extortionist, but not the overlord of vice Dewey claimed. Despite this, in his final address to the jury Dewey claimed that Luciano was "the greatest gangster in America" and, as we shall see, his publicist, Hickman Powell, concocted stories a few years later to make this claim believable.

The New York *Daily Mirror* greeted the guilty verdict by calling Luciano "the czar of chain store vice," and announcing "the definite beginning of the end of gangsterism, terrorism, and commercialised criminality throughout the United States." Much more bombast greeted the verdict in the popular press as Luciano's conviction gave the misleading impression that forceful law enforcement provided the answer to vice and racketeering everywhere. Luciano had received a 30- to 50-year sentence for alleged pimping. Dewey had satisfied a need to blame specific targets for problems that law enforcement could not solve, notably enforcement laws against consensual activities.

In the process of convicting Luciano, Dewey had pioneered tactics that were later rolled out as a model for organized crime control around the world, and that are still in use today. These involved surveillance and wiretapping, inducements for criminals to become prosecution witnesses, and laws that made it easier to convict for conspiracy. An American adaptation of Mussolini's tactics in Sicily, in fact.

Dewey had put dozens of illegal gambling operators, loan sharks and industrial racketeers behind bars, but the popular accounts of his courtroom triumphs left out some uncomfortable details. He manipulated public opinion, he coerced reluctant witnesses, he illegally used wiretaps against political opponents and he failed to make an impact on wholesale illegal profit-making in New York. In 1940, Benjamin Stolberg in the *American Mercury* commented that Dewey's conception of criminal justice had no place for constitutional rights and instead "resembled that of a psychologist who builds a labyrinthian trap for rats, to learn whether or how soon they can get out of it."[132] In the following decades, as we shall see, the US government constructed a labyrinthian trap of global dimensions.

Dewey and his staff were great press manipulators and the press were happily complicit for the sake of good crime stories. Most journalists did little investigating themselves and lazily adapted material prepared by Dewey's staff. The trials made Dewey an ideal subject for popular magazines such as *Time*, *Collier's*, *True Detective*, the *Saturday Evening Post* and *Women's Home Companion*. An image was created for the young Midwesterner that helped elect him as governor of New York State in November 1942 and made him twice an (unsuccessful) Republican presidential candidate, in 1944 and 1948.

10
From Gangbusters to Murder Inc.

By the end of the 1930s, Cummings, Hoover, Dewey and their imitators throughout the country had successfully waged war against organized crime, at least according to their cheerleaders in film, radio and print.

At the same time, popular movies and such radio shows as *Gang Busters* and *Mr District Attorney* reflected the theme that the war on organized crime was being won. The film *Roaring Twenties* (1939), a nostalgic look back to the Prohibition decade, stressed how things had changed for the better. "Eddie, the days of the racket are over," says the operator of a dingy saloon to the main character played by Jimmy Cagney. Or as Cagney says to a fellow gangster played by Humphrey Bogart: "It's a new kind of setup, you and I don't belong." Earlier gangster movies had tended to end with a shootout with the criminal hero dying with memorable last lines. "Mother of mercy, is this the end of Rico?" were Edward G. Robinson's last words in *Little Caesar*. The climax of *Angels with Dirty Faces* (1938), by contrast, was a scene in which a priest comes to death row to ask Rocky, played by Cagney, to destroy his own popular hero image by dying like a coward. Cagney complies with the destruction of his romantic image by having to be dragged to the electric chair crying like a baby.[133]

A syndicated front-page headline at the end of 1939 summed up the triumphalist theme: "Organized Crime Took the Rap – Right Down the Line in 1930–1940 Decade." "The challenge of organized killers, kidnappers and bank robbers in the Thirties was probably the most brazen in American crime annals," the story began, "But by the end of the decade, so smashing were the onslaught of Federal, state and city police, virtually all of the 'big shot' gunmen and 'big ransom' kidnappers were in prison or dead." Capone, Dillinger and other gangster "stars" were then listed.[134]

The triumphalist "gangbusting" mood was sustained throughout the war. The successful prosecution of a number of contract killers and their alleged "boss," Louis "Lepke" Buchalter, competed for headlines with news from the war in Europe and the Far East. Buchalter, a New York garment industry racketeer, was accused of operating a nationwide killing service given the title "Murder Inc." by reporters. The idea of contract killing across the United States being a centralized and even corporate national enterprise began to take hold with the press accounts of the testimony against Buchalter and others given by a Brooklyn gangster, Abe "Kid Twist" Reles, in the early 1940s, and was strengthened by the publication and success of *Murder Inc.: The Story of "The Syndicate"* by Burton Turkus and Sid Feder in 1951. Turkus had been a prosecuting attorney on the Buchalter case and Feder was his ghostwriter. They made their case by quoting hyperbolic claims about career criminals, such as: "It's just like Bethlehem Steel. It has a board of directors, a treasurer ... and runs like a big syndicate." The authors claimed, in a way that was already becoming familiar, that the syndicate was "an octopus of lawlessness."[135]

Alan A. Block, a historian of organized crime, made a study of the relevant "Murder Inc." trial transcripts and extant internal documents and came to very different conclusions from those of Turkus and Feder. Block wrote:

> What Turkus and Feder described and concluded was simply not what Reles related. For instance, when Reles talked about cooperation in the Brooklyn underworld, Turkus and Feder called it organization. When Reles talked about favors being done by one racketeer for another, Turkus and Feder wrote about orders and a smooth chain of command. When Reles talked about the geographical mobility of various criminals, Turkus and Feder held it as proof of the national scope of the cartel. When Reles talked about the innumerable mobs that populated the New York underworld, Turkus and Feder interpreted it as proof of the confederation of organized crime. When Reles talked about murder using the underworld argot of contract, Turkus and Feder concluded that murder was a real business conducted in the interest of the National Crime Syndicate and carried out by a special group of enforcers. And finally, when Reles talked about the shifting, changing, bickering, competitive, murderous social world of organized crime, Turkus and Feder surmised that this untidiness was only the

inevitable and necessary fallout of the consolidation of organized crime. Everything, no matter how counter-factual, led to the big conspiracy, The Organization.[136]

The Murder Inc. conspiracy interpretation of organized crime was soon forgotten, however. The alleged leader, Buchalter, had already been convicted and was executed in 1944. Buchalter, and most of his associates, were Jewish American, and identifying organized crime primarily with Jews at this time was a non-starter in the Holocaust-aware context of the times. Italian Americans became the chosen scapegoats. By a similar process to the one that Block described in relation to the Murder Inc. conspiracy interpretation of organized crime, the Mafia conspiracy interpretation of organized crime became the conventional wisdom. The difference was that the federal government, aided by many in the media and some in the academic community, gave unjustified credibility to the Mafia interpretation.

PART II

Lies about Criminals: Constructing an Acceptable "History" of Organized Crime

Introduction

Opinion makers, including the editors and journalists of newspapers, magazines and television news companies, convey misleading information about the past for a number of reasons. First and probably most frequently they unwittingly repeat past lies – they are pressed for time and work from clipping files or book-length accounts of their chosen subject. Some make up implausible details of past events because made-up versions of the past are often more interesting than mundane realities. Some politicians lie about the past to boost their chances of election to positions of power and influence. Some public officials lie to boost the power and resources of their agencies, or to cover up the failures of their agencies. Some defense lawyers and accountants lie because their job is to serve their clients, rather than to tell the truth. Many prosecutors lie (or at least bend the truth) to secure convictions, and this often takes priority over truth-telling. Some, and probably most, criminals lie as part of a deal with prosecutors to secure more lenient treatment from the courts. If enough people lie in a consistent manner their tales will be believed and may, as in the case of organized crime control, help shape government policy in ways that the great majority of people accept. All of the above combined to create and perpetuate the myths surrounding the Atlantic City gangster "conference" of 1929 and the subsequent nationwide "purge" of old-style Mafia gangsters in 1931, called melodramatically the "Night of the Sicilian Vespers" by one journalist making a nonsensical reference to a thirteenth-century Sicilian rebellion. The impact of these lies taken together served the purpose of creating influential foundation myths for the phenomenon known as organized crime in America and, in the process, helped justify the building of America's national security state.

1
The Genesis of the Atlantic City "Conference" Legend

The Atlantic City gangster "conference" story began life as a credible account by Al Capone of a trip he made to the New Jersey resort in May 1929. The newspaper and magazine reports of this visit at the time were based almost entirely on Al Capone himself as a source. There have been countless reconstructions since, in books, articles, television documentaries and the HBO series *Boardwalk Empire*, yet Capone remains the only known source for the story.

Capone was arrested for carrying a gun in Philadelphia on May 16, 1929, a day after he had been in Atlantic City, and told police investigators the following:

> I have tried hard to stop all this killing and gang rivalry. That was my purpose in going to Atlantic City. It was a peace conference. I engineered it. Some of the biggest men in the business in Chicago were there. ... "Bug" Moran, leader of the north side gang, ... and *three or four other Chicago gang leaders were there* [emphasis added]. We talked over our trouble and at the end agreed to sign on the dotted line, bury the past and forget warfare for the general good of all concerned.

This was reported on 18 May in the *Atlantic City Daily Press*, the *Philadelphia Inquirer*, the *New York Tribune* and the *Los Angeles Times*.[1] So, that was the word on the Atlantic City "conference" from the only known witness consulted. Capone and three or four other Chicagoans talking about peace. The *Chicago Tribune* claimed that it had identified the "three or four" others at the conference – beyond Capone and Moran – as Joseph Aiello, Earl McErland, Joe Saltis and John Torrio, although it did not substantiate this claim.[2]

The exaggeration of Capone's account began with the publication of a book by Walter Nobel Burns, *The One-Way Ride: The Red Trail of Chicago Gangland from Prohibition to Jake Lingle*, in 1931. Burns upped the number of conference attendees to "about 30 veterans" of Chicago gang wars from the "North, South and West Sides" of the city.[3] Other journalists would by then have taken note that Burns' inflation of the numbers was not challenged.

The fictionalization of Capone's account had already begun in November 1929 with the publication of a short story by Damon Runyon in *Cosmopolitan* magazine. Runyon was by then one of the most popular American authors, turning out mainly tales of New York low-life for the Hearst publication group. In the story "Dark Dolores," his narrator relates how he was "persuaded" by "Dave the Dude" to catch a train to Atlantic City to attend a "big peace conference" to settle a gang war going on in St. Louis between three rival mobs. It would have been clear to readers that St. Louis stood for Chicago and that one of the mob leaders, "Black Mike" – "an Italian with a big scar on his face" – stood for Capone. The popularity of Runyon's stories would have assured that the conference entered popular consciousness.[4]

After Runyon's story the fictionalization process took a big step forward with the printing of a photograph in the *New York Evening Tribune* on January 17, 1930. It showed Capone walking next to the political boss of Atlantic City, Enoch "Nucky" Johnson. The picture looks fake – Capone's wearing heavy winter clothes, Johnson's in light summer clothes. However, the alliance between corrupt politics and gangdom implied by the juxtaposition of the nation's most notorious gangster with a machine politician chimed with the dominant perspective on organized crime at this time.

* * *

There was little more published about the Atlantic City "conference" until Hickman Powell's *Ninety Times Guilty* in 1939. Powell was the first author to claim that Runyon's imaginary "interstate" conference was actually true. He wrote: "In May 1929, Al Capone went to a peace conference in Atlantic City," and elaborated that "The last year had been bloody. There had been the killing of Frank Yale in Brooklyn, the Valentine's Day massacre in Chicago, and various minor killings."

"Frankie Costello, the slot machine man," he continued, "who has never been one to encourage violence, arranged the meeting and spent twenty-five thousand dollars of his own money on it. Various gang chieftains were entertained for several days at the Hotel President."[5] Powell does not mention a credible source for these claims.

Powell went further than merely paraphrasing a fictional account. He sowed the seeds of what became the mainstream interpretation of organized crime history, supported by most writers, film directors and – most damagingly – by the US government. "The aim of the Atlantic City conference," he claimed, "was to establish peaceful co-operation in the underworld instead of warfare." He then launched a bizarre theory that he dubbed "the Americanization of the underworld." "One disturbing element had been a group commonly called 'greasers' who were very influential in the Unione Siciliano – old-line, unassimilated Italian leaders and recent immigrants."[6] Popular journalists would later transform the "Unione Siciliano" he referred to into the allegedly all-powerful and centralized Mafia that many opinion-makers claimed would come to control organized crime in the whole of the United States and, for good measure, in much of the rest of the world.

Powell put the New York gangster, Charles "Lucky" Luciano, at the heart of his analysis. Luciano, he claimed, *may* have been one of those at the Atlantic City "conference" but he was in any event "close to Capone and closer still to others who were rising to succeed Capone in racket power." "For leader(s) of the Italian gangs, Lucky was the candidate of those who were out to 'Americanize' the underworld."[7]

By the time Powell wrote this book he had become a speechwriter for Dewey, the New York prosecuting attorney who, in the late 1930s, was campaigning for high office in New York State with a view to an eventual tilt at the presidency. Dewey had secured the conviction of Luciano on the charge of "compulsory prostitution," on 90 counts, hence the title of Powell's book. Luciano had received a 30- to 50-year sentence – an unprecedented sentence for being in effect a pimp.[8]

After claiming that Luciano may have been present at the Atlantic City "conference," Powell added that it was followed by "doubtless many meetings" between "various big underworld leaders" and that at one of these – "held late in 1931 or early in 1932, in a Brooklyn hotel" – the "Combination" was formed. "Underworld sources" told him that

"The power of Charlie Lucky had a lot to do with that. Through the underworld he and his allies spread the Pax Siciliano."[9]

Reviewers were convinced of the authenticity of the book. The *Springfield Republican*, for example, wrote that "the author tears off the veil that hides from the ordinary citizens' eyes the world of the gangster, the prostitute and the dissolute ... Although the book is sensational, a reading of it would tend to sober public thought."[10] The book sold well and is still in print.

Four months after *Ninety Times Guilty* was published it was revealed that Powell – in addition to being Thomas Dewey's speechwriter – was the ghostwriter for Dixie Davis, "the racketeer lawyer" whose name was used as the author of a hugely influential series of articles in *Collier's Weekly* – a magazine with a circulation in excess of two million. Powell's dual identity as Dewey's "spin doctor" and someone passing himself off as an underworld insider was revealed in short "buried" stories in a number of publications, but only the obscure but independent *Evening Standard* of Uniontown, Pennsylvania, came close to revealing the duplicitous significance of the *Collier's* series.

Under the headline "Nice Propaganda for Brother Dewey," its story went as follows:

many *Standard* readers have perused the recently concluded "bad man" confession series of Dixie Davis, the notorious New York shyster lawyer who was the professional "mouthpiece" for the Manhattan gangs.

It didn't take the reading of all installments of the lurid Davis tale for the intelligent reader to perceive that while the stories were published under the Davis "byline" that someone else, someone with a cultivated, fluid, graphic writing style had really spun the yarn into the type that the public saw.

This now turns out to have been the case.

Nor did it take the intelligent reader very long to perceive that the so-called "inside story" of the gangster lawyer was in reality a piece of lurid, sensational "exposé" used as a vehicle for publicizing and boosting the energetic, ambitious and spotlight-seeking District Attorney Tom Dewey.

Again and again in the recital of the past few years ... there appears in the story at frequent intervals a word or a paragraph of praise for Mr. Dewey.

"What a grand guy this Dewey is" was the sum and substance of the alleged Dixie Davis memoirs.[11]

The Dixie Davis memoirs, in other words, were part of the "selling" of candidate Tom Dewey to a statewide and soon afterwards a national constituency.

Davis' (in reality spin doctor Powell's) references to Dewey in the articles go from the admiring, "Dewey was a bad guy from our standpoint, for I had seen him operate as a prosecutor in federal court," to the groveling, "I knew I was in the presence of a great guy." Indirectly Davis (Powell) enhanced Dewey's reputation by grossly exaggerating the importance of Luciano, adding spurious substance to Dewey's claim at the 1936 trial that Luciano was "the greatest gangster in America." Powell, as Davis, was able to give an "insider" account of the alleged reorganization of the underworld that followed the Atlantic City "conference." As Davis he was able to paraphrase the claims he had made in *Ninety Times Guilty* without the need to qualify his assertions. Powell as Davis was now therefore claiming that Luciano *did* organize the conference rather than *may* have organized the conference. The Unione Siciliano was, in the articles, "the mysterious, all-pervading reality," which organized the underworld on a national scale during and after Prohibition. Its leader, Salvatore Maranzano, was shot dead on September 10, 1931, and "at the very same hour there was about ninety guineas knocked off all over the country." After orchestrating this purge, Luciano, according to Powell as Davis, "set up a system of underworld co-operation that spread from coast to coast." Luciano was then compared to "Hitler developing the system of axis powers."[12] This was the origin of the "Night of the Sicilian Vespers" story, to which we shall return.

It had been a fantastic story in *Ninety Times Guilty*, but given spurious substance by Dixie Davis as participant observer it was made much more convincing. Countless writers have repeated versions of it, sometimes referencing Powell's book but more often just retelling the Atlantic City "conference" story as if it was an unchallenged fact.

Collier's paid Powell, Davis and Davis's wife, Hope Dare, $20,000 for the articles.[13] Powell remained a Dewey employee for the rest of his career. Dewey, once he became governor, gave him a job in New York State administration. Powell kept it until he took his pension. Davis and "Red headed showgirl" Hope Dare bought an ice cream parlor in Los Angeles and, as far as is known, stayed there.

2
Consolidating the "Conference" Legend

On December 10, 1940, the Hearst newspaperman Jack Lait made a reference to the mythical Atlantic City meeting, as he praised the efforts of the IRS against "syndicate" criminal and corrupt politicians. "There's a convention in New York ... Its [sic] a gathering of top gangsters and racketeers of the nation. Such get-togethers are not uncommon. They have been held in Chicago, Miami, Atlantic City, Phoenix, Providence and other points."

It must have been a lengthy New York convention since he repeated the column almost verbatim on July 22, 1949 – nine years later.[14] The only difference was a subeditor's correction to Lait's omission of an inverted comma in the first version: "It's a gathering of gangsters and racketeers ..." The federal policing agencies were singled out for praise as the only answer to such evidence of nationwide organization and super-government among hoods:

> And a shudder of fear has the mob geniuses shaky. They haven't forgotten what happened to Al Capone, "Lucky" Luciano and "Nucky" Johnson ... They know that whenever the Feds really try, they can get these malefactors of great stealth, for they are all venal and vulnerable, they have influence beyond calculation, but when the G-boys are ordered from up above to close in, nothing can help them.

This was the first time the politician Johnson was mentioned in connection with the Atlantic City "conference," albeit indirectly, and it was not as the host in the way later writers embellished the story.

In 1950, the year after the second of Lait's reports on the alleged conference, Senator Kefauver read and later endorsed a book that Lait co-wrote with another journalist, Lee Mortimer: *Chicago Confidential.*

Kefauver was preparing for an influential investigation of organized crime.[15] He was impressed enough to write a testimonial letter to the book's publisher, William Randolph Hearst.

In 1959, Frederic Sondern, a journalist who relied on agents from the FBN for his sources, made the claim that not only were Atlantic City "conference" gangster delegates from across the whole of the United States, but that they were all members of the Mafia. In *Brotherhood of Evil: The Mafia*, he made the unsourced claim that Capone had beaten the brains out of three gangsters seated at a dining table, and continued:

> A few weeks later Capone issued invitations to the senior capi Mafiosi of Chicago, Detroit, New York, Philadelphia and several other big centers to meet in Atlantic City in May 1929. ... It was the Atlantic City gathering that made underworld and Mafia history ... The Sicilians listened as Capone explained a project on which he had been working for some three years – a nationwide syndicate and organization, not only for bootlegging but gambling, prostitution, labor racketeering and various kinds of extortion as well ... At Atlantic City a series of peace treaties for the Chicago, New York and other areas was hammered out and ratified – without documents and signatures but with a validity that lasted a long time. It was the fundamental design and unwritten constitution of the modern American Mafia.[16]

Sondern had taken Hickman Powell's imaginative reconstruction of the Atlantic City "conference" and made all the significant participants Italian American in line, as we shall see, with the FBN's propaganda contention that organized crime in the US was controlled by a single Italian entity.

In 1965, one of America's best-known journalists, Walter Winchell, added his prestige to the Atlantic City "conference" mythology. Winchell was in a sense the voice of the "gangbuster" since he was the narrator of the popular *Untouchables* television series. In his syndicated column, he wrote:

> It was Capone who organized the nation-wide crime syndicate ... In May 1929 the mob chiefs gathered in Atlantic City at

Capone's invitation ... There they organized their operations on a more business-like level ... They operated like any big business ... Recognized leaders, standard rules of procedure and periodic meetings. ... If the black flag of the underworld were to unfurl atop one of the tallest skyscrapers in New York it would be a fit symbol of how the Mafia has gained control of that building and many other real estate holdings.[17]

By this time most of the American law enforcement community, as well as the rest of the America media, shared the kind of interpretation articulated by Winchell, and given official sanction by President Lyndon Johnson's Commission on Law Enforcement and the Administration of Justice in 1967. "Today," according to the Commission's report, "the core of organized crime in the United States consists of 24 groups operating as criminal cartels in large cities across the Nation. Their membership is exclusively Italian, they are in frequent communication with each other, and their smooth functioning is insured by a national body of overseers."

The report offered very little historical substantiation for its claims besides the following short paragraph:

The present confederation of organized crime groups arose after Prohibition, during which Italian, German, Irish and Jewish groups had competed with one another in racket operations. The Italian groups were successful in switching their enterprises from prostitution and bootlegging to gambling, extortion, and other illegal activities. They consolidated their power through murder and violence.[18]

The only known source for a "history" that implied that only immigrants participated in organized crime was Sergeant Ralph Salerno of the New York Police Department. Dwight Smith has detailed the ways in which Salerno provided as much historical and analytical substance as the commission required in its efforts to justify a large increase in policing resources and powers to combat what it saw as a security threat to the United States. Accuracy was not the commission's concern.[19]

The commission's work culminated with the Organized Crime Control Act of 1970 that, as we shall see, was significant nationally and internationally. In a book published in 1969, Salerno and his co-writer, John S. Tompkins, confirmed an acceptance of Atlantic City "conference" mythology. After detailing Capone's conviction and imprisonment on tax evasion charges in 1931 and the shootings of John Dillinger and other bank robbers, they asserted that, "Unnoticed during all of the hoopla about sending Capone to prison and the FBI's war on crime, major crime itself was organized at a meeting in Atlantic City in 1931, and the details worked out over the next few years."[20] By moving the mythical meeting from 1929 to 1931, the authors had managed to prevent the only known source for the alleged convention or conference – Al Capone – from attending it altogether.

By the 1970s there was no limit to the imagination and deceit of "true crime" writers when it came to descriptions of the Atlantic City "conference." In 1971, Hank Messick devoted six pages to the event in *Lansky*, a biography of the Jewish American gangster businessman who founded something Messick called the National Crime Syndicate. Lansky, Messick claimed, was the real inspiration for the gathering of mobsters – not Capone, Luciano or Costello. Messick embellished the story by:

1. Adding claims and details on Enoch Johnson. Instead of just being the subject of the probably doctored photograph walking along the city's Boardwalk beside Capone, Johnson now "ruled a criminal-political empire" in the resort who could be depended upon to "entertain the boys in style."
2. Faking conversations between Lansky, Luciano and others that happened four decades earlier and could have no other source than Messick's imagination. One example being Luciano saying the following to Lansky: "Masseria's going to be sore as hell if I go (to the conference) and he ain't invited. He's got a lot of trouble on his hands now with this bastard Maranzano. Any day now he's going to order a purge."
3. Giving names to the previously unnamed "gang chieftains from all over the East and Middle West" who were, according to Messick, at the conference.

Messick's new guest list was as follows:

> The New York delegation included Adonis, Costello, Luciano, Lansky, Lepke, and various minor characters such as Larry Fay and Frank Erickson. In addition to Capone, Guzik was there. Cleveland sent Lou Rothkopf and Moe Dalitz, along with Chuck Polizzi whose real name was Berkowitz. Joe Bernstein led a delegation from the Purple gang in Detroit ... King Solomon came down from Boston. Nig Rosen and Max "Boo Hoo" Hoff were there from Philadelphia. ... John Lazia from Kansas City. New Jersey was represented by ... "Longy" Zwillman.[21]

Messick's imaginative reconstruction of the conference was soon outdone by Martin Gosch and Richard Hammer in *The Last Testament of Lucky Luciano* (1975). The book project was initiated by Gosch, Hammer was a crime journalist brought in later. Gosch is usually described as a film producer, but his boss, Barnett Glassman, was probably more accurate when he described him as "just a hustler in the film business, conning guys all over the place."[22]

According to Gosch's account, Lucky Luciano himself had told him that he was the central player in the Atlantic City "conference." Luciano had asked him to be his "Mr. Boswell" in 1961, a year before he died. The heart attack happened, appropriately and, in terms of publicity, profitably, when Luciano was meeting Gosch at Naples airport on January 26, 1962. The 1961 deal, according to Gosch, was for Luciano to record his life story to Gosch on tape and for it to be written up and published ten years after his death. According to Gosch, Luciano said he wouldn't "hold back nothin'" and that the money gained would be "an annuity" for Gosch and his wife, Lucille.[23]

The paperback rights of *Last Testament* were auctioned for $500,000, a serialization appeared in *Penthouse* magazine the year before publication and the book was chosen as the main selection by both the Book-of-the-Month club and the *Playboy* Book Club. Its success was based largely on the publisher's claim that it was the life story of Lucky Luciano as dictated by the Mafia boss himself before his death in 1962.

Tony Scaduto and other writers doubted the *Last Testament's* authenticity. In Scaduto's biography, *Luciano* (1975), he noted the non-existence of actual tapes and listed many of the book's errors. He added that Gosch did not even make notes of those so-called conversations until long after the talks were supposed to have taken place. Gosch, Scaduto reported, was sued by his former boss, Glassman, since Glassman was the only one of the two who had a signed contract with Luciano. This was because Luciano had wanted his story to be told as a film. The publisher Little, Brown, wrote Scaduto, "paid Glassman a lot of money to drop the suit with the agreement that much more would be paid if the *Last Testament* would be turned into a film itself."[24]

Last Testament was a fake, based mainly on hearsay accounts written by Hickman Powell and others. It quotes Luciano as saying that he was at meetings and events during the time that he was in prison – it even quotes him talking about an event that happened two years after he died.[25] Gosch himself did not benefit from the hoax since he died just before the book was published. There was, however, clearly "an annuity" for his wife.

Gosch and Hammer added several more gangsters to Messick's list: "Purple Gang" leader, Abe Bernstein, Willie Moretti from New Jersey, John Torrio, and Dutch Schultz, Albert Anastasia, Vince Mangano and Frank Scalise. Gosch and Hammer, like Messick, invented dialogue and put Nucky Johnson at the center of events that followed the alleged refusal of one hotel to let the imaginary group of lowlifes in, "So Nucky picks Al up under one arm and throws him into his car and yells out, 'All you fuckers follow me!'" Johnson then, according to Gosch and Hammer, laid on "a constant round of parties, with plenty of liquor, food and girls." This is quite a leap given the only evidence of Johnson's presence was a photograph showing him in summer clothes walking besides Al Capone in winter clothes on the Atlantic City boardwalk. The Atlantic City "conference" was a good base for a story, however, as the author of *Boardwalk Empire* (2010), "The true story that inspired the HBO series," must have realized. He uncritically used *The Last Testament* as one of his main sources.[26]

3
The Purge that Wasn't

Returning to the account in *Ninety Times Guilty*, Hickman Powell, as
well as inventing the Atlantic City "conference," offered his readers the
first account of an alleged "purge day," that lay the foundations of what
became the most widely accepted explanation for the evolution of
organized crime in America. Powell related that the "greasers" or "cold
hard Sicilian gunmen" got together in July 1931 at Coney Island "and
elected their own chief, one Salvatore Maranzano ... Maranzano set
about challenging the power of the Combination" and "on September
10 1931 ... Maranzano ... was thoroughly riddled with bullets and
stabbed with a knife until dead." He continued:

> There were plenty more gunmen abroad that day. Maranzano was
> only one of the victims marked for slaughter. I got the story from
> two men, one of whom was associated with Lepke in these years, and
> another of whom was an intimate of Bo Weinburg's. [Weinburg was
> one of the alleged assassins of Maranzano.] The more conservative
> version is that thirty of Maranzano's followers were murdered
> *within the next few days* [emphasis added]. The other one, probably
> nearer the truth, is that ninety of Maranzano's recruits and old-line
> "greaser" leaders were wiped out in cities all over the country, most
> of them within the same hour as that in which Maranzano was
> killed ... At any rate, the Maranzano minority was exterminated. It
> was a purge. The underworld had been "Americanized."[27]

In 1951, the previously mentioned Turkus and Feder elaborated on
Powell's claims. In *Murder Inc.: The Story of the Syndicate*, they narrated
that "The day Marrizano [*sic*] got it ... Some thirty to forty leaders of
Mafia's older group all over the United States were murdered that day
and in the next forty-eight hours." After making a number of other
unsourced claims, they concluded, "These early developments have
been chronicled, since it is from ... the purge of the Mafia, and Lucky's

[Luciano's] resultant coronation, that modern gangdom – Murder Inc., the national crime organization – may be traced."[28]

The significance of these unsourced claims only recently became apparent when the US government made available on the internet documents that had previously only been available to FBI agents. The so-called "Mafia Monograph" was a secret document prepared by the FBI's Central Research Section meant only for limited distribution among federal law enforcement officials. It was a "study" of the origins, nature and activities of the Mafia in Sicily and the US and became a "bible" for the top echelon of federal law enforcement, including, of course, J. Edgar Hoover.[29] The monograph highlights the significance of "purge day" but its only source for this "evidence" for the alleged centralization of power in America's underworld is the book by Turkus and Feder, described earlier as almost complete invention. After "Marrizano [*sic*] was shot," the Monograph paraphrased, "and his throat cut ... within a period of several days, some 30 or 40 other older leaders of Mafia groups throughout the country were murdered."[30] The FBI's Central Research Section even repeated Turkus and Feder's misspelling of Salvatore Maranzano's name. From that time on the federal government's almost desperate efforts to "prove" its centralization of organized crime thesis lay behind the development of organized crime control policy.

In 1963, a congressional committee chaired by Senator John McClellan held televised hearings to highlight a witness to the foundation, structure and function of what it called the Cosa Nostra,[31] instead of using the more familiar Mafia label. McClellan asked a small-time New York criminal called Joseph Valachi how many men were killed on "purge day." Valachi responded, "four or five Senator." McClelland's committee then asked Sergeant Ralph Salerno if he knew of any more than four or five New York murders on September 10, 1931 – Salerno answered that he had no record of any other murders on that day.[32] This did not, as we shall see, prevent the committee, and all federal government officials, including J. Edgar Hoover, coming to the same conclusions as Powell, Turkus and Feder regarding the national organization of organized crime by a select group of Italian American criminals.

In 1968, Peter Maas' bestselling book, *The Valachi Papers*, based on Valachi's testimony and written with the active cooperation of FBI officials, claimed that:

The murder of Maranzano was part of an intricate, painstakingly executed mass extermination engineered by the same dapper, soft-spoken, cold-eyed Charley Lucky Luciano ... On the day Maranzano died, some forty Cosa Nostra leaders allied with him were slain across the country, practically all of them Italian-born old-timers eliminated by a younger generation making its bid for power.[33]

Millions of filmgoers worldwide saw the slaying re-enacted in the 1972 movie *The Valachi Papers*, starring Charles Bronson. The following year a "true crime" book – *Mafia!* – repeated Powell's "grandiloquent" title for the purge, the "Night of the Sicilian Vespers" mentioned earlier. Claims that were based on nothing more than the puffery of Thomas E. Dewey's publicist.

Valachi had only mentioned the possibility of four or five murders on "purge day" and no more than that were ever named in the "true crime" literature. In the 1970s, the historian Alan A. Block set out to check the truth of the purge story. He did a survey of newspapers in selected cities beginning two weeks prior to Maranzano's death and ending two weeks after. He looked for any stories of gangland murders that could be connected, even remotely, with the Maranzano case. Although he found several accounts of the Maranzano murder, he could only locate three other murders that might have been connected. Two of the dead men were Louis Russo and Samuel Monaco, both in New Jersey, and mentioned by Valachi in his testimony. There was also the Pittsburg murder of Joseph Siragusa on September 14, 1931. "The killing of four or five men does not make a purge," concluded Block, "and certainly the killing of three of four men in the New York Metropolitan area and one man in Pittsburgh does not make a national vendetta." The rest, according to Block, were "the fictional members of the Mafia's legion of the damned."[34] The nationwide purge story, although fictional, had given credibility to the idea that lay behind the Organized Crime Control Act of 1970 and thus a set of organized crime control policies that have since been exported to the rest of the world. Organized crime, according to this idea, had been centralized and was thus a national security threat justifying a draconian response. This kind of analysis derived from Dawes, Mussolini and Hickman Powell and didn't help the US government combat something it clearly didn't understand.

4

The US Government's History of Organized Crime

Evidence that the federal government remained committed to Powell's tall stories can be found in evidence presented before a Senate committee in 1988. At the hearing, entitled "Organized Crime: 25 Years after Valachi" a "Chronological History of La Cosa Nostra in the United States" was presented by the Justice Department's Organized Crime Intelligence and Analysis Unit. Consisting mainly of dates of gangland killings, the following derived from Powell's unsourced claims:

May 15, 1929
Al Capone, boss of the Chicago crime family, was arrested by the Philadelphia Police Department on a charge of carrying concealed weapon shortly after leaving what he described as a 3-day "peace conference" of leading mobsters in an Atlantic City, New Jersey hotel ...

April 15, 1931
Giusseppe Masseria, "boss of all the bosses,"
was shot to death in a Coney Island, New York restaurant ...

September 10, 1931
Salvatore Maranzano, successor to Masseria, was shot and stabbed to death in his Manhattan office building by 4 members of Meyer Lansky's Jewish mob posing as police officers ...

October 15, 1931
... Following the death of Salvatore Maranzano, a wave of gangland slayings, known as the "Sicilian Vespers" swept the country.[35]

This evidence, and the recent release of the FBI's 1958 Mafia Monograph, explain the misplaced certainty behind statements issued on organized crime by federal officials, and help to explain the failure of organized crime control methods based on a flawed understanding of the problem.

* * *

After Block's debunking of the "purge day" story, commentators adjusted their narratives about the origins of organized crime in America. Claire Sterling published a sequence of books as the international community was moving towards harmonizing national law enforcement systems on the American model. As we shall see in Part IV, Sterling was the "historian" who emerged to narrate the rise of the "Mafia," the "Octopus" or the "National Crime Syndicate," and America's eventual triumph against it to the international community. *The Mafia: The Long Reach of the Sicilian Mafia* (1990) and *Thieves' World: The Threat of the New Global Network of Organized Crime* (1994) demonstrate a mixed-up reliance on the worst of an earlier generation of "true crime" writers. "Luciano murdered," she wrote in *The Mafia*, "the two Sicilian bosses currently killing each other's soldiers off in New York – Joe 'The Boss' Masseria and Salvatore Maranzano – and became The Boss himself." She then quoted from the hoax account by Gosch before concluding that, "The event was celebrated at Chicago's Blackstone Hotel in the autumn of 1932. Al Capone played host, and delegates came from all over the nation. Lucky Luciano was acclaimed as the undisputed leader of a modern, managerial crime corporation, nationally organized and distinctly American in outlook."[36] She had clearly mixed up the Atlantic City "conference" with a meeting in Chicago which may or may not have happened. Capone was by then in prison, however, and could not have been the host.

The sleight of hand that allowed the federal government to claim success against organized crime is only convincing if people believe the phony history of organized crime constructed by the likes of Hickman Powell, Burton Turkus, Sid Feder and many more commentators who took their imaginative claims as the truth.

The US government still has Luciano's alleged centralization of organized crime at the heart of its analysis as can be demonstrated by the FBI website.[37] Consulted on July 28, 2016, the "official" history of organized crime suggests a continued reliance on mythical assertions. Its account begins by repeating the notion that organized crime in America arrived when Sicilians immigrated at the end of the nineteenth century, then moves to the idea that Luciano centralized organized crime in America:

> By the end of the '20s, two primary factions had emerged, leading to a war for control of organized crime in New York City. The murder of faction leader Joseph Masseria brought an end to the gang warfare, and the two groups united to form the organization now dubbed La Cosa Nostra. It was not a peaceful beginning: Salvatore Maranzano, the first leader of La Cosa Nostra, was murdered within six months ...
> Charles "Lucky" Luciano ... became the new leader. Maranzano had established the La Cosa Nostra code of conduct, set up the "family" divisions and structure, and established procedures for resolving disputes. Luciano set up the "Commission" to rule all La Cosa Nostra activities. The Commission included bosses from six or seven families ... With Maranzano out of the way, Luciano become the most powerful Mafia boss in America and used his position to run La Cosa Nostra like a major corporation. He set up the LCN Commission, or ruling body, composed of seven bosses, and divided the different rackets among the families.

Like other distortions, the Atlantic City conference and "purge day" stories have served many purposes beyond the obvious need for writers to present stories interesting enough to be published and bureaucracies claiming a knowledge of the past. By elevating ordinary gangsters like Capone, Luciano, Costello and Lansky to the level of omnipotent masterminds, attention is deflected away from corruption within the various business, law enforcement and criminal justice systems within the United States.

Government officials chose not to base their interpretations of organized crime on research. Instead there was an emphasis on nationwide criminal conspiracy. The fragments of evidence they collected about gangsters knowing other gangsters did not prove their claims, as the historian William Moore explained:

> Important figures involved in liquor manufacture and distribution or gambling, as in other business or professional activities, might

well become acquainted; similar interests such as racing, resorts, and possibly joint investment ventures would occasion meetings for both pleasure and planning. In some cases, ethnic and family ties might strengthen these relationships. Certainly underworld businesses, like upperworld business, did not proceed in a vacuum.[38]

In the imaginations of government officials, however, thousands of acquaintances, deals and relationship ties were conflated together to form a conspiracy theory that gave the American and international public an explanation appropriate for Cold War propaganda purposes – organized crime, the explanation went, was a big problem, but it was a big problem not of America's making.

The Atlantic City "conference" story – one that still only has a single credible source in Al Capone – was transformed from a meeting involving a handful of Chicago gangsters into a meeting that divided underworld territory throughout the entire United States under the auspices of a quasi-national government of crime. The mythical conference thus gave organized crime in America a start date: May 15, 1929. Another story which began with no credible sources at all gave the idea of the Mafia as a centralized organization a start date: September 10, 1931. For a variety of expedient reasons, many journalists and law enforcement officials began to use fragments of information to jump from the undeniable to what should have been the unbelievable – failed businessmen like Capone, Luciano and Lansky constructing a government equivalent to the US government and a corporate edifice comparable to US Steel and General Motors.

Inset 3: "Lucky" Luciano and a Life in Exile

On January 20, 1953, the world's most famous living gangster businessman, known as Charles "Lucky" Luciano or Salvatore Lucania, wrote this desperate and poorly spelled letter to the governor of New York State, Thomas E. Dewey:

Via Tasso 464
Napoli Italy
I hope you dont mind the way this letter is written, and also that I am writing to you, it is the best I can do, and also my only hopes for some relief.

Till this last election I thought they wanted to knock you out of politics, but after election I see that they dont want to let up, the agents that Anslinger has here are stooping to everything to get me.

I wish you would take some interest in this matter, because I never gave it a thought in going into the dope business, direct or indirect, and if it wasn't so I wouldn't be writing to you.

If you dont believe me I make a sujestion, and that is to have the Attorney General appoint one investigator to investigate the Narcotic Division there and all the European Interpol, including me. I have another sujestion if you want to. I could send direct to you my side of the story, of what I know, which I would like it much better.

Governor, since I left the U.S.A. I haven't had a day in peace, and there isn't any let up in sight.

If you dont want to do it for me, please do it for yourself, that you didn't let out of jail an international dope smuggler.

That great power that the Narcotic Division has, is in the wrong hands.

Sincerely
Salvatore Lucania[39]

Dewey, as a special prosecutor in New York City nearly 20 years earlier, had secured the conviction of Luciano on the charge of compulsory prostitution. Luciano had received the exceptionally long sentence of 30 to 50 years in prison. On January 2, 1946, as

Governor of New York, Dewey had commuted Luciano's sentence conditional on his deportation to Italy on the grounds that Luciano had contributed valuable assistance to the American Second World War effort. Speculation with minimal evidence as to the nature of this help formed the basis of many print articles and a book published in 1977, called *The Luciano Project: The Secret Wartime Collaboration of the Mafia and the U.S. Navy.*

In the letter Luciano was reacting to the attention being heaped on him by Harry Anslinger and his agents of the FBN. Luciano clearly had no idea how American government worked – the idea of a state governor asking the US Attorney General to examine the activities of a federal agency on behalf of a suspected criminal was naïve.

At the end of the Second World War, Anslinger had worked hard to reframe drug use and addiction as a war between good and evil to be fought just as relentlessly as the recent hostilities against Germany, Italy and Japan. He reworked an old moralist theme to tell *True Detective* magazine in 1946, for example, that "With the coming of peace our country faces a foe that can be just as deadly as the enemy in the field of battle."[40]

It was difficult to portray illicit powders and pills as a convincingly frightening foe, and so Anslinger and his allies began to make absurdly exaggerated claims about Luciano's power and influence, and to concoct a history of organized crime in America based on the assertion that Luciano's organization, "The Mafia," had achieved almost total underworld dominance. Top FBN agent, Colonel Garland Williams, began this process in 1947 when he told news reporters that "Luciano has been the suspected head of international dope traffic since 1930 or thereabouts."[41] News reports derived from Williams and other FBN agents in the early 1950s had Luciano as "the czar of a vast and secret underworld government"[42] and "the kingpin of narcotics traffic in the United States and Italy."[43] One newspaper piece in 1955 claimed that: "Luciano has increased your taxes and the cost of goods and services; has corrupted your unions, your police, your politicians; has organized your criminals and flooded your country with narcotics."[44]

The two journalists who served Anslinger's interests best were Jack Lait and Lee Mortimer, columnists for Hearst publications and joint authors of a series of bestselling *Confidential* exposés. Luciano, they wrote, was the head of the Mafia, which was "the super-government which now has tentacles reaching into the Cabinet and the White House itself, almost every state capital, huge Wall Street interests, and connections in Canada, Greece, China and Outer Mongolia, and even through the Iron Curtain into Soviet Russia."[45] It controlled, they wrote, "all sin" and "practically all crime in the United States." Not surprisingly given the power and reach of "his" organization, Luciano was "the richest man in Italy" who paid off "half the government and most of the cops."[46]

Drew Pearson, another influential columnist, repeated the same message about the exiled Luciano. Like Lait, Mortimer and many other commentators on organized crime, he acknowledged his debt to the FBN. In 1950 Pearson used claims about Luciano as a key part of what was becoming the commonly accepted version of the history of organized crime in America. "Few people," he wrote, "realize the tremendous power" of the Mafia "or that its head, Lucky Luciano, directs its affairs from Italy." "The history," he elaborated, "of these strange underground rulers goes back to the 18th century when the Mafia was organized in Sicily to oppose the tyranny of the Bourbons." In America, he continued, "With the advent of prohibition the Mafia woke up to the realization that there was money to be made easily: and it worked hand in hand with the Jews who had the ready cash to start businesses. Furthermore, the Jew, who is seldom a killer, used the Mafia to great advantage to protect himself against intrusions and hijacking ... those [Mafia] members who went into partnership with the Jews in bootlegging prospered financially by leaps and bounds." "The Jew" was thus an important part of Pearson's analysis.

Variations of the remainder of Pearson's narrative and "analysis" have been repeated so many times in print on or film that few people today doubt their authenticity. After a couple of years of Mafia gangsters killing each other in the early 1930s, Pearson claimed, Luciano brought about "pacification" and, "From that time, the Mafia has cornered every racket promising easy money – narcotics, pinball machines, slot machines, prostitution, gambling of every form and description." Pearson's closing line was that "Lucky Luciano, the international head, still exercises a mysterious control over the American underworld from Italy."[47] The Jews Pearson had in mind as co-founders of modern organized crime were Arnold Rothstein and Meyer Lansky. Pearson was building on decades of xenophobia that would be given spurious legitimacy by a succession of government committees and commissions and federal police reports.

After writing his sad letter to Governor Dewey in 1953, Luciano continued to live in Italy until he died. Despite almost constant surveillance by the FBN and the Italian police, and regularly being linked with drug traffickers, no conclusive evidence was ever found. As a medium dollar-rich American in an Italy whose economy was broken by years of fascist corruption and wartime devastation, he didn't have to work. The following description of his final years by his most recent biographer is convincing: "Luciano wasn't making a fortune in Italy from illicit heroin smuggling. He was still living off the money his friends continued to send him from the United States, and that was getting to be less and less as they came under pressure themselves. He was always thinking of little business projects, but these usually came to nothing."[48] He went to the movies or the races and he had girlfriends, but mostly he sat in bars and restaurants, often American-themed bars and restaurants, where he was keen to talk to American reporters and tourists when he could. Commenting on the press attention he was getting, Luciano told one journalist, "I'll tell you, they got me accused of starting the Second World War and they'll get to that, you'll see."[49]

His saddest projects involved efforts to get films made of his life and career, where he appeared to only have succeeded in boosting the fortunes of Martin Gosch and the many writers who later chose to make *The Last Testament of Luciano* a legitimate source.

In 1964, two years after Luciano's death, the US Senate's Permanent Subcommittee on Investigations investigated the role of organized crime in the illicit traffic in narcotics and they found evidence that contradicted claims about the hierarchical structure of drug trafficking almost completely. Instead of an organization with the likes of Luciano in control, they found vast networks of criminal entrepreneurs that transcended state borders, ethnic identity, culture, religion and other social variables. These networks had over 400 actors spread across Marseilles (20), Le Havre (4), Paris (21), Milan (8), Genoa (2), Naples (4), Rome (4), Sicily (23), Turkey (13), Beirut (11), Montreal (25), Toronto (10), Buffalo (8), Boston (9), New York City (86), Connecticut (6), Philadelphia/Camden (4), Baltimore (3), Washington, DC/Fairfax County (9), Miami (12), Atlanta (4), New Orleans (6), St. Louis (3),

Cleveland (5), Detroit (6), Chicago (36), Omaha (3), Kansas City (11), Tulsa (1), Dallas (5), Houston (8), Brownsville (1), San Antonio (1), El Paso (1), Denver (4), Seattle (4), Portland (4), San Francisco (15) and Los Angeles (13).

The criminologist Jeffrey Scott McIllwain has analyzed these actors and found that they were: "the producers, refiners, distributors, importers, exporters, wholesalers, retailers, pushers, financiers and enforcers involved in an inherently extensive transnational criminal enterprise based on a myriad of relational ties formed within an extensive, international social system of organized crime."

According to McIllwain, these varied roles did not take account of the networks' relational ties to upperworld allies such as corrupt cops, politicians, customs officials or judges and other underworld actors in Asia, the Caribbean, Mexico, and Central and South America. The actors composing these networks came from Lebanese, Sicilian, Italian, French, Corsican, Armenian, Turkish, Chinese, French Canadian, African American, Mexican, English and Irish backgrounds. They were Jewish, Moslem, Christian and Buddhist. Some were related by blood or by marriage. Some grew up together in the same neighborhoods or met in prison. Others shared ethnic backgrounds or met in the social context of local underworlds.[50]

The evidence overwhelmingly pointed to a lack of hierarchy in the organization of international drug trafficking, but US officials chose to ignore all evidence that did not support notions of a big super-criminal government of crime headed by the likes of Luciano.

PART III

Covering up Failure: Constructing an Acceptable Response to "Organized Crime"

Introduction

The nonsensical but widely believed falsehoods described in Part II were in line with Cold War thinking and helped give Americans the impression that the business and government institutions of the United States were fundamentally faultless. The problems of organized crime were seen as external – the result of a foreign conspiracy. The real but usually separate activities of Italian American gangsters in different cities were conflated to provide a catch-all explanation of American organized crime problems.

By the 1960s most commentators went along with the idea that American systems of government and business were themselves fundamentally sound but faced threats from a hierarchically organized criminal conspiracy known as the Mafia or sometimes the Cosa Nostra. The Mafia, according to politicians, law enforcement officials and the media, threatened the integrity of local government. The Mafia, they repeatedly said, corrupted police officers, lawyers and legitimate businessmen, and thus framed discourse so that perpetrators became victims. Richard Nixon put the weight of the presidency behind the Mafia conspiracy interpretation and ensured the almost unchallenged passage of the Organized Crime Control Act of 1970. Thus an analysis that shifted blame from many of those actively involved in organized crime had meant that organized crime control strategies could be developed that did not require any questioning of the prohibition laws or America's business and political systems.

Beginning in the late 1960s, a number of journalists and academics pointed out the almost complete absence of evidence and logic behind mainstream analyses of organized crime. They established beyond doubt that Mafia gangsters in America were not part of a coherent, national organization that controlled illegal markets, and instead offered analyses of organized crime that called into question the entire thrust of the government's response.

From the 1980s, even the US government accepted that the idea of one "super-government" of crime was no longer credible. However, it simply pluralized its analysis and began to support claims that were equally dubious. According to these claims, the Mafia had once been all-powerful, but it was now challenged by other "super-governments" of crime such as Triads from Asia or drug "cartels" from South America. The Reagan administration set up a presidential commission into organized crime that provided superficial substance for such unproven assumptions. A large number of Mafia gangsters were successfully prosecuted during the Reagan era and anti-money laundering laws were added to the government's organized crime control armory. Many more organized crime problems were, however, either created or ignored by misguided policies set in stone during these years.

1
Mafia Mythology and the Federal Response

As we saw in Parts 1 and 2, the idea of organized crime as a specifically Italian import had taken root in America after a series of incidents that followed the unsolved killing of New Orleans Police Chief Hennessy in 1890. In the 1920s the Chicago-based politician Charles G. Dawes introduced the idea of a foreign super-government of crime, and successfully shifted attention away from business criminality. Prominent Americans, notably the publisher, William Randolph Hearst, found in Benito Mussolini's campaign against the Sicilian Mafia a response to organized crime based on repression of selected criminals that did not threaten the status quo. Hyperbolic reporting of the influence or alleged influence of Al Capone in Chicago and Lucky Luciano in New York was given substance and shape by the likes of Hickman Powell, Drew Pearson and Hearst commentators Jack Lait and Lee Mortimer. Powell, it should be noted, was a publicist for a politician on the rise, the others claimed authenticity by acknowledging their debts to the FBN. The agency then pressured for an approach to drug control based primarily on crushing the foreign conspiracy they claimed controlled the traffic. At mid-century the alien conspiracy interpretation of organized crime was given another immense boost by the aforementioned senate investigative committee chaired by Estes Kefauver during 1950 and 1951.

The Kefauver Committee held televised hearings in Chicago, New York, New Orleans and other cities and its reports gave undeserved substance and respectability to notions about organized crime that should have been dismissed as conspiracy theories.

The committee's *Third Interim Report* borrowed a narrative from the likes of Lait, Mortimer and Pearson and traced the history of the Sicilian Mafia and its "implantation" into America, reflecting the assumption that Mussolini's campaigns in the 1920s and 1930s had been successful:

> The various drives against the Mafia in Sicily which were made by Italian governments from the 1870s down to Mussolini's time, were ... largely ineffective in destroying the Mafia. However, these drives had the effect of causing large numbers of Mafia members to migrate to the New World and many of them came to this country ... The Mafia became established in New Orleans and other cities. Moreover, like many underworld organizations it became rich and powerful during Prohibition and since that time this organization has entered every racket promising easy money. Narcotics, pinball machines, slot machines, gambling in every form and description are some of its major activities at the present time.

The committee's report then made the following frequently quoted but usually unexamined assertions:

> There is a nationwide crime syndicate known as the Mafia, whose tentacles are found in many large cities. It has international ramifications which appear most clearly in connection with the narcotics traffic.
>
> Its leaders are usually found in control of the most lucrative rackets of their cities.
>
> There are indications of a centralized direction and control of these rackets, but leadership appears to be in a group rather than in a single individual.
>
> The Mafia is the cement that helps bind the Costello-Adonis-Lanksy syndicate of New York and the Accardo-Guzik-Fischetti syndicate of Chicago as well as smaller criminal gangs and individual criminals throughout the country. These groups have kept in touch with Luciano since his deportation from this country.
>
> The domination of the Mafia is based fundamentally on "muscle" and "murder." The Mafia is a secret conspiracy against law and order which will ruthlessly eliminate anyone who betrays its secrets. It will use any means available – political influence, bribery, intimidation, etc. – to defeat any attempts on the part of law enforcement to touch its top figures or to interfere with its operations.[1]

The Kefauver report did not attempt to substantiate the crude analysis contained in these excerpts. Once the report had been issued, however, it, rather than the cheap sensationalism of journalists, became a significant historical source adding the illusion of weight and coherence to the idea of organized crime as a centralized entity and alien implant.

None of the evidence the committee actually produced indicated centralized national control, but the weight of a prestigious Senate investigative committee had been put behind an alien conspiracy interpretation of organized crime. This interpretation featured, in the words of the committee's chief counsel Rudolph Halley "the Mafia criminal super-government in America."[2] Halley's words echoed the claims of Charles Dawes two decades earlier.

Despite a great deal of hopeful effort, no evidence was produced at the hearings to support the view of a centralized Sicilian or Italian organization dominating organized crime in the United States. The committee said they were surprised when Italian American racketeers denied they were in an organization called the Mafia. These, if they testified at all, were constantly prodded, probed and encouraged by committee members and counsel to admit that they were in the Mafia, but none did so. This effort became farcical when Halley asked New Jersey racketeer Willie Moretti whether he was a member of the Mafia. Moretti answered with another question: "What do you mean by a member, carry a card with Mafia on it?"[3]

The only evidence the report offered for its Mafia conclusions were a number of drug trafficking stories supplied by the FBN involving Italian American gangsters. Neither these stories nor any testimony at the hearings were at all convincing about the idea of a centralized organization dominating or controlling organized crime. In fact, virtually all of the hard evidence produced by the committee contradicted its Mafia conclusions. The committee found men with different ethnic origins at the head of criminal syndicates around the nation, with frequent contact and cooperation between different ethnic groups. The ethnic origins of the suspected syndicate figures called before the committee were fairly equally divided between Jewish, Irish and Italian. Even in the committee's own choice of the two most powerful syndicates in the country – the Costello-Adonis-Lansky syndicate of New York and the Accardo-Guzik-Fischetti syndicate of

Chicago, which were somehow bound together by the Mafia "cement" – Jacob Guzik and Meyer Lansky were Jewish, and Frank Costello, Joe Adonis and Charles Fischetti had parents who originated in mainland Italy. Presumably Tony Accardo represented the Sicilian "cement." All of the major gangsters had been born or at least nurtured in America. The networks of illegal activities that the committee described cut across ethnic designations and always depended on the compliance of local officials. The evidence the committee uncovered showed that gambling operators in different parts of the country had sometimes combined in joint ventures, in the same way as businessmen everywhere, and had made a lot of money for themselves and for public officials.[4]

The committee made 22 recommendations to combat crime in interstate commerce. These included a number of acts tightening up existing anti-gambling legislation, the establishment of a Federal Crime Commission and proposals related to the regulation of immigration and deportation. Most of the proposals for new legislation generated little enthusiasm in Congress and were dropped. The Kefauver Committee was essentially a show put on to maintain support for existing anti-gambling and anti-drug policies, and it produced only one recommendation that had any long-term significance. The Committee's Recommendation XII reads:

> Penalties against the illegal sale, distribution, and smuggling of narcotic drugs should be increased substantially. There is an alarming rise in the use of narcotics, particularly among teenagers, who begin with marijuana and gradually become hopeless addicts to heroin and cocaine. The average prison sentence meted out to narcotics traffickers is eighteen months, and, as Narcotics Commissioner Anslinger told us, "short sentences do not deter." The committee endorsed the commissioner's recommendation that the law be amended to fix a *mandatory* [emphasis added] penalty of at least five years' imprisonment for dope peddlers and others engaged in commercial aspects of the narcotics traffic, on conviction for a second offence. Passage of such a bill has been recommended by the House of Representatives' Ways and Means Committee.[5]

This recommendation was in support of Congressman Hale Boggs, a white supremacist from Louisiana. Boggs had introduced a bill to increase all drug-offense penalties, with mandatory minimums of two years for a first offense, five years for a second offense and ten (to 20) for third and subsequent repetitions. Making the length of prison sentences for drug offenses mandatory diminished the role of judges, hit black and minority defendants hardest because enforcement was directed mainly at them, and eventually, as we shall see in Chapter 9, led to prisons that were overcrowded and incubators of the prison gang phenomenon.

The fate of an epileptic Mexican American named Gilbert Zaragoza was an early example of the harshness of the mandatory minimum policy. Poorly educated and with a pathetic record of minor brushes with the law, Zaragoza was trapped, at the age of 21, selling heroin to a 17-year-old addict-informer who worked for the FBN in Los Angeles. Both Zaragoza and the Bureau's "special employee" were addicts, and Zaragoza's selling activity was the easiest, and perhaps the only, way for him to obtain his own supply. He was charged and prosecuted under a sale-to-minors section of a successor law to the Boggs Act, and received a life term from a federal judge.

According to the mandatory terms of the law and his sentence he became an inmate of the federal prison system for the rest of his natural life with no possibility of parole. He had made two heroin sales that had earned him $27.[6] According to Rufus King's account in *The Drug Hang-Up*:

[Zaragoza] and the stream of thirty-, forty-, and fifty-year inmates who followed him into the federal institutions, who were barred from parole and therefore had no incentive to take part in rehabilitative programs, played havoc with enlightened prison administration throughout the federal system. But in the eyes of lawmakers that was seemingly a trifling price for the political benefits that are always believed to flow from posturing as relentless warriors in the battle against dope.[7]

Anslinger and Kefauver had got the Boggs Act passed by making organized crime a national security issue. This had the effect of closing off discussion about different approaches to drug control.

The Kefauver Committee had concluded that, while federal agencies could not be a substitute for state and local enforcement in dealing with organized crime, the federal government must provide leadership and guidance, establish additional techniques for maximum coordination of law enforcement agencies, take a positive approach in using its power to fight organized crime and seek legislation when its powers were insufficient. Given that organized crime was by then mainly associated with gambling operators and drug traffickers, the committee was effectively arguing the case for increased federal involvement in the enforcement of the gambling and drug laws. Kefauver and his colleagues had set an important process in motion. The US government, failing to learn any lessons from Prohibition, was more and more committed to the policing of illegal markets.

The committee's lack of evidence for its Mafia conspiracy theory did not matter since its aim was to reduce the complexities of organized crime to a simple "good versus evil" equation. The committee had accepted the arguments against gambling and drugs and no serious consideration was given to the possibility of government regulation and control of these activities. The public had to be convinced that prohibitions were the only option and prohibitions had to be made effective. Enforcement had to be seen as the only answer. The committee thus chose to put the weight of its opinion behind a bizarre and unsubstantiated interpretation of America's organized crime problems. Because organized crime was seen as a centralized foreign conspiracy, alternative ways of regulating and controlling gambling and drugs were out of the question; that would be a capitulation to powerful and alien criminal interests. The only solution, according to the committee and a growing consensus of opinion in the law enforcement community and among opinion makers, was increased federal commitment. This involved the enactment of more laws and the establishment of a federal law enforcement capacity that was capable of succeeding where local authorities had failed. By some means, according to the new line, people had to be prevented from indulging in activities that filled the coffers of the Mafia.

These were mythical interpretations, magically stringing together disconnected fears, prejudices and hatreds about organized crime and foreigners. The idea of a foreign conspiracy dominating organized crime effectively absolved the United States from any responsibility for its drug and organized crime problems, but left it with a problem. It still had to police society.

* * *

Real events such as the meeting of around 60 Mafia gangsters at Apalachin in 1957, the association of the nation's top labor leader Jimmy Hoffa with Italian American and other gangsters, and the televised testimony of a minor career criminal, Joseph Valachi, in 1963 were interpreted in essentially the same way. They all were said to demonstrate that the Mafia not only existed as a centralized national organization, but that it dominated organized crime in America.[8]

After Apalachin, even J. Edgar Hoover of the FBI changed his tune about organized crime. Previously, he had publicly considered organized crime to be a problem most closely associated with local political corruption. He had never denied the existence of organized crime, but he stressed the role of corrupt local politicians and police in protecting organized criminal enterprises. In fact, this was an accurate assessment of gambling-related organized crime, the type of crime that concerned the American media and politicians most during the 1950s and early 1960s. Hoover, quite sensibly, kept his agency away from the corrupting and fruitless tasks of gambling control.

By the 1960s, however, Hoover joined the chorus of law enforcement officials and media commentators that were making the terms organized crime and Mafia virtually synonymous. In 1960, he wrote in the *FBI Law Enforcement Bulletin* that the Mafia was a "lawless legion" that "infiltrates through every loophole, its booty flowing into underworld coffers whether it be nickel and dimes from a juke box in a bar in the smallest town or from a multi-million-dollar stranglehold on large metropolitan centers obtained through the domination of a few dishonest labor officials."[9] From this time on, Hoover chose to go along with the consensus of law enforcement opinion and decided to reduce organized crime to a single conspiratorial entity.

* * *

The FBI now became the leading standard-bearer against what it called the "La Cosa Nostra," and Hoover began to repeat the new conventional wisdom about organized crime. This was stated most comprehensively in the 1967 report of President Lyndon Johnson's Commission on Law Enforcement: "The core of organized crime in the United States consists of 24 groups operating criminal cartels in large cities across the nation. Their membership is exclusively Italian, they are in frequent communication with each other, and their smooth functioning is insured by a national body of overseers." The Commission's report recommended a complete package of laws to combat the Cosa Nostra's subversion of "the very decency and integrity that are the most cherished attributes of a free society."[10]

One of the Commission's consultants, Donald Cressey, gave these notions a veneer of academic respectability. Cressey's 1969 book, *Theft of the Nation: The Structure and Operations of Organized Crime in America*, claimed that organized crime in the most powerful nation on earth, a nation then of 200 million people, was controlled by a single Italian entity. Cressey followed FBI practice and called this single entity the Cosa Nostra rather than the Mafia but the analysis was the same. Cressey's final recommendation for the control of organized crime was to call for the federal government to come to an understanding with "Cosa Nostra's Commission in the way the Department of State has come to an understanding with the Kremlin." The Cosa Nostra, according to Cressey, controlled illegal gambling among other things, and an understanding with the government had the potential of eliminating the corruption and violence associated with gambling and "subject the organization to reasonable governmental regulations such as those pertaining to all corporations." It was a sadly misinformed acceptance of the idea that organized crime in America was governed by a super-government.[11]

* * *

Murray Kempton, one of America's leading columnists, was the first to see through the Cressey/FBI-style Cosa Nostra mythology. Reviewing Cressey's book alongside Ed Reid's *The Grim Reapers* (1969) and FBI transcripts of the eavesdropped words of Sam "The Plumber" DeCavalcante, boss of a New Jersey Cosa Nostra family, Kempton noted that the academic Cressey and the journalist Reid were "our chief sources of social misinformation."

Reid's book was an updated version of his first effort in writing organized crime history, *Mafia* (1952). This claimed that the Italian organization was "history's greatest threat to morality" and "the principal fount of all crime in the world controlling vice, gambling, the smuggling and sale of dope, and other sources of evil."[12] The first line of the 1969 book claimed that "The Mafia is a mailed fist on the scabrous arm of organized crime girdling the earth," and elaborated:

> The fist has its fingers in the very bowels of the human economy, on whatever level people are found: digging into the swank parlors of the White House; grubbing in the opium fields of Red China ... running the lives of the peoples of the world, the coinages, the factories, the shipyards, the docks, the mills, the farms ... killing or maiming people who stand in its way. No one is immune from its attacks. The innocent bystander, the honest cop, the crusading journalist, a thousand men ... all fall victim to the Mafia.[13]

Reid's work was another retread of Charles Dawes' claim that organized crime was a foreign super-government, or, as Reid put it himself, "The Mafia was a super-government of crime that is more powerful than any formally constituted government on earth."[14]

Kempton's review critiqued the Cressey and Reid notions by contrasting their fantastic claims with the mundane reality of DeCavalcante's existence. He juxtaposes, for example, Cressey's claims of "between $6 or $7 billion" going into the coffers of Cosa Nostra so "that any given member of Cosa Nostra is more likely to be a millionaire than not" with DeCavalcante's overheard complaint that "We got 31 or 32 soldiers. Most of them are old people who ain't making much. Those making money give me one third. Say one makes $600, then he gives me $200 and I don't split with anyone else." Clearly, Kempton states, after analyzing evidence of the paltry rewards of life in DeCavalcante's circles, it is "not an environment productive of millionaires."[15] The real world of organized crime revealed by the bugs in DeCavalcante's office was one of stresses and strains over who gets to carry the bricks on building sites, which bosses have to steal dresses from factories to make ends meet and the difficulties in getting tickets for the Copacabana nightclub.

Kempton was swimming against the tide of governmental and journalistic opinion while Cressey and Reid were going very much with the flow. In 1967, Johnson's Commission made over 20 recommendations for federal action against organized crime, most of which were making their way through Congress to be enacted as laws when Kempton's piece was published. Reid's hyperbole complemented Cressey's "reasoned" approach and was widely echoed in exposés that accompanied the progress of the new laws. In August 1969, for example, *Time* devoted eight pages to the Mafia and described it as "a huge, far-reaching dynasty of organized crime – a powerful octopus which administers not only illicit narcotics traffic, gambling and other rackets, but has been infiltrating legitimate unions, business and entertainment enterprises ... its puppets are to be found not only among police, but in the legislatures and even the courts." It was, according to *Time*, a national security threat, "Like the Soviet Conspiracy of Stalin's day, or Hitler's gang of cut throat [*sic*], it is utterly amoral, using terrorism, torture and assassination to bring the reluctant to heel." *Time* joined most of the media in calling upon Congress to push through the new "anti-crime bills."[16]

Before the 1950s, very few people would have associated organized crime exclusively with Italian ethnicity. By the late 1960s, thanks to endless claims by journalists and the phenomenal success of Mario Puzo's *The Godfather* (1969), the thousands of conspiracies that constitute organized crime were reduced to just one – the Mafia. Government officials were happy to supply journalists with the "facts" to support this explanation for the country's organized crime problem. The knowledge that some Italian American gangsters had become rich and powerful in their own cities, and had contact with other gangsters in other cities, was distorted into something far more mysterious and menacing.

There is no doubt that Italian American gangsters have been prominent in US organized crime since the Prohibition years. The disputes are over the identification of organized crime almost exclusively with Italian Americans, the suggestion that organized crime is some sort of alien transplant on to an otherwise pure political and economic system, and the alleged monolithic nature of the Mafia itself. Many people, in every part of the world, not just in America, came to believe that something called the Mafia ran organized crime in the United States. Mafia mythology took a firm grip on people's imagination, by constant repetition of an image.

The phrase organized crime had thus become common by the 1960s, signifying a hierarchically organized criminal conspiracy. Organized crime was now seen as a criminal army far away from earlier perspectives that emphasized the involvement and responsibility of "respectable" society for the pervasive problem of organized crime activity in the United States. This new conceptualization of "organized crime" thus got public officialdom and private business interests off the hook.

Since it was now commonly accepted that a foreign conspiracy was corrupting the police, the police had to be given more power to fight this conspiracy. It didn't matter that police corruption was a key part of the problem of organized crime – increasing police powers was the only serious solution considered. Reconsideration of the laws governing gambling and drug-taking was out of the question. The only answer was increased law enforcement capacity and more laws to ensure the swift capture of gambling operators and drug traffickers behind whom the Mafia or Cosa Nostra was always supposed to be lurking.[17]

By the 1960s, Mafia mythology had provided US officials and politicians with an easy-to-communicate threat to the nation. Mafia mythology helped to limit people's awareness of the flaws in an approach to organized crime based exclusively on giving the government more power to combat threats to America's morally authoritarian and business-dominated system.

The Mafia never did control or even dominate organized crime in America, although Mafia families certainly had a great deal of influence in some areas in some cities. Serious journalists, historians and criminologists, as we shall see in Chapter 3, would, like Kempton, demonstrate the almost complete absence of evidence and logic lying behind Mafia mythology, but they were ignored.

2
President Richard Nixon and Organized Crime Control

US government officials got the power they claimed would enable them to fight the Mafia conspiracy in the Organized Crime Control Act of 1970. Organized crime control provisions now included: special grand juries; wider witness immunity provisions for compelling or persuading reluctant witnesses; witness protection measures; extended sentences for persons convicted in organized crime cases; and the use of wiretapping and eavesdropping evidence in federal cases. One of the most significant parts of the package was the Racketeering Influenced and Corrupt Organizations Act, or RICO, which made it illegal to acquire, operate or receive income from an "enterprise" through a "pattern" of racketeering activity. Any individual or group who committed two or more indictable offenses characteristic of organized crime within a ten-year period, as part of a continuing criminal enterprise, could receive extended prison sentences, fines and asset forfeitures. With concurrent anti-drug legislation, a far stronger policing presence was established in America.

Organized crime control policy added superficial substance to the tough law-and-order image Nixon had been trying to cultivate since his narrow presidential election victory in 1968. In many ways it was appropriate that Richard Nixon was the man who presented the paradigm of organized crime control to the American people. He was dishonest, morally authoritarian, expedient and corruptly indebted to the big business interests that had paid for his campaigns.

In the process of getting the 1970 act passed, Nixon articulated the law enforcement consensus on organized crime. He gave the Mafia conspiracy theory the seal of presidential approval in a message to Congress on April 23, 1969. He described the Mafia's influence as "more secure than ever before," and warned that its operations had "deeply penetrated broad segments of American life." "It is vitally important," he continued, "that Americans see this alien organization for what it really is – a totalitarian and closed society, operating within an open and democratic one. It has succeeded so far because an apathetic public is unaware of the threat it poses to American life."

He claimed that gambling was "the lifeline of organized crime" and would thus be the focus of the administration's efforts. Gambling, he elaborated, "provides the bulk of the revenues that eventually go into usurious loans, bribes of police and local officials, 'campaign contributions' to politicians, the wholesale narcotics traffic, the infiltration of legitimate business and to pay for the large stables of lawyers and accountants and assorted professional men who are in the hire of organized crime."[18]

In the same month as he made these claims, Nixon directed a group of presidential advisers to examine the effectiveness of the executive branch in combating organized crime. Nixon's advisers focused their study on the effectiveness of the federal anti-organized crime program in nine mainly north-eastern cities. After reviewing it with more than 100 federal, state and local state criminal justice and law enforcement personnel, they came to the damning conclusion that federal organized crime control was failing badly. The advisers made many recommendations for improvement, but their mandate restricted them to suggestions for structural and administrative changes in the executive branch. These they made, but they also included the following comment which would have seriously undermined Nixon's line on organized crime had it been made public: "We would be negligent, however, not to emphasize that organized crime flourishes in today's legal and social environment. Even with administrative improvement, organized crime will continue to thrive so long as the community relies primarily on criminal sanctions to discourage gambling and the use of drugs."[19]

The Nixon administration paid no heed to the report's conclusions and recommendations, making sure that its findings were classified and ordering the destruction of all copies. Egil Krogh was the White House administrator responsible for the order and although the rest may have been destroyed he failed to destroy his own copy, which remained in his Watergate file.

During and since the Nixon years the US government began a "war" against drugs and therefore, as the presidential advisers had predicted, organized crime continued to thrive. Domestically, the Nixon administration's main legislative innovation was to secure the passing of the Comprehensive Drug Abuse Control Act of 1970 – a statute that brought together everything Congress had done in the drug field since curbs on opium smoking in 1887. The law gave the Department of Justice an array of powers over licit and illicit drugs covering possession, sale and trafficking. Drug offenders faced severe sanctions including life for those engaged in "continuing criminal enterprise" or who qualified as a "dangerous special drug offender." Treasury funds were to be made available to enforcement agents to hire informants, pay for incriminating information and make purchases of contraband substances. Agents were given the power to seize on sight any property they thought was contraband or forfeitable, and execute search warrants at any time of the day or night, with a new "no-knock" procedure if a judge had authorized it. We shall return to the destructive consequences of such an aggressive drug prohibition policy.

The Nixon administration's efforts against gambling were the final futile chapter in this part of America's program of moral reform. By the mid-1970s the increased federal effort against gambling had subsided with little accomplished despite the enormous expense involved in surveillance and prosecution. There were a few, pointless prison sentences achieved after expensive and time-consuming policing operations. A former strike force chief later told the *Wall Street Journal* that gambling cases had become something to keep the statistics up: "We would investigate a couple of low grade bookmakers, call them organized crime figures and go after them."[20]

By the middle of the 1970s the trend towards a regulatory approach to gambling was well established. Pompous lectures about the evils of gambling, and deceptive claims for the potential of anti-gambling measures, could no longer halt a re-examination of policy by many state and local authorities looking for ways to increase revenue and influenced by an expanding corporate gambling sector. Casino and other forms of gambling in the United States still have problems with racketeering and fraud but no more so than in other corporate-dominated sectors.

Most gangster owners of Las Vegas casinos had sold out to corporate interests by the 1970s. In 1967, for example, Meyer Lansky was thought to have collected $1 million as his share of the sale of the Sands Hotel.

This might seem a lot of money, but as his biographer Robert Lacey has pointed out, the new purchasers had picked themselves a bargain:

> In the course of the next decade, Las Vegas casinos multiplied many times in value and came to change hands for hundreds of millions of dollars. It was like the legal state lotteries that proliferated in the 1970s and 1980s, instantly dwarfing the numbers games they mimicked. The corporate inheritors of Las Vegas have proved that the legitimate world can run a racket better than any crook.[21]

The same point can be made with regard to the rise of online gaming in the last decade.

3
Challenging the Orthodoxy

Following Kempton's dissection of the Valachi- and DeCavalcante-based Mafia mythology, a number of academics and commentators began a sustained critique of claims about the Mafia's centralized structure and criminal omnipotence, characterizing them as representing an "alien conspiracy" analysis of organized crime. They were right but mainstream politicians, government officials and journalists refused to engage with organized crime analysis that had been based on serious research.

Joseph Albini published a study of organized crime in Detroit that contradicted the portrayals of established hierarchies and centralized national control. In *The American Mafia: Genesis of a Legend* (1971), he wrote, "rather than being a criminal secret society, a criminal syndicate consists of a system of loosely structured relationships functioning primarily because each participant is interested in furthering his own welfare. [Since] relationships in syndicated activity are extremely flexible and constantly changing, it would be futile and unrealistic to attempt to chart or give limits or boundaries to the multitude and types of those relationships."[22]

Albini's insight was based on interviews with organized criminals as well as law enforcement officers. When the book came out it was ignored by most of the press but he was invited on television shows to promote it. On one of these he was asked, "Is it true the Mafia paid you to write this book?"[23] Albini has written that his first response was laughter, thinking it was a joke. But Albini quickly realized that the interviewer was sincere because he was so under the spell of Mafia conspiracy theory that he honestly believed that anybody who questioned its existence was an accomplice to its plots. Albini also recognized that he, as an Italian American messenger, may have influenced the interviewer's calculus. "The fact my name ended in an 'I' apparently lent credence to his belief."[24]

Albini faced similarly uninformed criticisms from members of his own ethnic group. One approached him at a book signing in Detroit and asked why Joe didn't want to say there was a centralized Mafia. "Look, it's the only thing we've got," the man complained. "If these cake-eaters respect us at all, it's because they know we can dump them in the river. Take away that and the Italians will really eat dirt."[25]

Two contemporaries of Albini, ethnographers Francis and Elizabeth Ianni,[26] also found that the US government had little or no knowledge on organized crime. The Iannis carried out extensive fieldwork among one New York Mafia family and its associates. They focused on the behavior and power relationships within the family and identified a number of rules of conduct that guided family members. They concluded that secret societies such as the Mafia were not really formal organizations in the way the federal government had for decades claimed they were. "They are not rationally designed and consciously constructed," argued the Iannis, "they are responsive to culture and are patterned by tradition. ... They are not hierarchies of organizational positions which can be diagrammed and then changed by recasting the organizational chart; they are patterns of relationship among individuals which have the force of kinship and so they can only be changed by drastic, often fatal action."[27]

Dwight C. Smith, in *The Mafia Mystique* and in subsequent work, also made an effort to move away from the organized crime control community's unproductive focus on ethnicity and hierarchy in the study of organized crime.[28] Instead he proposed "a theory of illicit enterprise" as an invitation to further research and study. He meant by "illicit enterprise" the "extension of legitimate market activities into areas normally proscribed, for the pursuit of profit and in response to latent illicit demand. In this context, the loan shark is an entrepreneur in the banking industry; the drug or cigarette smuggler is a wholesaler and the fence a retailer; and the bribe-taker is a power broker." "These observations," he argued, "reflect two fundamental assumptions: that the range of activity in any marketplace is continuous in character, from the very saintly to the most sinful; and that organizational concepts ordinarily applied only to legitimate businesses are applicable to that entire range of activity."[29] Smith was arguing that the workings of the market system have to be understood in order to construct an organized crime control policy that worked.

There was also a significant challenge to "Godfather" mythology in Gay Talese's *Honor Thy Father*,[30] an "insider" account of the New York Bonanno crime family. This made a point that had been lost by other "true crime" writers: "the Mafia is merely a small part of the organized crime industry."

Talese's insights were based largely on information given to him by Bill Bonanno, son of Mafia boss Joseph Bonanno. Talese describes the younger Mafiosi reaction to the aforementioned DeCavalcante transcripts thus:

> Bill Bonanno was immediately angered at being described unflatteringly; but he also felt, after a second and third reading, that the tapes clearly reconfirmed what he and his father had concluded – the brotherhood was now overpopulated with braggarts and mini-mafiosi, and if President Nixon needed $61 million from Congress to combat such insignificant characters it surely must represent the greatest example of law enforcement feather-bedding in history.[31]

Referring to New York's Mafia "commission" of bosses attempting unsuccessfully to bring some order to their chaotic world, Bill felt that it "was no wonder that that his father had become incompatible with the commission and had refused to be guided by the dictates of old men approaching senility and middle-aged men hardly competent."[32]

For journalists and government officials, New York remained at the center of the supposed national conspiracy. Few understood that a succession of slayings of Italian American gangsters in New York hardly suggested a coherent and disciplined environment. Nevertheless, every shooting was followed by examples of what Jack Newfield called "The Myth of Godfather Journalism," ill-informed speculation about who ordered the hits and who benefited by rising up the Mafia hierarchy.

Newfield was writing in July 1979 after the shooting of Carmine Galante; a drug trafficker fancifully promoted to *capo di tutti capi* ("boss-of-all-bosses") by the newspapers. Newfield described most Mafia reporting as "consumer fraud," with the need to "name new godfathers with the frequency of new Miss Subways" and an overreliance on clipping files and speculative leaks from law enforcement agencies. The agencies' motive to exaggerate were "bigger budgets derived from greater publicity," but their knowledge of organized crime was in fact very limited, as reflected in their inability to control any of the criminal activities. An FBI agent admitted that in truth, "It's all bullshit. We don't really know what's going on. It's all tribal warfare with shifting alliances." Newfield concluded: "There is no one Mafia godfather. There is no capo di tutti capi. There are just law enforcement agencies trying to arrest gangs of career criminals. And newspaper publishers trying to improve circulation. The rest is hype, the rest is myth."[33]

Jimmy Fratiano, the most famous gangster informant of the 1970s, made a similar point. Fratiano had been a successful hitman but an unsuccessful criminal entrepreneur, earning the less than impressive nickname "The Weasel." He was associated with the small and weak Los Angeles "Mafia family." He did, however, help produce a number of significant convictions, testifying against three New York gangsters, one Los Angeles gangster and Rudy Tham, an important San Francisco Teamster official.

Fratiano thought that most Mafia journalism was a joke and poured scorn on the presentation of the Mafia as a tightly knit national organization controlling organized crime. In an interview with crime writer Ovid Demaris, Fratiano revealed what he thought of a May 1977 article in *Time* magazine. The article was entitled, "The Mafia – Big, Bad and Booming," and began with a brief description of the organization and its chain of command: "The Mafia is overseen nationally by the commission, a dozen or so dons who, usually, but not always, defer to the dominant boss in New York because he controls the most men and rackets."[34]

The story claimed that the Mafia was in a state of unrest since the death of "Don Carlo Gambino," the *capo di tutti capi* who had brought a measure of peace to the nation's Mafia families "through guile, diplomacy and strong-arm discipline." Fratiano's reaction to this was, "How they liked this boss-of-all-bosses bullshit."

The article, in the usual way, then "supported" its assertions with a list of Italian American gangsters including Tony Spilotro, one of Fratiano's associates. Spilotro, according to *Time*, controlled loan-sharking, prostitution and narcotics along the Las Vegas Strip, and its assertions were supported with a quote from an unnamed Justice Department official. Fratiano's first-hand knowledge of Spilotro and Las Vegas was different: "Spilotro was nothing but a strong-arm errand boy. The thought that he could control loansharking, prostitution and narcotics along the Strip was mind-boggling. It would be like trying to control three tidal waves with a machine gun."[35]

In 1986, Spilotro was found beaten to death in an Indiana cornfield. Since then writers and law enforcement officials have continued to make highly speculative claims about his importance without offering much by way of substantiation.[36]

Nicholas Pileggi's *Wiseguy: The Shocking True Story of Life in a Mafia Family* (1986) stands out in the Mafia "true crime" oeuvre. Tracking the experiences of an informer, Henry Hill, it provided a convincing account of day-to-day New York Mafia life as being one of treachery, chaos and betrayal rather than the ordered world of Godfather mythology. The film version, *Goodfellas*, directed by Martin Scorsese in 1990, captured much of the tackiness and uncertainty of career criminality in an environment where the US state ultimately had the power.

The work of critical analysts of organized crime such as Albini, Smith, Block and the Iannis, and critical journalists such as Kempton and Newfield, was dismissed and largely forgotten. If their work was referred to at all it was claimed that they denied the existence of the Mafia, when in reality they had simply exposed poor research and faulty conclusions.

The alien conspiracy idea persisted for nearly two decades after the 1970 Organized Crime Control Act. As a result, federal police and prosecutors focused mainly on the task of putting Mafia bosses behind bars.

They met with little success throughout the 1970s, while another of the key aspects of Mafia mythology was exposed as a fraud by properly conducted research at the beginning of the 1980s. An in-depth study of illegal gambling operations made it abundantly clear that no centralized Mafia had ever controlled illegal gambling in America. Peter Reuter's research in *Disorganized Crime: The Economics of the Visible Hand* was based on a vast quantity of materials seized in police raids and interviews with multiple informants. Unlike work based on the likes of Joe Valachi, none of Reuter's critical assertions rested on the unconfirmed statements of a single informant. At a local level, Reuter found that Mafia groups in some parts of New York "had acquired the defining characteristic of the state, namely monopoly of coercive force." However, he also stressed that "The existence of a much more powerful state ... limits the coercive powers of the Mafia and lessens its internal cohesion." "The Mafia," he concluded, "is less centrally coordinated than legend and popular ideology would have us believe. Internal informants and poorly defined property rights within the Mafia prevent it from tapping the potential returns from its dispute settlement role."[37] Taken together Kempton, Albini, Smith, Reuter, Newfield, Bonanno and Fratiano had demonstrated beyond any doubt that although Mafia "families" did have influence in some businesses in some cities, and some significant influence in some trade unions,[38] the Mafia was not a coherent national organization that controlled or even came close to dominating organized crime in America.

4
Sustaining and Updating Mafia Mythology

By the 1980s the US government was faced with mountains of evidence, logic and analysis that showed that the idea of a centralized organization controlling gambling, drugs, labor racketeering and other organized crime activities in a country with a population of 300 million people was nonsense. Mafia mythology needed shoring up, particularly for the international audience, and it got an immense and defining boost through a series of court cases against Mafia bosses Anthony "Fat Tony" Salerno, Carmine "Junior" Persico and Anthony "Tony Ducks" Corallo. These cases came to be known as the "Mafia Commission trials" and marked the peak of federal police and prosecutorial success against Mafiosi during the 1980s and 1990s.

The Mafia Commission trials of 1986 and 1987 have historical significance but not, as usually claimed, in marking the successful dismantling of the Mafia's long-established hierarchy of five New York family leaders who adjudicated on various issues. The significance is rather in giving the US government a success story that they could then sell to the world, in ways reminiscent of Mussolini's propaganda tactics of the 1920s and 1930s.

This effort against the leaders of five New York Mafia families began in 1980 with "Operation GENUS," as James Jacobs relates in *Busting the Mob: United States v. Cosa Nostra*, and "coordinated federal, state and local agencies: FBI agents, New York City detectives and officers, assistant US attorneys, as well as New York State Organized Crime Task Force attorneys and investigators."[39] More than 200 agents and attorneys were assigned to the task of building cases against each of the families, based on the RICO Act of 1970.

With evidence gathered through witnesses, informants and electronic devices, government prosecutors began by making much of the history of Cosa Nostra with the intention of setting a damning context. They traced the Mafia Commission's history from the 1957 Apalachin meeting of crime bosses through the testimony of former surveillance agents and state troopers. These officers were, of course, able to testify that the meeting happened but, since they were not actually at the meeting, they could not have known what was discussed in the meeting itself. Just as countless "true crime" books had used speculation about the event by people who were not there, the commission trial jury were similarly informed by people who were not there. From the fragmentary evidence given by witnesses to an event that happened 30 years earlier, Rudolph Giuliani, the lead US attorney in the trials, jumped to conclusions about events alleged to have taken place 25 years *before* Apalachin. He claimed that "boss Charles 'Lucky' Luciano started the commission 56 years ago to divide territories and settle conflicts among the families."[40] Newspapers supported the idea of the 1931 foundation date referred to by Giuliani. The *Springfield Gazette*, for example, reported that Corallo, Persico and Salerno were convicted of "sitting on or working for the commission established by Charles Lucky Luciano in 1931 after a bloody mob war."[41] Or, as the *New York Daily News* put it, "Three Mafia 'godfathers' were convicted yesterday of belonging to a national 'commission' that has ruled organized crime with an iron fist since the days of Al Capone."[42] "The case," claimed the *Springfield Union*, "proved for the first time the existence of a panel that oversees the Mafia's national operations ... and kept organized crime organized since the Prohibition days."[43] The press reports had thus jumped from hearsay about the long-dead Luciano to claims that local New York gangsters controlled organized crime in America.

Mainstream British journalists chose not to challenge these notions, as most of them simply assimilated the idea of an Italian-dominated centralized American underworld. The *Guardian* journalist, Michael White, for example, claimed that the murder of Mafiosi "Big Paul" Castellano, "prompted fears of a renewed surge of Mafia warfare for control of his $1 billion empire whose tentacles stretch from drugs, gambling to labour racketeering," adding the derivative claim that Castellano had been regarded "as the most important 'Capo di tutti capi' in the American underworld."[44] Janet Daley, an influential columnist for the *Independent*, and later the *Times* and *Sunday Telegraph*, wrote the following in 1990:

early this century came a great wave of Sicilians who brought with them their own family industry. The Mafia gained a hold in America at a time when law enforcement was nominal ... Few British casual observers seem to have any idea how wide and comprehensive the influence of organized crime is in the US. Having its roots in the Little Italy of New York, it now runs the gambling, prostitution and drug empires of America.[45]

As we shall see in Part IV, these kinds of misguided historical assumptions informed British policymakers as they sought to replicate American "success" against organized crime.

The evidence at the commission trials showed there certainly was a commission, but it also showed the limits of "commission" power. Old men meeting in dingy social clubs could approve new Mafia members and could resolve some of the conflicts among their associates, but they could not direct or control criminal activity in New York, let alone nationally. All five of the commission members were from New York and it was clear that New York's gangster setup was very different from the setup in other parts of the country. They were certainly gangsters, but they were definitely not part of a tightly knit, all-powerful national syndicate.

Judging from their recorded conversations, the New Yorkers feared and mistrusted gangsters from other cities. "I think," as Salerno told some of his associates in one intercepted telephone conversation in 1984, "these fuckin' Chicago guys are going to knock my brains in."[46]

Another conversation, this time between Salerno and Corallo, recorded in the Palma Boy Social Club on December 12, 1984, again indicates more insecurity than strength. Salerno is complaining about the lack of respect shown him by a younger gangster:

SALERNO: Fuck that shit ... I won't take orders from the guy.
CORALLO: ... the rest of the guys you got around here that you, you, like, that you made.
SALERNO: They'll always be here. Listen, Tony, if it wasn't for me, there wouldn't be no mob left. I made all the guys. And everybodys' a good guy. This guy don't realize that? I worked myself. Jeez, how could a man be like that, huh? ... I go over and talk to him ... like,

like the first time, the argument I had with him in the barbershop ...
that day. So he says, "Fat Tony ..."

CORALLO: No, I know the way he talks, I've been in meeting
with him.

SALERNO: Oh [moans].

CORALLO: ... I seen the way he talks, "Fuck him, shoot him."
Tony, he's, he's, he's ... One thing, get rid of them, shoot them, kill
them, but then, you know, you can't go on. It's disgusting. Well,
here's to your health, and fuck everything.[47]

In November 1986 both were given 100-year-long prison sentences
and both died in prison.

John Gotti was the next gangster in the hyped-up tradition of
Capone and Luciano. From the time of the Salerno/Corallo trials in
1986 his name kept appearing in the newspapers as the government's
most wanted "Godfather." Variously called "Dapper Don" because of
his expensive dress sense, or "Teflon Don" because of the inability of
government charges to stick, Gotti "strutted through the pages of
the New York tabloids," even making it to the cover of *Time*. The
Guardian went beyond the hyperbole of American newspapers and
referred to Gotti as "Boss of the USA," using mythical numbers to
claim that, "in New York, the Mafia makes $600 billion a year. Most
of it ends up with John Gotti."[48]

Gotti's rise and fall undoubtedly had drama. He was born in the
South Bronx, the fifth of 13 children, dropped out of high school at 16
and soon began to get arrested. Before 1969, he faced charges of street
fighting, drunkenness, car theft, gun possession and burglary, serving
short sentences in county prisons.

In 1969 he was sentenced to three years in federal prison for a
bungled truck hijacking at John F. Kennedy International Airport. In
1973 he took part in the barroom killing of an Irish gangster called
James McBratney. The case went to court in Staten Island where the
district attorney generously offered Gotti the chance to plead guilty to
the charge of attempted manslaughter. He got out in 1976. Towards
the end of 1985, he took over as boss of the Gambino family after
the shooting of "Big Paul" Castellano. From then the US authorities
pursued him relentlessly, bringing him to trial unsuccessfully twice

and recording enough on tape to provide much of the substance for his eventual conviction in 1992.[49]

On the tapes Gotti frequently incriminated himself in murder and racketeering activities. On January 17, 1990 he was also recorded in an apartment above the Ravenite Social Club in Little Italy, Manhattan, at a ceremony in which new members of Cosa Nostra were "made." Gotti gave the following speech:

> And this is gonna be a Cosa Nostra till I die. Be it an hour from now or be it tonight or a hundred years from now when I'm in jail. It's gonna be a Cosa Nostra. This ain't gonna be a bunch of your friends are gonna be "friends of ours," a bunch of Sam's friends are gonna be "friends of ours." It's gonna be the way it's gonna be, and a Cosa Nostra. A Cosa Nostra! ... I wanna see an effort. I gotta see an effort for, starting now, a Cosa Nostra. I don't need a guy who come, tell, tell me, "I feel sorry you got trouble." And I don't mean the cops. I mean the people who can make this a joke. You know what I mean? That's not a fucking joke. And I (inaudible) some guys. See even, even, even some guy, some of the people downstairs now. You know I know whose fucking stomach is rotten. And I know whose stomach ain't rotten. You think I, could smell it. The way a dog senses when a guy has got fear in him, you know what I mean?[50]

On other occasions he made it clear that, for all the oaths of unquestioning loyalty and eternal silence, there was neither unity nor silence in the world he lived in. Gotti's words scarcely revealed the leader of a coherent organization.

Gotti also turned out to be not such a good judge of character as he imagined he was with all the talk of rotten stomachs. One of the men he was addressing was Salvatore "Sammy Bull" Gravano, whose testimony in 1992 probably did more than the tapes to sway the jury towards convicting him. Gravano admitted to 19 murders himself and told of Gotti's sponsorship of the killing of Castellano.

The jury found Gravano's testimony and Gotti's recorded words convincing enough to find Gotti guilty on 43 federal charges of racketeering, multiple murders, loan-sharking, gambling and jury tampering. He was guilty, in effect, of being a racketeer in a city full of racketeers.

The taped conversations should have ended the idea of an organization with almost unlimited national and global power. Gotti was "a cheap thug, and not a particularly bright one," according to Ronald Goldstock, director of New York's Organized Crime Task Force.[51] But most commentary left analysis aside and heaped praise on the government for its success.

The FBI, and other law enforcement agencies, have made many successful investigations of the 20-plus Italian American crime "families" that undoubtedly existed. The court evidence showed that many Mafiosi swore masonic-type oaths of allegiance, used murder and intimidation to protect territories, markets and operations, and New York bosses were sometimes asked to adjudicate on conflicts involving families away from that city.[52] But the evidence also showed the limits of Mafia power and the limits of the government's campaign against them. It showed that bosses, even in cities where Mafiosi were plentiful, such as New York, could not direct or control criminal activity in their own city let alone nationally. They were certainly powerful gangsters, who made an impact on local economies, but not part of a tightly knit, all-powerful national syndicate that could centralize control of illegal markets and therefore constitute a national security threat as was being claimed.[53] James B. Jacobs, a law professor who has written extensively and favorably on federal government campaigns against Italian American gangsters, acknowledged that there was little or no evidence of the existence of a ruling national commission of Mafia bosses. "It is best to think of Cosa Nostra," he wrote, "as a mélange of locally based crime families, each of which has exclusive jurisdiction in its territory."[54]

Evidence from the Mafia trials and from the popular genre of books about Mafia members turned FBI informers suggests a treacherous and often not very well organized Italian American underworld. Although some Mafiosi found themselves lucrative niches in the legal and illegal economies of these cities, studies in recent decades have made it clear that no one organization or cartel could possibly control illegal markets, notably the illegal markets that concerned Americans most: gambling and drugs.

As the New York arrest of over 120 alleged Mafiosi in 2011 showed,[55] Italian American career criminals are continuing either to operate separately or compete or cooperate on occasion. They will also continue to be collectively called the Mafia and be much overrated in films and newspaper articles wishing to applaud government successes. No neat and tidy hierarchy of *capos*, *consiglieres* and soldiers can explain the tidal wave of crime and violence associated with gangsterism and other forms of systematic illegal activity. Mafiosi only participated in a much larger and more complex criminal environment encompassing both legal and illegal markets, but there was no reason to believe that locking up scores of ageing patriarchs or younger bosses made even a marginal impact on organized crime activity in America.

The clear implication of the Mafia supremacy assumption was that the way for the rest of the world to control organized crime was by using the methods that the US government had pioneered in the control of organized crime in America. This meant that the US at the same time as it was trumpeting success against the Mafia, had to revise its understanding of organized crime so that continued failure could be explained and a stepped-up law enforcement response both at home and abroad could be justified. The alien conspiracy explanation for organized crime was therefore replaced by the "pluralist revision" explanation for organized crime.

5

From Super-Government to Super-Governments: The Pluralist Revision of Organized Crime

On October 14, 1982, President Ronald Reagan announced a plan intended to "end the drug menace and cripple organized crime." To do this he announced the creation of a panel of "distinguished Americans from diverse backgrounds and professions with practical experience in criminal justice and combating organized crime." This nationwide investigation was to last for three years, "analyze and debate the data it gathers," and "hold public hearings on the findings." Apart from legislative recommendations, the intention was "to heighten public awareness and knowledge about the threat of organized crime and mobilize citizen support for its eradication."[56] On July 28, 1983, Reagan formally established the President's Commission on Organized Crime, to be chaired by Judge Irving R. Kaufman and composed of 18 other men and women, mainly from the law enforcement community.

The commission's stated intention was to investigate the power and activities of "traditional organized crime" and "emerging organized crime groups." By then, despite the hoopla caused by the FBI drive against the Mafia, it was clear that gangsters from every racial and ethnic origin were involved in systematic criminal activity, and that making organized crime synonymous with Mafia was no longer viable or even desirable for the law enforcement and criminal justice bureaucracies. There was a need to adapt Mafia mythology to a new age.

At the first hearing in November 1983 the nation's top law enforcement officers articulated a new federal perspective. The commission's deference to the Reagan administration was illustrated from this first hearing. The main speakers were Attorney General William French Smith, FBI Director William Webster and Drug Enforcement Administration (DEA) Administrator Francis Mullen, and each identified "traditional organized crime" exclusively with

Italian Americans or "the La Cosa Nostra." They all highlighted that organized crime was no longer synonymous with one group and stressed the importance of "emerging groups," mentioning motorcycle gangs, prison gangs and "foreign-based" organizations. At the hearing, drug trafficking was identified as the most profitable organized crime activity and the problem that most needed addressing.[57]

At a hearing held on October 23–5, 1984, the commission's counsel, James D. Harmon, outlined the US government's direction of travel for organized crime control and international organized crime control. "While it is true," he testified, "that the specifics of the commission is to examine organized crime in this country, it is equally true that what is occurring in the United States is linked to the events of organizations of an international character and that organized crime must be attacked, for the attack to be successful, on an international basis." He then referred to US law enforcement successes against "traditional organized crime" before implying that US techniques should be replicated elsewhere in the world but particularly in Asia since, as he testified to the commission in New York hearings, "The tentacles of the Chinese Triad Societies run from the hills of Burma to the financial centers of Hong Kong, the many streets of this and any other American cities."[58]

After three years' superficial investigation of its identified problem areas of drugs, labor racketeering, money laundering and gambling, the commission added very little to the government line outlined at the first hearing. It did, however, help in the effort to adapt Mafia mythology to a new age by adding its weight to an idea already circulating in the national and international media. The Mafia, according to the new conventional wisdom, had once been the dominant force in US organized crime, but was now being challenged by several crime "cartels," "emerging" among Asian, Latin American and other groups. *Guardian* journalists dutifully represented this perspective in a 1986 article reporting on the Mafia Commission convictions, entitled "Gangs Set to Usurp Mafia." The dramatic convictions of a group of Mafia dons in New York," the account began, " will force basic changes in the way crime is organized, according to federal and New York authorities." "The new gangs are composed of different ethnic groups – Hispanics, blacks, orientals, Russians and Jews," and of these, the reporter continued, "The most important ... are made up of Hispanics who deal in narcotics trafficking," referring specifically to "the Medellin Cartel,"[59] accepting uncritically the preferred US government name for a number of drug smuggling groups operating from the city of Medellin in Colombia.

US officials, under the auspices of the Kaufman Commission, had thus made a seamless transition from a Mafia conspiracy interpretation that couldn't be exported to parts of the world that did not have significant Italian populations to a more pluralist interpretation that, as we shall see in Part IV, could be exported anywhere on earth. The commission's recommendations on "Foreign Assistance" included the following indication of the direction of travel to be followed: "The willingness of a country to engage in and actively implement drug-related extradition and mutual assistance treaties should be a primary consideration in the ultimate US policy decision regarding foreign assistance to that country."[60]

Gary Potter, in his book in *Criminal Organizations*, argued that the federal government had successfully adapted the alien conspiracy interpretation rather than overhauling official thinking about organized crime. The argument remained the same: forces outside of mainstream American culture threatened otherwise morally sound American institutions. Potter described the new official consensus as the "pluralist" revision of the alien conspiracy interpretation.[61] The notion of a foreign "super-government of crime" that Vice President Charles Dawes had frightened Americans about in 1926 had become the "super-governments of crime," and could thus evolve into an international security issue.

Despite the evidence of continuing failure, the commission did not challenge the essential correctness of the law enforcement approach to organized crime control – based, as it was, on long-term investigation, undercover operations, informants, wiretaps and asset forfeiture. Throughout the hearings, successes against the Mafia and the need to "stay in front" of the emerging "cartels" were emphasized.

In sum, the commission concluded that the government's basic approach to the problem was sound but needed a harder line on all fronts, including international fronts: more wiretaps, informants and undercover agents in order to get more convictions which would require more prisons. Witnesses who might have pointed out the deficiencies of this approach were not consulted. The American people, and most of those who covered organized crime in the international press, had by then been conditioned to see organized crime as groups of separate and distinct gangsters rather than as the more fluid, varied and integrated phenomenon portrayed by earlier commentators and contemporary researchers. The commission therefore did not consider corruption within the system as part of the problem of organized crime, and by the 1980s they did not have to. Years of information about organized crime based on false assumptions had conditioned people not to ask questions.

The Kaufman Commission's understanding of organized crime was representative of a pervasive dumbing down since the business community, the police and the politicians had defined themselves out of the problem. Early thinking on the issue of organized crime had focused on defects in American laws and institutions and found them responsible for America's organized crime problems. Kaufman's group, following a path that had been taken since the Kefauver Committee, focused on different groups of criminals and found them responsible for America's organized crime problems. The logic of early conceptualizations suggesting the repeal of unworkable laws and the honest and effective enforcement of the rest was lost. The Kaufman group's restricted understanding of organized crime allowed it to avoid confronting failures in policy and faults in institutions, notably the difficult issues of corruption and the existence of powerful prison gangs.

The commission, however, did make a significant contribution to the armory of powers held by the government in the name of organized crime control. It produced the first draft of the Money Laundering Control Act of 1986, to be discussed in Chapter 6.

6
The Origins of the Anti-Money Laundering Regime

The practice of legitimizing ill-gotten gain by laundering or simply managing criminal money is as old as wealth. Within the US, the corrupt, harmful and often illegal acquisition of wealth by hundreds of American businessmen, and the rendering of all this wealth respectable, was well documented by, among others, Gustavus Myers in *History of the Great American Fortunes*.[62] This practice did not begin to be called "money laundering" until the 1960s and 1970s, mainly in articles about crime in the Caribbean, and in Watergate-era descriptions of corporate donations to Nixon's campaigns.

Ironically, Nixon's corrupt administration had begun the criminalization of laundering by supporting the Bank Secrecy Act of 1970, which required that a Currency Transaction Report must be filed by financial institutions whenever a currency transaction was more than $10,000. Prosecutors and police soon began reporting difficulties in cases involving money laundering, and after a decade of botched cases the Kaufman Commission responded by making money laundering its first order of business. In an October 1984 report entitled *The Cash Connection: Organized Crime, Financial Institutions and Money Laundering*, the commission concluded that:

The effectiveness of such prosecutions ... is limited because Federal statutes do not grant law enforcement authorities use of all the investigative tools they need ... forms of electronic communications ... play a vital role in facilitating and maintaining such schemes. At present, however, a criminal violation of the [Bank Secrecy] Act does not constitute an offense on which the Justice Department can predicate an application for court authorized electronic surveillance. ...

Finally ... the civil and criminal penalties imposed by the Act are far too lenient to discourage money laundering ... the risk to the launderers is negligible when contrasted with the seemingly limitless financial potential of laundering.[63]

In his letter to President Reagan introducing this report, Kaufman stated the rationale behind the recommendations, with laundering replacing gambling as "the lifeblood of organized crime":

> As our study reveals, money laundering is the lifeblood of organized crime. The Commission believes that its recommendations, when implemented, will arm the financial community and law enforcement authorities with the weapons needed to strike at the very heart of the narcotics trade and other activities engaged in by organized criminal groups. The driving force of organized crime is the incentive to earn vast sums of money; without the ability to freely utilize its ill-gotten gains the underworld will have been dealt a crippling blow.[64]

The *Cash Connection* report made it clear that it was the government's intention to protect the financial community rather than police it:

> Money Laundering invariably has a deleterious effect upon the financial community. By corrupting officials and employees of financial institutions in furtherance of laundering schemes, money launderers undermine the integrity of those institutions and, if discovered by law enforcement agencies, can vitiate the reputation of those institutions for soundness of prudent judgment ... the mere fact that money launderers saw fit to use that institution may seriously affect the public's perception of the institution.[65]

The report's Executive Summary invited the response of the banking community to their recommendations and proposed legislation. "Constructive dialogue," the report stressed, "is essential to the development of new procedures and legislation which will deny money launderers access to financial institutions for their illegally generated profits."[66] There was thus no acknowledgment that the banking community actually profited from dirty money.

The intention of the commission's proposed Money Laundering Control Act of 1986 was, in the report's words "to make it possible for the Federal Government to develop a fully coordinated national strategy to combat money laundering." "If money laundering" it continued, "is the keystone of organized crime, these recommendations can provide the financial community and law enforcement authorities with the tools needed to dislodge that keystone, and thereby to cause irreparable damage to the operations of organized crime."[67] As things turned out, little or no damage was done to the operations of organized crime. Many have been convicted on money laundering charges but, as we shall see, vast amounts of dirty money continued to be laundered.

From the time of the Kaufman Commission, America put itself in the vanguard of an international effort to combat money laundering which in effect provided a smokescreen to disguise continual failure.

One of the provisions of the 1986 Act required the chairman of the Federal Reserve Board, at that time Paul Volker, to meet with central bankers in the forum of Group of Ten (G10) industrialized countries in order to begin focusing international attention on money laundering. Growing from these consultations, the Group of Seven heads of state and government agreed in 1989 to form the Financial Action Task Force (FATF), to coordinate anti-money laundering programs globally. According to Raymond Baker's account in *Capitalism's Achilles Heel: Dirty Money and How to Renew the Free-Market System*, FATF took its cues from the US and "focused its early efforts almost exclusively on drug trafficking, tiptoeing around corrupt money and burying consideration of tax-evading money."[68] As we shall see, this blind-eye approach doomed the anti-money laundering regime from the outset.

Inset 4: Meyer Lansky and the Origins of Money Laundering History

The legend of Meyer Lansky is still fresh in those people's minds who watched the TV series *Boardwalk Empire*. In the final episode he's shown sitting at a round table listening to Charles "Lucky" Luciano announcing the beginnings of the "Commission" of multi-ethnic gangsters that would run organized crime in America after Prohibition.

Organized crime mythology always has a function – Al Capone mythology justified the federal government moving into law and order matters previously reserved to the individual cities and states. Luciano mythology helped justify the Hale Boggs act of 1951 that introduced the concept of mandatory minimums for drug offenders into law. Luciano mythology also lay behind the Organized Crime Control Act of 1970 which was the template not only for organized crime control efforts in the US itself but also for similar efforts around the world. Meyer Lansky mythology helped justify the Money Laundering Control Act of 1986 which criminalized money laundering.

Fables about Lansky populate the money laundering literature. He is usually credited as being a kind of "founding father" of the practice. Take this example:

> The origins of money laundering are imprecise but we know that the activity began to develop on an industrial scale in the United States in the middle part of the twentieth century as Mafia bosses recognized the need to demonstrate that their enormous pools of wealth had developed from "legitimate" sources. Meyer Lansky, known as the "Mob's Accountant," developed a significant gambling empire that stretched across the U.S. to Cuba. He was able to successfully utilize casinos and race tracks to place and launder criminal money.[69]

Or this, from the first of Jeffrey Robinson's bestselling books on money laundering: "Lansky not only built the financial skeleton for postwar organized crime, he opened Caribbean eyes – wallets, safe deposit boxes and secret bank accounts – to the delights of tax havens. He helped show the island nations how to become the world's biggest collection of sinks."[70] In *The Sink* he repeated the point when he claimed Lansky was "a thief with a blueprint" who "invented the world's first offshore financial haven" in Cuba.[71]

Lansky's spurious reputation for criminal control and innovation had begun in the 1960s. *Time* magazine in 1969, for example, in an article entitled "The Conglomerate of Crime," claimed that "Lansky, the 'gang's leading financial wizard' was 'being overly modest' when he claimed in 1966: 'We're bigger than US Steel'." "Measured in terms of profits," the article continued, "Cosa Nostra and its affiliates are as big as US Steel, the American Telephone and Telegraph Co., General Motors, Standard Oil of New Jersey, General Electric, Ford Motor Co., IBM, Chrysler and RCA put together."[72]

Two journalists, Hank Messick and Nicholas Gage, getting their information in part from the IRS and in part from their own imagination, established Lansky's reputation as the organizer of organized crime and the founding father of money laundering. Messick began the process in 1965 with a series of articles. "Lansky Rules Crime Cartel from Florida"[73] is a representative headline. He followed these up with the bestselling *Lansky* in 1971, which opened with the following claims about him made by the mainstream American media:

"The most powerful leader of organized crime in the country." *Wall Street Journal*

"One of the richest and most powerful men in the United States." *The Atlantic*

"He is Public Enemy No. 1." *The Readers Digest*, "quoting a leading Mafia expert."

Gage made similar claims in his 1971 book, *The Mafia is Not an Equal Opportunity Employer*. "Lansky," he wrote, was "the main architect of the giant conglomerate that is organized crime in the United States." Gage claimed that Lansky's personal fortune was "somewhere between $100 million and $300 million." "It was Lansky," he added, "who developed the worldwide system of couriers, middlemen, bankers and frontmen that allows the underworld to take profits from illegal enterprises, send them half-way around the world and then have the money come back laundered clean to be invested in legitimate business."[74]

Although *Time* was an international publication and the Messick and Gage books sold well in US and international markets, such ideas about Lansky were much more widely spread by the Hollywood movie *The Godfather Part II* (1974). A global cinema audience saw Hyman Roth, the Lansky character, narrow his eyes and whisper, "Michael! We're bigger than US Steel!"

According to Lansky's most diligent biographer, Ronald Lacey, the quote derived from a misinterpretation of transcribed FBI bugs. Lansky was recorded on tape by FBI agents during the early 1960s, and spent much of the time discussing his medical problems. The tapes were running on the evening of May 27, 1962 when Lansky was recorded making a comment to his wife on a television studio discussion of organized crime. Lansky sat in silence through the discussion, according to the FBI report, until one of the panelists "referred to organized crime as only being second in size to the government itself." Lansky remarked to his wife that "organized crime was bigger than US Steel."[75] The comment reported by the FBI was thus very different from the paraphrased versions in *Time* and the *Godfather Part II* movie.

Lacey's research makes it abundantly clear that Lansky's deals and operations were not remotely comparable to those of corporations and he was not the founding father of money laundering. He examined Lansky's finances and found that:

> None of the tax returns of Meyer Lansky showed foreign interest payments, or any transactions that might be interpreted as money laundering. Nor did he hide behind the "miscellaneous income" headings to which lawbreakers often resort. With the ending of his Cuban income in 1960, Meyer listed simple, American sources of revenue on his tax returns ... All were thoroughly investigated and confirmed by the IRS.

However, Lacey found that Meyer Lansky did cheat on his taxes: "From some date quite early in the 1960s, he started sending money abroad, and it ended up in Switzerland in a classic numbered account. But his money did not return "laundered" to America. Meyer seems to have treated his new Swiss bank account as an elaborate version of cash under the bed."[76]

Lansky died in 1983. David May reported his death in the *Sunday Times*, repeating claims in the American press that his "secret fortune" was estimated at over $300 million.[77] Hank Messick had been the first to publicize this figure and explained it thus: "Whenever people have contacted me to confirm this," he stated, "I have always told them it was not my figure. It came from an expert who was supposed to know what he was talking about."[78] In other words it was a mythical figure.

When Lacey investigated these claims he found Lansky's estate to be far closer to zero than $300 million, and noted that Lansky's disabled son "Buddy" was approved for Medicare payments in 1989.[79] Buddy's death in relative poverty was not reported in the international press.

Many of those writing in the money laundering control literature continue to derive their understanding of the past from anti-Semitic stereotyping. It has saved many writers from having to admit that "money laundering" has characterized outwardly respectable fortunes for centuries, as Gustavus Myers in the *History of Great American Fortunes* (1937) and many other historians have documented. Having Lansky as a mythical founding father of the practice helped towards acceptance of an anti-money laundering regime that has scarcely impacted on the fortunes of a growing band of criminal money managers.

7
Informants, Liars and Paranoiacs

Not all the battles won by law enforcement against criminal syndicates were as clear-cut as they appeared at the time. In an environment that continued to be corrupt, US organized crime control measures were often misdirected, inadequate and counterproductive.

The conduct of the FBI's Boston office since the 1960s has come under particularly damning scrutiny. Robert Kennedy and J. Edgar Hoover's drive against the Mafia in New England focused on the crime bosses Raymond Patriarca and Gennaro Angiulo. To help bring them down, the FBI relied on "turning" some of their criminal associates against them, notably Joseph "The Animal" Barboza. Barboza was a contract killer and, as it turned out, a compulsive liar, who was more than willing to give uncorroborated testimony to the government in return for lenient treatment by the courts. In 1968 the FBI allowed Barboza to commit perjury for the government in the case against Joseph Salvati and five others. These were accused of murdering a New Bedford gangster called Edward Deegan in 1965. Deegan was found dead in an alleyway in Chelsea, Massachusetts, slain, according to the newspapers, in "gangland fashion." Documents released in 2002 showed that the FBI agents were aware that five gangsters, including Barboza, were involved in the "hit." They decided to keep silent, however, and allowed Barboza to testify against several innocent men, including Salvati, who served nearly three decades for the crime, unjustly imprisoned and cruelly separated from his wife and children.

Salvati's lawyer, Victor Garo, later summarized the case: "The FBI determined who got liberty, the FBI determined who got justice, and justice was not for all ... What Constitution? What Bill of Rights? What human rights? What human decency? We're the FBI? We don't have to adhere to these principles so long as we have a good press and so long as we get convictions. That will show that the ends justify the means."[80]

Barboza was freed and entered the newly created Witness Protection Program. He was given a new identity and life in California. He briefly worked in a legitimate occupation but had a fall, and as a result acquired $18,500 in workman's compensation. He used this money to traffic in drugs before killing a fellow drug trafficker and receiving a five-year sentence for the crime. While in prison he claimed he had proof that Frank Sinatra was a Mafia puppet, which was one of many conspiracy theories circulating in the right-wing media of the time. Barboza was invited by a government investigating committee to repeat his charges in Washington. His government handler, John Partington, clearly knew his man and said to him, "Shit, Joe, you don't know nothing about Sinatra, you're just making that shit up!" Barboza, according to Partington, just laughed and said, "It gets me out of the joint for a while, don't it?" At the committee's hearings Barboza testified that Sinatra was a front man for Raymond Patriarca in the ownership of the Sands casino in Las Vegas and a luxury hotel in Miami. Sinatra was forced to defend himself and made the point that Barboza was a "bum ... running off at the mouth." No evidence was turned up to support Barboza's charges but mud tended to stick when Sinatra was concerned. After serving his sentence Barboza made some money extorting San Francisco bookmakers before someone shot and killed him in 1976.[81]

Barboza was only one of many gangster informants recruited by the FBI during their war against the Mafia. Others in Boston were James "Whitey" Bulger and Stevie "The Rifleman" Flemmi who were handled by FBI agent John Connolly. Between the 1960s and 1990s, Bulger, in particular, used his protected status as an FBI informer effectively. He was able to run loan-sharking, gambling and drug rackets in south Boston with virtual immunity. He was told whenever his phone was about to be tapped or his operations were about to come under surveillance. Most disturbingly, he was also told who was informing on his crimes. Several killings resulted. All the time his criminal competitors were being investigated, wiretapped and prosecuted by federal government officials. Eventually, Bulger and Flemmi were charged with 21 murders, eleven of them committed while they were cooperating with the FBI. Three of the victims had been talking to the FBI. Connolly was convicted in May 2002 on charges relating to his mutually enriching relationship with Bulger.

In 1994 he had leaked word of a federal grand jury indictment to Bulger who then went on the run until 2011 when he was arrested at the age of 81. Flemmi was convicted in 2004 on racketeering charges and admitted to his role in ten murders carried out by him and other members of the Bulger gang.[82] Two years earlier, in May 2002, Congressional investigators discovered a 1965 memo to J. Edgar Hoover informing him of four innocent men imprisoned for life for a murder committed by FBI informant Flemmi. The memo also stated Flemmi would likely kill again, but added revealingly that "the informant's potential outweighs the risks."[83]

These and other memos written between 1964 and 1987 showed that the Bureau senior staff knew and condoned much of what Connolly and other Boston agents were doing. Evidence also suggests that Boston was just one of many cities where agents used and protected violent criminals as informants.[84] After evading capture for more than two decades, Bulger was found guilty in August 2013 of eleven murders and on 31 racketeering counts.[85]

Commenting on the Bulger case, Professor Sean Patrick Griffin of the Citadel University noted that the deluge of Mafia mythology, from the Valachi hearings through to *The Godfather*, was the proximate cause of the scandal. "In its myopic zeal to bring down Italian Organized Crime," he noted, "the FBI for decades permitted Bulger to do all sorts of things."[86] "The onslaught of Mafia imagery," Griffin continued, "became a complicated mess of life imitating art, where public opinion – driven by mass media and by government propaganda – began dictating law and public policy, which served to create a vicious cycle from which we have never gotten out." He elaborated:

> If you interviewed an FBI agent today (as I have done – I also lectured hundreds of agents over years in the 2000s), their sense of organized crime is no different than it was in the 1960s. It is remarkable (and problematic!). I had an Assistant US Attorney years ago tell me that his challenge was that juries (because of the social construction of organized crime as hierarchical and Italian) EXPECT to hear certain things in an organized crime prosecution. So, he told me (and my class), if a jury expects X (even if it's all mythology and BS), that's exactly what they'll get! Which, of

course, reinforces the nonsense with the jurors and with the media and with those who read/view the coverage and so on.[87]

The end result of this was that US government was able to claim victories against organized crime in general even if it was either protecting or ignoring active and murderous non-Italian organized criminals.

As the economist R.T. Naylor has also pointed out, information received from informants like Bulger and lesser criminals is not to be trusted:

> The criminal milieu has more than its share of pathological liars and acute paranoiacs, not to mention people who have lived so long in the shadow world of deceit and deception that they cease to recognize any border between fact and fantasy. The credibility of the information is especially dubious when informants have a vested interest (in terms of direct payment, license to continue their own rackets, or reduced sentences) in exaggerating the importance of the information they are peddling.[88]

Organized crime control techniques tend to be overly dependent on criminals whose main interest is in serving themselves.

8
Seizing Assets to Fund the Crime War

The US government has been seizing the assets of criminals since 1789 and the birth of the nation, but developments since the Organized Crime Control Act of 1970 have made asset forfeiture much more part of the crime control armory. The tendency has been to make the seizure of assets easier. US authorities therefore had the means to get much richer without the need to ask for extra taxes.

In 1978, a civil forfeiture law was enacted, declaring "All moneys used in, and all assets acquired from, the illicit drug trade belong to the United States government and are subject to civil seizure under the forfeiture power." The importance of this law is that the burden of proof is much less for civil law than for criminal law.

Previously the government had to prove guilt before depriving people of their property; from the 1970s it was up to the individual to demonstrate that the seized property is actually "innocent" of facilitating a drug crime – or that it was not obtained through criminal activity. If the claimant fails to satisfy a judge or jury that the property is "innocent" of the alleged drug crime, then the goods are forfeited to the government. Usually the seized property remains unclaimed because the legal fees involved are prohibitive and people are unlikely to risk criminal charges being brought against them.

With this new tool the DEA was able to seize drug assets totaling $268 million in just three years between 1979 and 1982. These figures then continued to increase, boosted by the passage of the Comprehensive Crime Control Act of 1984. This act strengthened and streamlined all federal forfeiture laws and created a new amendment that provides for the equitable transfer of property forfeited federally, to either state or local law enforcement agencies, or both, which participate in investigations. In other words, every American police officer now had a financial motive for seizing assets. Between 1985 and 1992 the total value of federal asset seizures increased over 1,500 percent to over $2.4 billion.[89] More recently, in the 2014 fiscal year alone, Justice Department agencies made a total of $3.9 billion in civil asset seizures, much greater than that collected by criminal asset seizures. In most years since 2008, civil asset forfeitures have accounted for the lion's share of total seizures.[90]

Under forfeiture laws the government could seize property based solely on probable cause to believe that the property was used unlawfully. Probable cause can be as little as hearsay or innuendo. The government therefore does not have to prove criminal guilt to obtain a forfeiture judgment over someone's property.[91]

The thinking behind asset forfeiture was once persuasive, according to two of the federal officers who led the government's efforts during the 1980s, John Yoder and Brad Cates: "Seize the ill-gotten gains of big-time drug dealers and remove the financial incentive for their criminality. After all, if a kingpin could earn $20 million and stash it away somewhere, even a decade in prison would have its rewards. Make that money disappear, and the calculus changes."[92]

As we have seen, this was also the rationale behind the Money Laundering Control Act of 1986. From then on not only cash earned illegally could be seized but also purchases or investments made with that money, creating a whole scheme of new crimes that could be prosecuted as "money laundering." Yoder and Cates also explained that the property eligible for seizure was further expanded to include "instrumentalities" in the trafficking of drugs, such as cars or even jewelry. More than 200 crimes beyond drugs came to be included in the forfeiture scheme.

Law enforcement agents and prosecutors began using seized cash and property to fund their operations, supplanting general tax revenue, and this led to the most extreme abuses: law enforcement efforts based upon what cash and property they could seize to fund themselves, rather than on an even-handed effort to enforce the law. Critics see asset forfeiture as a means by which the state can take the bulk of the proceeds of criminal activity, and a good deal of the proceeds of honest activity.

Police agencies across the country have certainly got richer through asset forfeiture. Federal, state and local authorities soon began to use the proceeds from forfeiture cases to help fund everything from extra prosecutors and police officers to new supplies of vehicles and other law enforcement equipment, including high-tech surveillance devices such as night-vision goggles, infrared heat-detection devices, helicopters, bulletproof vests, a semi-enclosed firing range and a wide range of sophisticated weaponry. Forfeitures have included a Chevrolet dealership, a recording studio, a 1,000-acre plantation and many homes, cars, boats and planes.[93]

In 1991 the *Pittsburgh Press* analyzed more than 500 asset forfeiture cases nationally and found that 80 percent of those who lost homes, cars, boats or money to the authorities were never charged with a crime. The articles showed that people were often targeted because of their appearance or actions. Some were stopped and searched in an airport because they paid cash for a plane ticket or simply because they were black or Hispanic. On one occasion, a ticket agent informed on Willie Jones, an African American, who operated a nursery in Nashville, Tennessee, because he paid cash for a plane ticket. As a small grower he preferred to deal in cash and he was carrying just under $10,000. Federal agents simply seized the money. Jones failed to get his money back and was nearly driven out of business.[94]

In the decades since, little has changed. While drug dealers have learned how to protect themselves from forfeiture, the innocent take no such precautions and suffer the consequences. A 2015 case involved Joseph Rivers, a young black entrepreneur who boarded a train at Albuquerque, New Mexico to go to Los Angeles to make a music video. DEA agents asked to see his bag and found $15,000 in cash. The agents found nothing in Rivers's belongings that indicated that he was involved with the drug trade. He was not arrested or charged with a crime. They took the money anyway under the authority of the Justice Department's civil asset forfeiture program.[95] The Anti-Money Laundering Act of 1986 had made it possible to describe such cash amounts as "instrumentalities," as we have seen. At the time of writing Rivers has employed a lawyer to contest the forfeiture.

Writing in the *Huffington Post*, Radley Balko described the corrupt reality of asset forfeiture in the US. "Police in some jurisdiction," he wrote, "have run forfeiture operations that would be difficult to distinguish from criminal shakedowns," and continued:

Police can pull motorists over, find some amount of cash or other property of value, claim some vague connection to illegal drug activity and then present the motorists with a choice. If they hand over the property, they can be on their way. Otherwise they face arrest, seizure of property, a drug charge, a probable night in jail, the hassle of multiple return trips to the state or city where they were pulled over, and the cost of hiring a lawyer to fight both the seizure and the criminal charge. It isn't hard to see why even an innocent motorist would opt to simply hand over the cash and move on.[96]

"There's this myth that they're cracking down on drug cartels and kingpins," according to Lee McGrath of the Institute for Justice, commenting on asset forfeiture. "In reality, it's small amounts, where people aren't entitled to a public defender, and can't afford a lawyer, and the only rational response is to walk away from your property, because of the infeasibility of getting your money back."[97]

There have been efforts made to reform asset forfeiture practices but many American police forces have become dependent on the booty. "It's their bread and butter," as Vanita Gupta, of the American Civil Liberties Union, concisely summed it up.[98]

* * *

Asset forfeiture has done more than provide the bread and butter of American police forces. It has created a new form of commercial enterprise: informing for profit.

Organized crime control developments in the 1980s meant that informants could receive salaries and bonuses for information whether or not it leads to convictions, and up to 25 percent of profits if forfeiture efforts were successful.

Edward Vaughn of suburban San Francisco is one among many drug trafficking informants who have taken advantage of the government's largesse. He ran a multimillion dollar, international drug smuggling ring during the 1980s and served two terms in prison before arranging an early parole and paid informant deal with the government. From that point he earned $40,000 in salary and expenses between August 1989 and October 1990 working for the DEA, and was promised a 25 percent cut of any seizures. This information came out at a trial in

Pittsburgh in 1990 in which Vaughn's testimony resulted in one man being found guilty of dealing marijuana. The other defendant in the case was acquitted because the jury felt Vaughn had entrapped him by pushing him too hard to make a drug deal.[99]

A recent Department of Justice Report detailed the cost and extent of drug informant programs as well as its "unacceptably increased potential for fraud, waste, and abuse. ... Between October 1, 2010, and September 30, 2015, the DEA had over 18,000 active confidential sources assigned to its domestic offices, with over 9,000 of those sources receiving approximately $237 million in payments for information or services they provided to the DEA. ... the DEA did not adequately oversee payments to its sources."[100]

On the potential for fraud, waste and abuse, the report estimated that:

> during the 5-year period of our review, the Intelligence Division paid more than $30 million to sources who provided narcotics-related intelligence and contributed to law enforcement operations, $25 million of which went to just 9 sources. Additionally, we identified one source who was paid over $30 million during a 30-year period, some of it in cash payments of more than $400,000. We concluded the Intelligence Division's management and oversight of its sources was not commensurate with the large amount of payments it made to them.[101]

For all these and many more questionable outcomes, asset forfeiture never did, as promised, damage the profitability of drug trafficking. There are, of course, examples of successful forfeitures from significant criminals but they are far outweighed by a litany of fraud, waste and abuse that sometimes gets reported in the American news media but rarely gets covered internationally. Very little "difficult" information has been allowed to interfere with US efforts to export its organized crime control techniques worldwide as part of the "Americanization" of international law enforcement, discussed in Part IV.

9
Drug Prohibition and the Prison Gang Phenomenon

Racism was a motive for criminal justice developments set in motion by the Nixon administration. This was expressed, albeit awkwardly, in Nixon's comment reported in the diaries of his chief of staff, H.R. Haldeman. The "E" in the following excerpt stands for another White House aide, John Ehrlichman, and "P" stands for President Nixon:

Monday, April 28, 1969
Got into a deep discussion of welfare, trying to think out the Family Security decision, with E and me [welfare reform had been one of P's campaign issues]. P emphasized that you have to face the fact that the *whole* problem is really the blacks. The key is to devise a system that recognizes this while not appearing to ... Pointed out that there never has been an adequate black nation, and they are the only race of which this is true. Says Africa is hopeless, the worst there is Liberia, which we built.[102]

Haldeman and Ehrlichman were Nixon's closest domestic advisers. While researching a book on drug prohibition Dan Baum asked Ehrlichman about the Nixon war on drugs, and then narrated this response:

"You want to know what this was really all about?" he asked with the bluntness of a man who, after public disgrace and a stretch in federal prison, had little left to protect. "The Nixon campaign in 1968, and the Nixon White House after that, had two enemies: the antiwar left and black people. You understand what I'm saying? We knew we couldn't make it illegal to be either against the war or black, but by getting the public to associate the hippies with marijuana and blacks with heroin, and then criminalizing both heavily, we could disrupt those communities. We could arrest their leaders, raid their homes, break up their meetings, and vilify them night after night on the evening news. Did we know we were lying about the drugs? Of course we did."[103]

As a result of the war on drugs, declared by Nixon and continued by all of his successors, including Barack Obama, African American communities suffered from a phenomenon most often called "mass incarceration." Large numbers of African Americans were incarcerated, at percentages that exceeded any legitimate law enforcement interest. At the end of 1999, over half a million African American men and women were held in state and federal prisons. In 2000, the rate of incarceration for African American males nationwide was 3,457 per 100,000. In comparison, the rate of incarceration for white males was 449 per 100,000. This means, on average, African American males were 7.7 times more likely to be incarcerated than white males.[104] For Hispanic Americans the story is similar. "Rates of drug use and sales are more or less equal across racial and ethnic lines," according to the Drug Policy Alliance, but "drug law enforcement overwhelming targets black and Latino communities."[105]

Nixon's cynical and successful exploitation of the issue during his time in office has made it essential for all candidates for high office to appear tough on crime. Suggestions of "softness" on crime damaged the campaigns of George McGovern in 1972 and Michael Dukakis in 1988, for example. The political right has benefited most from the widely held belief that the poor were out of control in America and that the only viable response is increasingly draconian punishment for even minor offenses. This has led to the process of "governing through crime," according to the criminologist Jonathan Simon, as the United States and other advanced industrial societies have prioritized crime and punishment as the preferred contexts for governance.[106] Phrases like "Tough on Crime," "Zero Tolerance" and "Three Strikes and You're Out" were repeated endlessly to justify filling up the prisons.

As the market for drugs has increased in recent decades, so did the efforts of federal, state and local governments to suppress it. In 1969, $65 million was spent by the Nixon administration on the drug war. In 1982 the Reagan administration increased this commitment to $1.65 *billion*. In 2000 the Clinton administration massively increased this figure to $17.9 billion. In 2002 the Bush administration spent more than $18.822 billion. Under Obama, the rhetoric moved away from military analogies but the levels of spending remained immense; in 2015 it was $28.882 billion, rising to $30.560 billion in 2016.[107] States, cities and local governments also spent massive amounts to supplement the federal efforts.

The result of this effort has been a massive increase in arrests for drug violations. In 1973, there were 328,670 arrests for drug law violations according to the FBI Uniform Crime Reports. In 1989, there were 1,361,700 drug arrests, nearly 10 percent of all arrests. In 2002, that number rose to 1,538,813 – 45.3 percent of this figure was for marijuana arrests rather than for more dangerous drugs. In 2012, drug offenses remained the single most common cause of arrest. Of the 12.2 million estimated arrests in 2012, 1.55 million were for "drug abuse violations." Most of these arrests were for simple possession offenses rather than sale or manufacture.[108]

More than any other single factor, the succession of Nixon-style wars on drugs declared by Presidents Reagan and Bush (Sr.) fueled the largest and most rapid expansion of the US's prison population in its history. Between 1980 and 1994, the prison population tripled from 500,000 to 1.5 million. In 2002 the United States incarcerated 2,166,260 persons, some 701 per 100,000 of the national population. This compared with the United Kingdom's rate of 141 per 100,000 of the national population, which was the highest rate among European Union countries.[109] According to 2011 figures, the United States had the highest prison population rate in the world at 743 per 100,000 of the national population, followed by Rwanda (595) and Russia (568).[110]

One of the consequences of this war against the poor and the minorities has been the rise of prison gangs. Francis Ianni, the ethnographer of organized crime discussed earlier, made an accurate observation in his 1974 book, *Black Mafia*, about an issue that a generation of opinion makers and federal officials have consistently refused to engage with: "prisons and the prison experience," he found, "are the most important loci for establishing the social relationships that form the basis for partnerships in organized crime." Many people, he elaborated, "share incarceration as a common experience to the extent that they know each other before, during and after various jail terms." "In many cases," Ianni continued, "prison friendships can be very similar to the 'old school tie' in which an Etonian prime minister picks another Etonian to serve in his government because he knows that he can rely on certain values and standards of conduct from an earlier shared experience." Ianni was building on a wealth of observation over the centuries that showed that prisons were self-perpetuating institutions because they reinforced existing criminal attitudes and because they provided many opportunities for learning new criminal techniques. Ianni's studies revealed the great extent to which criminal partnerships were formed in prison and some of the mechanisms that operated in prison to promote the formation of these partnerships.[111] Unfortunately Ianni's research was ignored, and the costs of pursuing mass-imprisonment policies have maximized harms to the rest of society. The cost, in particular, was the multiplication of gangster partnerships.

US prisons gangs have been fighting or cooperating over prostitution, protection and drug trafficking rackets for decades in systems based on brutality, informants and staff corruption. Most of the gangs are organized along racial and ethnic lines and spend as much time fighting each other in wars based on race hate as in commercial ventures. During the 1970s and 1980s, some like the Aryan Brotherhood, the Black Guerillas, the Mexican Mafia and La Nuestra Familia were said to have achieved statewide and even interstate influence, but since that time there has been evidence of an increasing splintering of prison groupings.[112]

The most reliable repeated surveys, according to historian James C. Howell, "suggested that 12 percent of all federal and state prison inmates were members of prison gangs in 2003, and this figure grew to 19 percent in 2009, a substantial increase in just seven years." He stressed that "only about half of the validated members belonged to a gang prior to confinement, thus half join gangs after entering prison." Furthermore, given that prison gangs are well institutionalized in the largest state and federal correctional facilities, these are sure to remain strong in the foreseeable future.[113]

The pathway to prison gang membership, according to Howell's survey of recent research, begins in juvenile detention centers that serve as entry portals to long-term gang careers:

Confinement in a juvenile correctional facility is one of the strongest predictors of adult prison gang membership ... when gang members are released from custody, they generally return to their neighborhoods of origin and renew old associations in their original street gang. Having done time and handled it successfully, they earned "rep" on the streets ... If they resume prior criminal activity, the contacts made in the prison system will become more important. This amounts to a vicious cycle. More confinement of gang members increases the strength of prison gangs. This, in turn, expands prison gangs' influence on local gang violence, thereby generating more arrests, starting the cycle again.[114]

While the extent and efficiency of Mafia hierarchies have been exaggerated, there is no doubt that prison conditions favor the development of hierarchies. Prison gangs such as the mainly Hispanic Texas Syndicate and Mexican Mafia are hierarchically organized. Howell summarized research on these two prison gangs: "Each of these prison gangs was structured similarly, along paramilitary lines with a president, vice president, and chairman or general who overseas captains, lieutenants, a sergeant of arms, and soldiers." They both have constitutions which in the case of the Texas Syndicate consists of eight rules:

1. Be a Texan.
2. Once a member, always a member.
3. The Texas Syndicate comes before anyone and anything.
4. Right or wrong, the Texas Syndicate is right at all times.
5. All members will wear the Texas Syndicate tattoo.
6. Never let a member down.
7. All members will respect each other.
8. Keep all gang information within the group.

Death is the penalty for intentionally or unintentionally violating any of the established rules.

"Less well organized gangs," Howell continued, "have an uncomplicated structure, usually with one person designated as the leader who overseas a council of members who make the group's final decisions."[115]

Christian Parenti, in *Lockdown America* (2000), explained how the violence, corruption and general failure of the system, like many law enforcement defeats, served the bureaucracy of control better than victory ever could – "mayhem in prison is parlayed into empire-building." "The more 'deviance' the big house excretes," he continues, "the more the guards and administrators need new prisons, ... more gang investigators, further expansion into outside communities, closer cooperation with other agencies, better computers, more dossiers, new tracking software, better guns, more tear gas, more body armor ... and so on. Thus corrections bureaucracies grow, like most others."[116]

Despite the growing bureaucracies, violence is now more likely to be a central organizing principle in prisons than staff rules.

Since the 1980s the US government has been very coy about the prison gang phenomenon, often using jargon descriptive words such as "security threat group" instead of prison gang, for example, to discourage difficult questions and observations. In a story on the Universal Aryan Brotherhood, an Oklahoman offshoot of the broader Aryan Brotherhood, Michael E. Miller, writing in the *Washington Post*, concluded that the US government has never attempted to address let alone answer such questions as "How to defeat a gang that doesn't just openly recruit and operate inside Oklahoma's prisons, but practically *owns* the institutions? What to do when each arrest just adds to the organization's ranks?"[117]

In the last decade it has become clear that prison gangs, particularly in border states like Texas and California, are working ever more closely with Mexican drug groups for mutual benefit.

The California Attorney General's Office reported in 2014 that members of prison gangs and street gangs now took on roles as enforcers, drug sellers, arms smugglers and money launderers for Mexican groups. They were then able to get to buy their drugs in bulk from the major organizations, thus bypassing the middlemen and receive up to 50 percent discounts on wholesale drug purchases. This relationship allows the Mexican organizations to conduct operations without entering US territory, thus reducing their risks, and enabling the expansion of their distribution networks. US gang members offer the added benefits of being able to cross the border with less risk of detection and having an in-depth knowledge of the areas where they operate.[118]

The Mexican organizations, according to Seth Ferranti of *The Daily Beast*, identified and recruited talent in American prisons, seeking "free agents" to connect on their release with their south-of-the-border counterparts in the ever-expanding drug job market." The organizations were "recruiting American prisoners," he continued, "to increase their manpower, access to arms, distribution points, and trafficking abilities in a multifaceted strategy to keep drugs going north and money and weapons back south." "There's an awful lot of Mexicans locked up in the feds," Ferranti was told by a prisoner, "doing 20- to 30-year bids, effectively out of action for the cartels. So what they're doing is recruiting other prisoners, who are about to get out, to sell drugs for their people." "I'm telling you," Ferranti's source continued,

it's like a job fair in here. I'm at the end of a 10-year bid in the feds, and I got a couple of different Mexican dudes making me offers. They want to send me 20 keys right when I get out, on the front. It's crazy. I didn't want to go back to selling drugs, but 20 keys? I could come up quick and be set for life, you know what I mean?

"By recruiting those well versed in criminal knowledge and underworld tactics, the cartels are hedging their bets as they move everything north," the prisoner told Ferranti. "These Mexican dudes in here are looking for prisoners to sell drugs for them, dealers to connect to their people." "With aspiring drug traffickers filling our nation's prisons," Ferranti concluded, "the cartels have had no problem attracting new recruits." "A lot of these guys in here don't got no skills," the prisoner continued, "All they know is the drug life. And with these Mexican dudes selling them dreams and offering them the connect of a lifetime, they're in no position to say no. They all think they'll be the next Scarface. They want to feed their families and get on their feet. But even Tony Montana didn't last. That's the nature of the business. Still, the easy money is too big a temptation to ignore for most of these guys."[119] Most independent reports confirm Ianni's 1974 judgment that "prisons and the prison experience are the most important loci for establishing the social relationships that form the basis for partnerships in organized crime."[120]

* * *

The expansion of America's prison system itself has multiplied criminal opportunities, as an ongoing case involving two former Mississippi officials, including the head of the prison system, has demonstrated. The case raises questions about the involvement of the private sector in America's prison policy.

In February 2015, Christopher B. Epps, the former commissioner of the Mississippi Department of Corrections, and Cecil McCrory, a former state lawmaker who had become involved with the private prisons industry, pleaded guilty to federal corruption charges. Federal prosecutors accused the men of a scheme in which McCrory channeled more than $1 million to Epps, including cash and mortgage payments, in exchange for lucrative state contracts. Epps had already resigned as corrections commissioner, a position he had held since 2002, and gave up his assets, including $1 million, a large home, a Gulf Coast condo and two Mercedes.[121]

The logical conclusion from the prison expansion and prison gang story is that imprisonment is far from the answer to organized crime but logic, as we have seen, has scarcely impacted organized crime control policies, or crime control policies generally.

Politicians from both major parties have not addressed a problem that is directly related to the great expansion of drug arrests and convictions that have stretched penal institutions to breaking point. Although the full consequences of putting hundreds of thousands of young people in with career criminals will not be known until the prison gang phenomenon is addressed by an investigative commission. Spectacular substance has been added to the observation that prison serves best to train more efficient and determined criminals. The public has been conditioned by politicians and media and therefore few question a crime control solution based largely on arresting and locking up the poor or the mainly black and Hispanic minorities. This will continue to have disastrously counterproductive consequences, something that the contemporary "Black Lives Matter" movement continues to publicize.

As this discussion of prison gangs shows, prison helps criminals develop and network. This result has been well known for centuries. In 1777 the prison reformer John Howard detailed much of the corruption and many of the horrors of imprisonment in his book, *The State of the Prisons*. He was one of the first to note the importance of prisons as places of apprenticeship for would-be professional criminals, "in some gaols you see ... boys of twelve or fourteen eagerly listening to the stories told by practiced and experienced criminals, of their adventures, successes, stratagems, and escapes."[122]

American state myopia on the unintended consequences of imprisonment is now being shared by the UK and every other nation that chose to replicate its policies, particularly on drug prohibition.

10
Organized Business Crime: The Elephant in the Room

Prominent American commentators once saw organized crime in America as an unfortunate and avoidable product of unfettered capitalism. Charles Beard, Walter Lippmann, Murray Gurfein and other Depression-era writers called for more rigorous business regulation to lessen the opportunities for successful organized crime in legal markets. As we have seen, however, the term "organized crime" was reframed in terms of foreign conspiracy and this did not require more rigorous business regulation, only tough and very selective policing that focused mainly on minority groups.

Franklin Roosevelt's New Deal administration accepted the need for business regulation to the extent of putting significant checks and balances on capitalism and therefore on organized business crime. From the 1980s, checks and balances were watered down or removed and more opportunities for successful organized business crime opened up.

The cornerstone of New Deal banking reform, as we have seen, was the Glass–Steagall Banking Act of 1933 that addressed the regulatory void that had allowed crooked bankers to operate freely in many state systems. The new regulations restricted the speculative use of bank credits, secured private deposits with a government-run insurance program which required big banks to contribute to the security of small banks, and forbade commercial banks from engaging in the investment business. Glass–Steagall thus drastically curbed the ability of unscrupulous bankers to game the system in the ways that had contributed to the Great Depression. The measures helped to sustain stability in the banking industry for decades. This was reflected in a sharp decline in the number of bank failures after reform. Federal regulatory activity thus succeeded in reducing opportunities for fraud and thus protecting the savings of ordinary Americans.[123]

The Securities Act of 1933 and the Securities and Exchange Act of 1934 were intended to address another regulatory void. The one that had allowed rampant stock market fraud and wild speculation during the years of the 1920s Republican ascendancy. Wall Street before the 1930s was starved of information. Firms were not required to publish regular, properly audited reports and only a handful of investment bankers like J.P. Morgan could make sound financial decisions since they had a monopoly on the necessary information. Opportunities abounded for insider manipulation and wildcat speculation, and in the tradition of laissez-faire the main check on fraudulent activity was the clearly inadequate *caveat emptor* or "let the buyer beware!"[124] The Roosevelt administration intended to supplement *caveat emptor* with "let the seller also beware," making those who managed banks, corporations and other agencies handling or using other people's money accountable for this trust. The law, Roosevelt insisted in a message to Congress, must put "the burden of telling the whole truth on the seller," and called for a law that was designed to prevent fraud by requiring companies to register all new issues of stocks and bonds with the Federal Trade Commission. It required issuing corporations to make "full and fair" disclosure of all relevant financial information about the new issues and the companies involved in them.[125] In sum, the intention was to let in the light on stock market transactions.

The Securities Act and the Securities Exchange Act set up a five-person Securities and Exchange Commission (SEC) to enforce the new regulations. The SEC's investigative history since its establishment shows that corporate representatives, stock buyers and sellers, stockbrokers, investment advisers, accountants and attorneys are at least as likely to be thieves as those in less respectable jobs. The difference is they have greater opportunities.[126]

There were authoritarian sides to the New Deal, as discussed earlier, and bureaucratic empire builders, notably J. Edgar Hoover, exploited them. However, many of its laws and policies successfully transformed and cleaned up the banking and finance sectors of the American economy. The New Deal policed business in ways that restricted corporate powers, while creating new rights and protections for workers. "We were to use the ... powers of government," Roosevelt later explained, "to fight for [constitutional] ideals ... because the American system visualized protection of the individual against the misuse of private economic power, the New Deal would insist on curbing such power." Much of American history since that time has been about banks and corporations regaining the special privileges that Roosevelt had often railed against.[127]

Although New Deal reform showed what could be done to manage and contain crime and capitalism, the nation was still recognizably the America created by business interests. Despite the great effort put in by New Deal reformers there were still large areas of American life that allowed or even fostered opportunities for successful organized criminal activity.

Instead of continuing to make progress in addressing the structural deficiencies of American capitalism, the Second World War and the Cold War shifted the nation's attention away from internal reform and towards national security. As part of this shift, organized crime began to be redefined as already discussed – it went from being seen as an indication of problems in the management of American capitalism to being seen as a conspiratorial foreign entity – a threat to national security.

Studies demonstrating that ubiquitous organized crime did in fact indicate structural problems with American capitalism were ignored or, if necessary, buried. An early case involved a classic of American criminological literature, Edwin Sutherland's *White Collar Crime* (1949).

Sutherland's research found that the criminality of corporations was similar to the professional organized criminals he had previously studied. It was persistent, extensive, usually unpunished, most often deliberate, and involved the connivance of government officials or legislators. He cited cases of bribery, fraud, embezzlement, antitrust violations, false advertising and the theft of trade secrets by such major corporations as Armour & Company, Swift & Company, General Motors, Sears Roebuck and Westinghouse. In the steel and automobile industry he found evidence that corporations were often ready, willing and able to use violence to win industrial disputes or break unions. He also showed that the American "free enterprise" system was a misnomer since practically all large corporations engaged in the illegal restraint of trade.[128]

Sutherland also demonstrated that there were forms of corporate violence other than strike-breaking, using the Gauley Bridge disaster as an example. Researchers have since added detail to his insight.

In 1929 the New Kanawha Power Company – a Union Carbide subsidiary – chose the Rhinehart-Dennis Construction Company as the subcontractor to build a tunnel near Gauley Bridge, West Virginia. Rhinehart-Dennis recruited a mainly black workforce for the task and put them to work in deadly conditions. Immediately after dynamite was used to blast rock that was extremely high in silica content, workers were herded back into the tunnel. Rhinehart-Dennis foremen beat them with pick handles to get them to return. Increasing numbers of workers became progressively shorter of breath and then dropped dead. Rhinehart-Dennis contracted with a local undertaker to bury the African Americans in a field at 55 dollars per corpse. Three hours was the standard elapsed time between death in the tunnel and burial. In this way, the company avoided the formalities of an autopsy and death certificate. It was estimated that 169 African Americans ended up in the field, two or three to a hole.

An estimate of the project's final human cost put it at 476 dead and 1,500 disabled. Some survivors took Rhinehart-Dennis and New Kanawha to court to sue for negligence but the cases were sabotaged by public and private corruption in West Virginia. The chief of West Virginia's Mines Department testified that he had observed no dust in the tunnel in 1930 or 1931, although he had written letters to the company in 1931 urging them to do something about the dust condition. One of the jurors in the trial was found to be riding home every night in a company car and there were many more rumors of jury tampering. Eventually, 167 of the suits were settled out of court for a total of $130,000, with one-half going to the workers' attorneys. One of the workers' law firms was later found to have accepted a $20,000 side-payment from the companies. No punitive action was ever taken in the case against Rhinehart-Dennis, New Kanawha Power or Union Carbide.[129]

Sutherland's book showed an awareness of the problems involved in the exposure and prosecution of the organized crimes of the powerful in America. Just before publication he was made even more aware of the difficulties of "whistle blowing" on the powerful in America by his publisher's reluctance to allow the naming of the guilty corporations in case they took legal action. Lawyers had advised the publisher, Dryden Press, that it would be liable for damages because the book called certain corporations "criminal," although they had not been dealt with under criminal statutes. Sutherland had insisted that the white collar behaviors he detailed were criminal rather than civil offenses and that the persons who committed them ought to be punished as severely as persons who committed personal or property crimes. However, Sutherland finally agreed to drop the corporate names, after more pressure from his university's administrators. The book appeared in a form that would not offend the corporate criminals involved. Although *White Collar Crime* has now been read by generations of criminology students, its impact was thus massively reduced by what amounted to a form of censorship. The real names of the corporations were added to an uncut version of the book in 1983, long after the book could make any policy impact.[130]

Until the 1960s and 1970s very few criminologists or commentators chose to risk their careers by stepping outside the prevailing pro-business consensus and exposing pervasive organized crime in business. Sutherland had demonstrated that organized crime permeated the top of the American economic structure at least as much as the bottom, but the point would have been lost on most people by the late 1940s. It was considered unpatriotic in the early Cold War era to challenge the integrity of the American economic system, especially during the first two decades of the Cold War fight against communism at home and abroad.

An indication that the majority of Americans who believed that corporations were now "socially responsible" were wrong came in 1961 when a criminal conspiracy in the electrical industry of at least seven years' duration was revealed. During the 1950s many local authorities and public bodies used a sealed bid procedure to get the best prices when buying equipment from manufacturers. In mid-1959, however, officials from the Tennessee Valley Authority noticed they were getting lists of identical prices.[131]

These and other bids were too careless to avoid suspicion and eventually four grand juries were convened to probe price-fixing in the electrical industry. Twenty indictments were handed down, involving 45 individual defendants and 29 corporations. Most thought it best to plead guilty. Seven defendants were jailed for terms of 30 days, and fines amounting to $1,787,000 were set against the corporations.[132]

Evidence produced at the trials revealed that executives from supposedly competing corporations would regularly get together to fix prices and would go to some length to avoid suspicion. The officials spoke in code, calling their meetings "choir practice" and taking a "Christmas card list" of those attending.

A Senate investigating committee later asked one of the officials whether he knew that these meetings were illegal and got this response: "Illegal? Yes, but not criminal. I didn't find that out until I read the indictment ... I assumed that criminal action meant damaging someone, and we did not do that ... I thought that we were more or less working on a survival basis in order to try to make enough to keep our plant and our employees."[133] In fact, this price-fixing conspiracy cost American consumers millions of dollars involving theft from the American people of more money than was stolen in all of the country's robberies, burglaries and larcenies during the years in which the price-fixing occurred.[134]

The two corporations with the heaviest fines were General Electric ($437,500) and Westinghouse ($372,500), but as the criminologist Gilbert Geis pointed out, "a half-million dollar loss was no more unsettling than a $3 parking fine would be to a man with an income of $175,000 a year."[135] This conspiracy against the antitrust laws and the public was exceptional only in that it was revealed, and some perpetrators punished.

* * *

The corporate criminal activity that will possibly cause most damage in the twenty first century is the disposal of dangerous waste products from the chemical, oil and other industries. Until the 1970s most corporations treated their waste products as they would ordinary garbage and simply dumped tons of toxic materials wherever it was most convenient – often in coastal waters or landfills.

Several scandals involving the premature deaths of many cancer victims prompted federal legislation in 1981, outlawing disposal that endangered the water supply and public health. Penalties of five-year prison terms and fines for knowingly putting people at risk could now be imposed. From then on the illegal disposal of toxic waste became organized crime.

The practice continued after the new laws had been passed. Private waste-disposal companies, sometimes run by gangsters but more often by unethical businessmen, made themselves available to dispose of a corporation's toxic waste cheaply and often illegally. As James Coleman reported in the late 1980s:

> New Jersey, with America's largest chemical industry (and, not coincidentally, its highest rate of cancer mortality), is experiencing especially severe problems with such illegal dumping. Legal testimony indicates that some waste disposal companies send out tanker trucks in the dead of the night to find empty streets, vacant lots, or quiet streams, and simply open the valves and let their dangerous cargo pour out ... One illegal dumping site was discovered when an empty lot suddenly burst into flames. Another was discovered by a fire inspector who found that his shoes were being eaten away by the chemicals dumped in a lot he happened to walk across.[136]

Donald J. Rebovich, who completed an empirical study of hazardous waste crime in four states, found that criminals involved in disposal of hazardous waste had become increasingly able to corrupt or evade regulatory efforts. He uncovered a criminal world very different to that of popular perceptions. The world of the hazardous waste offender was one in which the intensity, duration and methods of the criminal act were more likely to be determined by the criminal opportunities available in the legitimate marketplace than by the orders of a controlling criminal syndicate. The criminal dumper, he concluded, was "an ordinary, profit-motivated businessman who operates in a business where syndicate crime activity may be present but is by no means pervasive."[137]

Major corporations have also continued to flout the disposal laws. There are many examples in the meat packing and slaughter industries, for example. In 1997, Smithfield Foods and two of its subsidiaries were fined $12.6 million for discharging illegal pollutants into the Pagan River in Virginia. The ruling found that Smithfield had committed more than 5,000 violations of permit limits for phosphorus, cyanide and other contaminants including fecal coliform. Fecal coliform is an organism found in animal and human waste that is associated with bacteria known to cause serious problems in humans. The violations had continued over a five-year period and "seriously degraded" two rivers and Chesapeake Bay. The ruling also found that Smithfield had routinely falsified documents and destroyed water quality records.[138]

Basing their conclusions regarding a confidential survey of the senior attorneys of more than 200 corporations, the *National Law Journal* found in 1993 that 66.8 percent of the respondents said that their businesses had operated in violation of federal or state environmental laws at least some time in the previous year.[139]

In terms of the environment, the oil companies, Exxon and British Petroleum (BP) have been particularly damaging. In 1991, Exxon Corporation and Exxon Shipping pleaded guilty to criminal violations of federal environmental laws and paid a $125 million fine related to the eleven million gallons of crude oil spilled from the *Exxon Valdez* oil tanker. This spillage polluted 700 miles of Alaska shoreline, killed birds and fish by the hundreds of thousands, and destroyed the way of life of thousands of native Americans. Exxon also joins a long list of corporations who have illegally poisoned American waterways, mostly with delayed effects but in the case of illegal discharges from a Marathon Oil refinery with explosive consequences. After a two-year investigation by the FBI, Marathon pleaded guilty to criminal charges in relation to an explosion and consequent house fire. The house had been situated downstream from the company's Indianapolis refinery which had been illegally discharging explosive pollutants.[140]

Research by Tricia Cruciotti and Rick A. Matthews, on the *Exxon Valdez* oil spill, demonstrated that executive agreements with regulators to relax safety standards amounted to collusion and state-facilitated crime. To begin their case, they made this point by quoting from the Alaska Oil Spill Commission's conclusion:

> Today's error-inducing system usually advances human error as the explanation for an accident. That argument effectively closes off any detailed analysis of the system itself by shifting the blame to the most convenient individual available, either the master, the watch officer or both. Blame is not attached to overall company policy that may have led to the accident – such as excessive work hours leading to officer and crew fatigue, route shortcuts to save time, and a general misunderstanding in the maritime industry of the overall advantages, disadvantages and effects of automation.[141]

Cruciotti and Matthews then documented the decisions that made the oil spill, and the environmental damage it caused, a likely outcome. They argued that the spill and the consequent damage were a result of deliberate decisions. "This series of oversight and failures to reprimand wrongdoing created an environment that, when coupled with a strong corporate profit motive, was conducive to an accident such as the grounding of the *Valdez*." They warned, "In spite of new legislation, environmental harm, and the large fines levied against Exxon as a result of the *Exxon Valdez* oil spill, problems within the oil industry in general have continued, ranging from oil spills to refusal to obey rules and lax regulations." Problems with the enforcement of regulations, they argue, are to blame for the ineffectiveness of legislation. Without mechanisms for enforcement, rules and regulations rarely restrained organizational actors from committing damaging violations.[142]

There is little evidence that the corporate actors involved in the Deepwater Horizon Oil Spill were restrained by rules and regulations. The spill began on April 20, 2010 in the Gulf of Mexico on the BP-operated Macondo Prospect. An explosion led to a sea-floor oil gusher flowing for 87 days, until it was capped. It is considered the largest marine oil spill in the history of the petroleum industry.

The explosion killed eleven people, injured 16, and caused great emotional trauma for the surviving crew members. Residents of the Gulf Coast states also suffered as the oil destroyed their economic livelihood, leading to increased psychological stress for many. The environmental harm done to the ecological systems of the Gulf of Mexico by the uncontrolled flow of oil was devastating.[143]

A federal investigation into the explosion and spill concluded that BP, although "ultimately responsible" for operations and safety on the rig, violated safety laws. The inquiry also criticized BP's drilling contractors, Transocean and Halliburton: "The loss of life at the Macondo site on 20 April 2010, and the subsequent pollution of the Gulf of Mexico through the summer of 2010 were the result of poor risk management, last minute changes to plans, failure to observe and respond to critical indicators, inadequate well control response, and insufficient emergency bridge response training." A series of decisions were made that saved money but increased risk. In November 2012, BP received the biggest criminal fine in US history as part of a

$4.5 billion (£2.8 billion) settlement related to their responsibility for the disaster.[144]

The following year, Walmart Stores settled a decade-long investigation into its hazardous waste practices by the Environmental Protection Agency when it pleaded guilty to criminal charges and agreed to pay $81 million. In cases filed in Los Angeles and San Francisco, Walmart pleaded guilty to six counts of violating the Clean Water Act by illegally handling and disposing of hazardous materials at its retail stores across the United States. The company also pleaded guilty in Kansas City, Missouri to violating federal law governing the proper handling of pesticides that had been returned by customers at stores across the country.

The conduct was alleged to have taken place at every single Walmart in the country.[145]

* * *

Corporate power lies behind the lack of an adequate government response to organized business crime in the United States. Corporate power bent regulatory law to its interests, as Marshall Clinard pointed out in *Corporate Corruption*:

> Corporate power has seen to it that in the event of a law violation, legislatures have provided besides or in lieu of the criminal law a wide range of administrative and civil penalties. These include warnings, injunctions, consent orders, and non-criminal monetary payments. Even where the criminal penalty is available, it is infrequently invoked ... Since corporate offenders are rarely seen or treated by the government as criminals, the public has developed the perception that most corporate violations are basically "non-criminal" and thus not serious in nature.[146]

Many corporate strategies for avoiding prosecution are completely legal but, as David Burnham pointed out, others are not, such as bribery or more subtle arrangements involving the "revolving door" between public and private service. In the case of the latter, a Justice Department lawyer may be promised a lucrative job in a private law firm representing a target company on the usually unstated assumption that he or she help achieve the law firm's goal of maximum leniency for the client.[147]

For these and other reasons, the main deterrents to corporate crime are fines that are generally so small as to amount to less than a fraction of the profits made by large corporations in one hour of operation – the same "flea bite" deterrent that Edward Ross noted at the beginning of the twentieth century.

Since Sutherland's pioneering study, many commentators have confirmed that corporate crime is organized crime. Russell Mokhiber, in *Corporate Crime and Violence* (1988), profiled 36 cases of corporate criminality and concluded that corporate crime is "more than just isolated instances of errant corporate behavior. Patterns emerge, including destruction of documents, suppression of dissent within corporate bureaucracy and intricate cover-ups and stonewalls."[148] James Coleman, in *The Criminal Elite* (1989), surveyed many examples of corporate crimes and concluded that "in many ways the organizations themselves, and not individual employees, are the real perpetrators of organizational crime." He elaborated that:

> In many cases, criminal activities are rooted in an organizational subculture and a set of attitudes that have developed over many years, and they cannot be traced to any single individual or group of individuals. Of course, individual actors must carry out the criminal deeds, but there is ample evidence to show that the attitudes and characteristics of those individuals are of little importance. Those who refuse to carry out the illegal activities demanded by their organizations are simply replaced by others that will.[149]

In sum, Frank Pearce's conclusion in *Crimes of the Powerful* (1976) continues to apply: "The corporations provide the most efficient and largest examples of organized crime in America."[150] Inadequate regulation allowed this to happen, deregulation allowed more of the same.

11
Deregulation and the Rise of Corporate Fraud

Just as Roosevelt set the reformist, regulatory agenda of the period between the 1930s and the 1970s, Ronald Reagan set the deregulatory agenda from the 1980s that has recently been reaffirmed by Donald Trump's 2016 presidential victory.

Reagan's inaugural address of 1981 was an early rehearsal of the arguments that would become the conventional wisdom. He spoke of the need to restore America's "dynamic economy." He blamed economic difficulties on "the intervention and intrusion in our lives that result from unnecessary and excessive growth of government," and pledged to roll back government bureaucracy, and reduce tax and government spending. In February 1981 he unveiled his economic program, which promised large tax cuts, particularly to the rich, various cuts in help to the poor through welfare programs, and sweeping deregulation to "unshackle" business.[151]

Many of Reagan's appointees were more committed to the laissez-faire ideology than federal controls. The *Wall Street Journal* pointed out that the president was "naming regulators who by virtue of attitude or inexperience are more likely to be nonregulators."[152] The president and his officials argued that reducing enforcement of "needless regulations" at both federal and state levels was necessary to reduce business costs, make American goods competitive in world markets, and liberate "the free market." Partly as a result of Reagan's economic policy changes, business did boom for some in the 1980s, but there were downsides. The deregulation of everything from airlines and telecommunications to finance opened up a flood of opportunities for large-scale organized business crime that damaged many people's lives, and contributed mightily to the 2007/8 financial "meltdown."

Reagan's deregulatory efforts began when he championed the Garn–St. Germain Depository Institutions Decontrol Act of 1982.

This, he claimed, released "the yoke of excessive regulation" from America's Savings and Loans (S&L) institutions. It also, however, allowed industry insiders to loot outrageous sums of money. The act was the culmination of a series of administrative and legislative changes allowing S&Ls to compete for more business, going beyond their traditional role of offering affordable mortgages to ordinary people. Officers could now invest up to 40 percent of their assets in almost any ventures they liked the look of with deposits that were insured by a government agency, the Federal Savings and Loan Insurance Corporation.

S&L operators took their government-insured deposits and went on a wild spending and embezzlement spree. Many S&L officials used their new freedoms to embezzle staggering sums of money. One type of deal involved "land flips" – transfers of land between related parties which in the process artificially inflated its value. One condominium project in Lake Tahoe, Nevada, was bought for less than $4 million and sold back and forth until it cost $40 million. The transactions often took place in the same room.[153]

A report on the S&L scandal by the General Accounting Office (GAO) summed up the wider extent of the criminality. It found that:

> Extensive, repeated and blatant violations of laws and regulations characterized the failed thrifts that we reviewed in each and every case ... fraud or insider abuse existed at each and every one of the failed thrifts and allegations of criminal misconduct abounded ... despite the fact that examination reports revealed critical problems at the failed thrifts, federal regulators did not always obtain agreements for corrective action. When they obtained them, they were in many cases violated, ignored, and in many cases it was years before resolutions were taken.[154]

Estimates made in 2009 as to the amount the thrift crisis had cost taxpayers were around $300 billion.[155] The average prison terms for convicted S&L fraudsters were around two years, to be served in minimum security federal prisons. [156]

*   *   *

In 1993 Bill Clinton took office as the first Democratic president since Jimmy Carter in the 1970s. Initially he tried to distance himself from what he called "a bunch of fucking bond traders in Wall Street."[157] It was not long, however, before Clinton was moving closer to the right and espousing free market ideology or neo-liberalism, as it began to be called.[158] His speeches echoed such themes as individual responsibility, free enterprise and the dangers of big government, and he committed his administration to continue the deregulatory policies of his Republican predecessors, Reagan and George Bush Sr. During Clinton's two terms of office, the SEC and the Department of Justice were notably ineffective in pursuing criminal prosecutions for financial fraud.

An intense lobbying effort by banking interests, who spent more than $300 million, helped push through the repeal of the Glass–Steagall Act in 1999,[159] the Depression-era banking reform that forbade commercial banks from engaging in the investment business and thus removed a major source for conflict of interest. Conflict of interest, of course, often leads to fraud or at the very least forms of interest-serving deception. The end of Glass–Steagall, along with the other business-interest-serving developments since Reagan, allowed the corruption of the late 1990s to encompass the entire American financial community. The financial markets now resembled "Swiss cheese," as Frank Partnoy put it in *Infectious Greed*, "with the holes – the unregulated places – getting bigger every year."[160] Bankers, brokers, lawyers, auditors and analysts joined in a feast of fraud that began to be partially revealed when one of the shining stars of the so-called New Economy went bust in 2002.

Enron was first set up in 1985 from the merger of two energy companies. Its CEO, Kenneth Lay, was an ardent deregulator who hoped to gain from the new opportunities made possible by the Reagan administration's moves to loosen government controls.

Even after an expensive fraud took place on his watch, Lay chose to continue his policy of minimal supervision, while Enron was refashioned so effectively by another free market enthusiast, Jeffrey Skilling, that it rose to become the seventh largest US company in terms of revenue by the end of the 1990s. Skilling first became president and then CEO of Enron, and with a new vice president of finance, Andy Fastow, plus scores of the best and the brightest young analysts and associates, accumulated millions of dollars in salary, bonuses and, of course, stock options. Things were going so well that an enormous banner was put up at the firm's state-of-the-art skyscraper headquarters in Houston. It claimed in big letters that Enron was "The World's Greatest Energy Company on the Way to Becoming the World's Greatest Company."[161]

All the while Enron was greasing the wheels of the political process by donating freely to both political parties. In 2000, $2.4 million of Enron's money was spent supporting candidates for public office in the US, mostly for the Republicans but with large amounts going to Democrat free market supporters.[162] These kind of sums put Enron in the vanguard of the successful effort to deregulate California's energy grid, which was so poorly managed as to end in widespread blackouts and exorbitant prices for Californian consumers during the state's energy crisis of 2000–1. According to transcripts of telephone calls released in 2004, Enron traders joked about stealing from grandmothers, and talked openly about manipulating the electricity market by creating congestion on transmission lines and taking generating units offline to pump up electricity prices.[163]

Fastow was the company's chief financial officer and thus the architect of the thousands of convoluted offshore partnerships that contributed significantly to Enron's final collapse. The partnerships were given names from *Star Wars* and other films, such as Chewbacca, Jedi, Braveheart, Raptor and Condor. Some of the deals involving these partnerships are best described as outright theft. In one case, Enron was trying hard to sell three barges that were generating power off the coast of Nigeria in order to boost its earning for the 1999 fourth quarter. The company eventually persuaded Merrill Lynch to buy the barges on the oral understanding that Enron would later unwind the deal after Merrill had collected its profits. Merrill bought the barges at a price that netted Merrill, as promised, a 15 percent annualized return. Enron had to pay one of its partnerships a hefty fee for this, but as far as the public was concerned Enron got to record a profit. Enron's proposition and Merrill Lynch's willingness to implement it represented a much more general sense of corporate corruption.[164] There were many more of these corrupt deals. Essentially Enron used its offshore partnerships to report profits it never made and cover up enormous losses. Between July 2000 and October 2001, for example,

Enron recorded $1 billion of profit it did not really earn.[165] Although it was confidence tricksterism on a grand scale, actually proving fraud in the courts was difficult, at least partly because Enron's accountants, Arthur Andersen, shredded a number of possibly damning documents. Revelations about Andersen's complicity in Enron's deceptions shed some light on the widespread and often corrupt collusion between executives and their accountants.

Shortly after Enron's collapse came a string of revelations, disclosures and bankruptcies that made very clear the fact that the Texas company was just part of a barrel full of rotten apples. By the end of 2002, companies were regularly admitting that their reported earnings were not as they should have been and there was the collapse of a billion-dollar company every few weeks. The range of financial malfeasance and manipulation was vast, according to Frank Partnoy's account: "Energy companies, such as Dynergy, El Paso, and Williams, did the same complex financial deals Andy Fastow had engineered at Enron. Telecommunications firms, such as Global Crossing and WorldCom, fell into bankruptcy after it became clear that they, too, had been cooking their books." These top energy and telecommunications firms did the most notorious transactions, Partnoy continued, "including questionable round-trip swaps with each other, many of which were arranged by Wall Street's top banks and blessed by Big Five accounting firms."[166]

Wall Street's accounting norms were a crucial ingredient to the development of the criminal corporate culture laid bare by the scandals involving Enron, WorldCom and others. According to the economist Robert Bremner, these norms legitimated virtually any trick in the book to pump up "pro-forma" earnings – those that are reported quarterly to stockholders and the financial community. It was only later that regulatory agencies required more realistic figures. "Needless to say," Bremner added, "this system of dual reporting invited abuses – for instance, exaggerating short-term earnings just long enough to sustain equity prices while corporate insiders unload their stock."[167]

Organized business crime paid more than any other form of crime, and contributed hugely to a mountainous redistribution of wealth achieved by American corporate leaders that has continued from the 1990s. Between 1995 and 1999, the value of stock options granted to US executives more than quadrupled, from $26.5 billion to $110 billion. In 1992, corporate CEOs held 2 percent of the equity of US corporations; ten years later they owned 12 percent. Between 1997 and 2001, insiders cashed in some $18 billion in shares, unloading more than half this total in 2000 at the peak of the telecoms bubble and thus avoiding the massive hits taken by less well-connected investors. This all ranked, Bremner rightly concluded, among the most spectacular acts of expropriation in the history of capitalism.[168]

The rise in market power of Enron, WorldCom and the rest owed a great deal to criminal activities. Their crimes had many victims, including shareholders who lost money and workers who lost jobs when revelations of fraud caused bankruptcies or "downsizing." WorldCom investors alone lost more than $200 billion in equity and bonds from the company's bankruptcy, while workers' pension funds lost at least $70 billion in equity alone. Added to this more than 22 states lost more than $2.6 billion in their public employee retirement funds as a result of the bankruptcy. Local government funds lost billions more at a time when state and local governments were already facing fiscal crises, thus threatening the retirement security of teachers, firefighters, police and other state and local government employees.[169]

The effort against corporate crime was, and continues to be, mainly directed against individual transgressors. There have been some cosmetic rather than structural reforms, but these are unlikely to be an adequate response to a crisis that in the words of political scientist Justin O'Brien was "not the result of deviance but rather the inevitable out-workings of a political and economic system, which pivots on the malign power of money to distort the deliberative process." It was the system itself, O'Brien continued, "that now stands accused of creating the circumstances for the morally challenged executives to thrive." It was not in the interests of the system, he concluded, to draw attention to this failure.[170] The winners were few, the losers were many, even before the financial crisis that began in 2007. This crisis so far has resulted in millions losing their jobs, homes and savings, and encouraged many disaffected Americans to put Donald Trump into the White House.

12
Fraud and the Financial Meltdown

The definitive account of the 2007/8 economic meltdown has been written by the Financial Crisis Inquiry Commission (FCIC). The FCIC was a ten-member commission appointed by the US government. It held hearings up to 2010 and heard testimony from bankers and persons in business, academia and government. It provides a great deal of evidence and analysis that supports the case that the crisis was caused in large part by organized frauds. Its recommendations were not taken up by the Obama administrations and to date have been ignored by the Trump administration.

A representative early paragraph in its encyclopedic report is as follows:

Nonprime lending surged to $730 billion in 2004 and then $1.0 trillion in 2005, and its impact began to be felt in more and more places. Many of those loans were funnelled into the pipeline by mortgage brokers – the link between borrowers and the lenders who financed the mortgages – who prepared the paperwork for loans and earned fees from lenders for doing it. More than 200,000 new mortgage brokers began their jobs during the boom, and some were less than honorable in their dealings with borrowers. According to an investigative news report published in 2008 between 2000 and 2007 at least 10,500 people with criminal records entered the field in Florida, for example, including 4,065 who had previously been convicted of such crimes as fraud, bank robbery, racketeering, and extortion. J. Thomas Cardwell, the commissioner of the Florida Office of Financial Regulation, told the Commission that "lax lending standards" and a "lack of accountability"... created a condition in which fraud flourished. Marc S. Savitt, a past president of the National Association of Mortgage Brokers, added that ... some loan origination firms, such as Ameriquest, were "absolutely" corrupt.[171]

In 80 percent of mortgage fraud cases, the report added,

> fraud involves industry insiders. For example, property flipping can
> involve buyers, real estate agents, appraisers, and complicit closing
> agents. In a "silent second," the buyer, with the collusion of a loan
> officer and without the knowledge of the first mortgage lender,
> disguises the existence of a second mortgage to hide the fact that
> no down payment has been made. "Straw buyers" allow their names
> and credit scores to be used, for a fee, by buyers who want to conceal
> their ownership.[172]

The FBI had been aware of what it called "an epidemic of mortgage
fraud" as early as 2004. It held press conferences to alert the nation
to the problem. The following year it issued the *Financial Crimes
Report to the Public* which noted that a "significant portion of the
mortgage industry is void of any mandatory fraud reporting" and that
"mortgage fraud is pervasive and growing." "Combating significant
fraud in this area is a priority," the report stressed, "because mortgage
lending and the housing market have a significant overall effect on the
nation's economy."[173]

However, William K. Black, formerly a regulator prominent in
exposing S&L frauds, told the FCIC that "after a brilliant start in
identifying the epidemic of mortgage fraud," the FBI went tragically
astray and its efforts to contain the epidemic failed." "The FBI," he
elaborated, "suffered from a horrific systems capacity problem. It did
not have the agents or expertise to deal with the concurrent control
fraud epidemics it faced this decade ... The most crippling limitation
on the regulators', FBI's and DOJ's [Department of Justice's] efforts
to contain the epidemic of mortgage fraud and the financial crisis
was not understanding of the cause of the epidemic and why it would
cause a catastrophic financial crisis."

The framing of the issue of mortgage fraud, Black explained, was
then controlled by the mortgage banking industry – the industry that
represents the lenders that caused the epidemic of mortgage fraud.
The Mortgage Bankers Association (MBA) "followed the obvious
strategy of portraying its members as the victims of mortgage fraud."
Black continued:

What it never discussed was that the officers that controlled its members were the primary beneficiaries of mortgage fraud. It is the trade association of the "perps." The MBA claimed that all mortgage fraud was divided into two categories – neither of which included accounting control fraud. The FBI, driven by acute systems incapacity, formed a "partnership" with the MBA and adopted the MBA's (farcically absurd) two-part classification of mortgage fraud (FBI 2007). The result is that there has not been a single arrest, indictment, or conviction of a senior official of a nonprime lender for accounting fraud.[174]

This epidemic of fraud, the FCIC's report summarized, led to a housing bubble and the "collapse of this bubble – fuelled by ... scant regulation, and toxic mortgages – that was the spark that ignited a string of events, which led to a full-blown crisis in the fall of 2007."

Trillions of dollars in risky mortgages had become embedded throughout the financial system, as mortgage-related securities were packaged, repackaged and sold to investors around the world. When the bubble burst, hundreds of billions of dollars in losses in mortgages and mortgage-related securities shook markets as well as financial institutions that had significant exposures to those mortgages and had borrowed heavily against them. This happened not just in the United States but around the world. The losses were magnified by derivatives such as synthetic securities.[175]

"As a scholar of the Great Depression," Federal Reserve Chairman Ben Bernanke told the FCIC, "I honestly believe that September and October of 2008 was the worst financial crisis in global history, including the Great Depression. If you look at the firms that came under pressure in that period ... only one ... was not at serious risk of failure. ... So out of maybe the 13 ... most important financial institutions in the United States, 12 were at risk of failure within a period of a week or two."[176]

Thus an epidemic of fraud sparked a recession that was, according to the commission, the worst on record, "as reflected in the speed and breadth of the falloff in jobs, the rise of the ranks of underemployed workers, and the long stretches of time that millions of Americans were ... surviving without work."[177] For millions of honest Americans, the report made clear, the financial crisis has been "long, bewildering, and painful." "Stores have shuttered; employers have cut jobs; hopes have fled. Too many Americans today find themselves in suburban ghost towns or urban wastelands, where properties are vacant and construction cranes do not lift a thing for months."[178]

Few businessmen and women involved in the financial crisis frauds went to prison. When, according to Lynn Parramore, writing for *Alternet* in 2013, "banks and financial firms rob, defraud and mismanage the money of Americans – and even cast them out of their own homes illegally – the worst that usually happens is a fine." Since the 2008 financial crisis some of Wall Street's biggest banks have faced fines from regulators reaching into billion-dollar territory. Parramore was one of the few journalists to follow the money trail of these fines. She lists some of the banks and financial institutions that have been subject to massive fines, including Goldman Sachs, Citigroup and Bank of America, then lists the regulatory agencies, including the SEC, the US Justice Department and a smorgasbord of state governments and other regulatory agencies. All these "have been fining financial institutions for everything from concealing risky products, to illegally kicking soldiers out of their homes, to trying to scam bailout money."

Then Parramore asked "the billion-dollar question," where does the money go? She found the answer was not always easy to come by. Most of the money appeared to go to the Treasury's general fund, and restitution for victims is rare. "What is clear," she concluded, "is that fines, even the biggest ones, do little to deter criminal activity. Big banks appear to be simply calculating fines into their business models: fines, after all, don't exceed profits, and in this scenario, what do you think the incentive is for banks to cease their fraudulent and criminal activity? If you answered, 'none whatsoever,' you are likely correct."[179]

Charles Ferguson, in *Inside Job: The Financiers who Pulled Off the Heist of the Century*, made the valid point that the RICO Act provides for severe criminal (and civil) remedies for operating a criminal organization, and was explicitly intended to cover organized financial crime as well as violent criminal organizations. A great deal of the behavior that occurred during the bubble and described in detail in his book "would appear to fall under RICO statutes." "However," he points out, "there has not been a single RICO prosecution related to the financial crisis, nor has a single RICO restraining order been issued to seize the assets of either any individual banker or any firm."[180] This contrasts with the seizure of assets from the powerless as discussed in Chapter 8.

Despite the hard work and intelligent analysis of the FCIC commission, nothing fundamental will change. As the criminologist Laureen Snider noted, "the media spotlight shifts onto the next crisis, a regulatory status quo ante returns. Regulatory agency budgets once again come under siege, and antigovernmental rhetoric and policies increase."[181] The minimal response of Barack Obama's administrations made her point, even before the antigovernmental – "Drain the Swamp" - rhetoric of Donald Trump helped win him the 2016 presidential election.

Snider illuminated the process that will guarantee more unpunished and routine business frauds:

> Throughout each reform period, the omnipresent army of business "enablers" – tax lawyers, accountants, and investment advisers – are kept busy figuring out new ways to evade, avoid, or nullify each new set of regulations. Their "innovations" proliferate unchecked until the next wave of financial meltdowns occurs and the cycle begins once more. The result is that regulators find themselves responsible for enforcing an ever-more complex mass of obscure and often contradictory statutes, provisions and instructions that provide income for the stable of lawyers who are retained to find loopholes for their deep-pocketed employers and produce mystification for almost everyone else.[182]

In such ways the failure to control organized crime will be perpetuated – the discourse framed since the era of Charles Dawes is such that the organized criminal behavior of respectable business networks and institutions is seen as illegal but not really criminal. Americans therefore are where they were at the beginning of the twentieth century when the sociologist Edward Ross wrote about the uselessness of the "flea bite" deterrent of fines. Organized business crime remains routine, fines are just part of the costs of doing business in a nation that sold its organized crime control policies to the rest of the world.

13

Hiding the Failure of
Organized Crime Control

The Government Accountability Office (GAO) was set up in 1921 as the General Accounting Office, a nonpartisan federal agency that acts as the investigative arm of Congress, making the executive branch accountable to Congress and the government accountable to US citizens.

In its statement on "Mission," "Core Values" and "Work" the GAO says that it exists to "support the Congress in meeting its constitutional responsibilities and to help improve the performance and ensure the accountability of the federal government for the benefit of the American people. We provide Congress with timely information that is objective, fact-based, nonpartisan, nonideological, fair, and balanced." The GAO advises "Congress and the heads of executive agencies about ways to make government more efficient, effective, ethical, equitable and responsive." Its "work leads to laws and acts that improve government operations, saving the government and taxpayers billions of dollars." The GAO, in theory, is an important part of the US government's system of checks and balances.

Between 1972 and 1989, the GAO issued 19 reports with the words "organized crime" in the title. An indication of their most consistent message can be gained from their titles such as: "War on Organized Crime Faltering: Federal Strike Forces Not Getting the Job Done" (1978), "Stronger Effort against Organized Crime Needed" (1981) and "Organized Crime: Issues Concerning Strike Forces" (1989). An indication that the GAO had accepted the pluralist interpretation of organized crime is in the title of the final report published during the 1972 and 1989 period: "Nontraditional Organized Crime: Law Enforcement Officials' Perspectives on Five Criminal Groups" (1989). Since 1989 there have been no relevant GAO report titles that included the words "organized crime," unless one includes a

2011 report, "Organized Retail Crime," about shop theft.[183] There is no evidence in the GAO reports that organized crime has been controlled in America, and yet the agency that America relies upon for government accountability has decided to look away.

* * *

The Kaufman Commission, discussed earlier in Part III, was the last national commission to examine organized crime in America, and by every account it did not do a good job. Half of the commission's 18 members co-authored a statement that described the commission's processes during its three-year existence as flawed: "The process of report review was characterized by circulation of massive volumes of very preliminary draft material, unrealistic time deadlines for comment, consistent resistance to the scheduling of meetings to discuss report drafts, and final drafts which were not even shown to commission members before publication."

The dissenters unambiguously made clear that the commission's procedures were not sound. "The true history of the President's Commission on Organized Crime is a saga of missed opportunity," continuing:

> Poor management of time, money and staff has resulted in the Commission's leaving important issues unexamined, most notably the questions of the effectiveness of federal and state anti-organized crime efforts ... We have failed to make a complete national and region-by-region analysis of organized crime. Further we have not done an adequate job in assessing the effectiveness of the Federal Government's response to organized crime. Neither have we assessed the nature and quality of state and local responses to the problem. These failures point up the desperate need for the systematic collection and analysis of organized crime intelligence from all corners of the nation.[184]

All the dissenters, however, would have agreed with Judge Kaufman's verdict on organized crime given at the commission's final press conference. The investigation had convinced him that "law enforcement has been tested to its utmost. But let's face it. It hasn't succeeded."[185]

He then went on to make the bizarre case that urine-testing for drugs was worth trying in the effort to control drug-related organized crime, but his verdict on law enforcement's failure is as valid today as it was in the 1980s. Evidence of America's failure to control organized crime, however, was ignored, buried in media accounts of the "war" on organized crime's occasional successes. The Mafia Commission trials, the trials of scores of other locally based gangsters, and the blind eye turned by the GAO and other government agencies, allowed American officials to proclaim that the United States had controlled or at least drastically curbed its organized crime problem. American failures in organized crime control rarely got reported by foreign media.

Successes, however, were trumpeted around the world in newspapers, magazines and television documentaries, even as thousands of organized criminals continued to prosper. The dominant message was crystallized in the titles of three books of the time: *The Good Guys: How We Turned the FBI Round and Finally Broke the Mob* (1997); *Gangbusters: The Destruction of America's Last Great Mafia Dynasty* (1999); and *Mob Nemesis: How the FBI Crippled Organized Crime* (2002).[186]

It is also worth noting that by this time the serious study of organized crime in America was in decline. This decline could partly be explained by the political nature of the most influential funding agency in the fields of criminology and criminal justice – the National Institute of Justice (NIJ). According to Jeffrey Ian Ross, an academic who worked for the NIJ between 1995 and 1998, scholarship had minimal influence on the institute's research agenda. Instead the agenda was set by those at high political levels in Congress or the White House.[187] After the Kaufman Commission's flawed efforts, top politicians and officials chose to turn a blind eye to evidence that America had failed to control organized criminality within its own borders.

By the 1990s, the work of scholars such as Joe Albini, Dwight Smith and Alan Block, who had challenged the orthodoxy on organized crime and its control, was largely dismissed or forgotten. The updated conventional wisdom was expressed by Rensselaer W. Lee III, a specialist in Latin American drug control, who claimed in 1999 that the "United States has largely contained or marginalized its organized crime problem."[188] Such claims have scarcely been challenged in the twenty-first century despite a tidal wave of evidence to the contrary.

The sleight of hand that still allows the US government to claim success against organized crime is only convincing if people believe the phony history of organized crime constructed by opportunist politicians and bureaucrats and their cheerleaders in the media. Among the people who continue to believe in this false history are federal officials, as is clearly apparent from the FBI website.[189] Consulted on July 28, 2016, as discussed in Part II, the "official" history of organized crime suggests an understanding that has not moved on from the 1950s alien conspiracy interpretation and its 1980s "pluralist revision."

The first member of the American "La Cosa Nostra," according to the FBI, was Giuseppe Esposito, who fled to America after the murder of several notable Sicilian landowners. Esposito "was arrested in New Orleans in 1881 and extradited to Italy." After giving organized crime in America a foreign origin, the FBI's history then gives a brief account of the Hennessey incidents that appears to exonerate the American lynchers, in the same way as the xenophobes had done since the nineteenth century.

The FBI repeats a variation on Hickman Powell's ideas about Luciano centralizing the Mafia, and thus organized crime; the site then gives details on the FBI's 1980s and 1990s successes against Mafiosi. This careless repetition of a mythological past is accompanied by a claim that organized crime remains alien to America. Today, the agency claims, organized crime includes: "Russian mobsters who fled to the US in the wake of the Soviet Union's collapse; Groups from African countries like Nigeria that engage in drug trafficking and financial scams; Chinese tongs, Japanese Boryokudan, and other Asian crime rings; and enterprises based in Eastern European nations like Hungary and Romania."

"All of these groups," the FBI notes, "have a presence in the US or are targeting our citizens from afar – using the Internet and other technologies of our global age. More and more, they are literally becoming partners in crime, realizing they have more to gain from cooperating than competing."[190]

Even in a nation of 300 million people, which includes thousands of home-grown organized criminal networks consisting of representatives of every racial and ethnic group, including many white

Anglo-Saxons, the FBI has difficulty finding a group indigenous to the US involved in present-day "organized crime." The problem, according to the official interpretation, began abroad and remains external or foreign to the US. It fits an interpretation that many people want to believe: the FBI had a slow start against organized crime but eventually developed methods to destroy the centralized conspiracy that controlled organized crime. Therefore, according to this version, the answer to organized crime is to continue to support these methods, however repressive and counterproductive, and, as we shall see in Part IV, export these methods to the rest of the world.

14

Repression as Organized Crime Control

Organized crime control laws have given federal and local police officers more scope to spy on and suppress political dissent as well as facilitating the control of scapegoated minority groups. This process began almost as soon as the Organized Crime Control Act of 1970 was passed. Nixon's administration used its new powers much more actively against anti-Vietnam war protestors than Italian American or any other gangsters. Between 1970 and 1974 in particular, grand juries, along with increased wiretapping and eavesdropping powers, became part of the government's armory against dissent. The list of abuses during these years includes: harassing political activists, discrediting "non-mainstream" groups, assisting management during strikes, punishing witnesses for exercising their Fifth Amendment rights, covering up official crimes, enticing perjury and gathering domestic intelligence.[191]

In 1982, President Ronald Reagan announced a plan intended to "end the drug menace and cripple organized crime." The plan did not achieve either aim, but the high-level corruption and suppression of dissent using organized crime control powers continued. Among the mountains of evidence of corruption uncovered during the Iran–Contra scandals, a Senate subcommittee in 1989 confirmed that the US-supported Contra rebels used drug money to support their fight against the Nicaraguan government. A Senate report confirmed this:

it is clear that individuals who provided support for the Contras were involved in drug trafficking, the supply network of the Contras was used by drug trafficking organizations, and elements of the Contras themselves knowingly received financial and material assistance from drug traffickers. In each case, one or another agency of the US government had information regarding the involvement either while it was occurring, or immediately thereafter.[192]

The extensive drug trafficking by America's chosen allies, in other words, was known to US government agencies ostensibly engaged in a war to suppress drug trafficking.

While the country was officially engaged in its ambivalent war against drugs and organized crime, Reagan administration officials used organized crime control powers to infiltrate church meetings and wiretap church phones in Arizona and Texas. The intention was to monitor the efforts of some religious groups to provide "sanctuary" to Central American refugees. These refugees were primarily from El Salvador and Guatemala, countries whose regimes had the active support of the US government despite much documented evidence of violent suppression of dissent. For a single set of indictments, 40,000 pages of secretly taped conversations involving priests and nuns were compiled. No prison sentences resulted but the harassment successfully intimidated the "sanctuary" movement.[193]

More recently, in 2012, FBI documents obtained by the Partnership for Civil Justice Fund (PCJF) using Freedom of Information Act requests revealed that from its inception, the FBI treated the Occupy Wall Street (OWS) movement as a potential criminal and terrorist threat even though the agency acknowledged in documents that organizers explicitly called for peaceful protest and did "not condone the use of violence" at Occupy protests. FBI offices and agents around the country were conducting surveillance against the movement even as early as August 2011, a month prior to the establishment of the OWS encampment in Zuccotti Park, New York, and other Occupy actions around the country. According to Mara Verheyden-Hilliard, executive director of the PCJF, "These documents show that the FBI and the Department of Homeland Security are treating protests against the corporate and banking structure of America as potential criminal and terrorist activity. These documents also show these federal agencies functioning as a de facto intelligence arm of Wall Street and Corporate America." On August 19, 2011, for example, the reports showed that the FBI in New York was meeting with the New York Stock Exchange to discuss the OWS protests that wouldn't start for another month. By September, prior to the start of the OWS, the FBI was notifying businesses that they might be the focus of an OWS protest. Other revelations were:

- Documents show the spying abuses of the FBI's "Campus Liaison Program" in which the FBI in Albany and the Syracuse Joint Terrorism Task Force disseminated information to "sixteen (16) different campus police officials," and then "six (6) additional campus police officials." Campus officials were in contact with the FBI for information on OWS. A representative of the State University of New York at Oswego contacted the FBI for information on the OWS protests and reported to the FBI on the SUNY-Oswego Occupy encampment made up of students and professors.

- Documents released show coordination between the FBI, Department of Homeland Security and corporate America. They include a report by the Domestic Security Alliance Council (DSAC), described by the federal government as "a strategic partnership between the FBI, the Department of Homeland Security and the private sector," discussing the OWS protests at the west coast ports to "raise awareness concerning this type of criminal activity." The DSAC report shows the nature of secret collaboration between American intelligence agencies and their corporate clients – the document contains a "handling notice" that the information is "meant for use primarily within the corporate security community. Such messages shall not be released in either written or oral form to the media, the general public or other personnel ..."

- Naval Criminal Investigative Service (NCIS) reported to the DSAC on the relationship between OWS and organized labor for the port actions. The NCIS describes itself as "an elite worldwide federal law enforcement organization" whose "mission is to investigate and defeat criminal, terrorist, and foreign intelligence threats to the United States Navy and Marine Corps ashore, afloat and in cyberspace." The NCIS also assists with the transport of Guantanamo prisoners.[194]

* * *

Alongside this use of anti-organized crime and anti-terror powers to suppress political dissent, repression in America was put on an assembly-line scale. The courts filled the prisons, as we have seen, mainly with African Americans and other minorities, from the poorer sections of society. Serious convictions for crime in the US, much of it drug-related, accelerated. State and federal legislatures hugely increased the penalties for criminal violations. In New York, for example, Governor Nelson Rockefeller pushed through the so-called "Rockefeller Laws," enacted in 1973. These dictated a minimum sentence of 15 years' imprisonment for selling just two ounces (or possessing four ounces) of heroin, cocaine or marijuana. In addition, the new, enhanced sentences were frequently made mandatory. The concept of mandatory minimum sentences with the consequent diminution of the judge's role in cases was, as noted in Chapter 1, introduced to the American system by white supremacist Hale Boggs with the support of anti-organized crime crusader Estes Kefauver.

In today's American criminal justice system there is an imbalance of power, argued a former judge Jed S. Rakoff, in *The New York Review of Books*, with the prosecutor having all of it during plea bargaining processes, the defender and the judge having none of it, and juries rarely consulted. A plea bargain, he writes, is much like a "contract of adhesion" in which one party can effectively force its will on the other party. "The result," he concludes, "is that, of the 2.2 million Americans now in prison – an appalling number in its own right – well over two million are there as a result of plea bargains dictated by the government's prosecutors, who effectively dictate the sentences as well."[195] The unintended consequence of mass imprisonment has been, as we saw in Chapter 9, the proliferation of prison gangs, and whichever way this form of organized crime evolves it is likely to be destructive.

* * *

Just as Alcatraz symbolized the war on crime during the 1930s, perhaps the warehouse in Chicago known as Homan Square best symbolizes the repressive policies associated with America's twenty-first-century wars on drugs and organized crime. Spencer Ackerman, writing in the *Guardian*, revealed that for more than a decade, Chicago's police brought thousands of people under arrest to their detentions and interrogations warehouse at Homan Square. This warehouse complex, headquartering narcotics, vice and intelligence units for the Chicago police, has also served as a secret facility for detaining and interrogating thousands of people without providing access to attorneys and with little way for their loved ones to find them. Chicago police, particularly from the bureau of organized crime, could use their headquarters for incommunicado detentions and interrogations without attracting significant public notice. Ackerman reported that:

> officers used physical force on at least 14 men already in custody at the warehouse ... Police used punches, knee strikes, elbow strikes, slaps, wrist twists, baton blows and Tasers ... The new information contradicts an official denial about treatment of prisoners at the facility. The injured men are among at least 7,351 people – more than 6,000 of them black – who, police documents show, have been detained and interrogated at Homan Square without a public notice of their whereabouts or access to an attorney.[196]

The practices have echoes of the Mussolini/Mori campaigns in Sicily during the 1920s. America now has incommunicado detentions, millions of convictions without juries, wholesale use of eavesdropping, wiretapping, entrapment techniques, urine tests, hair tests and much more in a country with a written bill of rights, guaranteeing the right to privacy and due process of law. These rights have been diminished by campaigns that manipulated public fears about organized crime and drugs.

* * *

Organized criminal activity has harmed Americans from the womb to beyond the tomb, as my earlier book *Gangster Capitalism* (2005) detailed. Fertility clinic fraud cheated couples desperate to have children out of much of their savings. E-rate fraud allowed major computer firms to cheat school systems and therefore school children out of millions of dollars worth of taxpayers' money. Corporate violation of health and safety laws, consumer protection and environmental protection laws killed thousands prematurely each year. Corporate fraud in the mutual fund business and the insurance business, in particular, as well as the tidal wave of corporate fraud in general jeopardized the funds that many Americans had been putting away to educate their children or sustain a reasonable standard of life in their retirement. Rip-offs and abuse in private nursing homes showed that there is often no respite for many Americans facing death. Funeral fraud showed that wholesale larceny and abuse went on after death. Finally, gruesome revelations concerning a booming illegal trade in the remains of humans, mainly to supply a demand for the medical profession, shows that organized criminal activity affects Americans even beyond the tomb.

The list can be endlessly updated, just by consulting the kind of reports in American newspapers that rarely reach the media outlets of other nations. Yet the nation with these organized crime problems and many more besides sets the agenda on international organized crime control. The United States told other nations and international organizations, notably the United Nations (UN), how to control organized crime at the same time as so much of its business activity could be defined as simple fraud and therefore a form of organized crime.

PART IV

Selling Failure: Setting the Global Agenda on Drugs,
Organized Crime and Money Laundering

Introduction

The American approach to organized crime, based as it was on a limited understanding of the problem, failed to address many problems associated with systematic criminal activity and actually succeeded in perpetuating many others, most obviously those related to the trade in drugs. When, in the 1980s, the American government began to export its ideas about organized crime control to other countries, and through international organizations, it was the only nation to have a coherent, if painfully counterproductive, control plan. Government ministers, diplomats and civil servants of other nations either meekly went along with policies they didn't know had already failed or eagerly grabbed the opportunities presented by organized crime control policies for more repressive and intrusive policing techniques.

1

Losing Corporate Criminality
from Transnational Crime

Among its many crimes, President Nixon's administration was involved in corrupt alliances with the giant multinational International Telephone and Telegraph (ITT), in an episode that had devastating consequences for the people of Chile. The story of Nixon–ITT gave an early indication of some of the costs involved when the world's greatest power put the interests of capital over the rights of humans.

ITT were among Nixon's largest financial supporters and clearly expected special treatment in return. In 1971, ITT offered a large contribution to Nixon's campaign effort at the same time as it was engaged in negotiations over whether the corporation had violated the antitrust laws. On April 19 of that year, Nixon made the following revealing point to John Ehrlichman, recorded by the White House taping system: "I don't know whether ITT is bad, good or indifferent. ... But there is not going to be any more antitrust actions as long as I am in this chair ... goddam it, we are going to stop it."[1]

Nixon continued to act in ITT's interests in helping to remove Chilean president Salvatore Allende in 1973. ITT and other American multinationals had become increasingly worried about their Chilean interests from the late 1960s, when it became apparent that Allende and his socialist party were capable of winning electoral power and thus potentially harming corporate interests through programs of nationalization. In 1970, John McClone, a member of the ITT board of directors and former CIA head, contacted the agency to offer $1 million in anti-Allende efforts. Without directly accepting the money, the CIA advised the company on "secure" funding channels to Allende opponents. Despite these efforts, Allende narrowly won the 1970 elections. ITT then urged the CIA to take tough action against Allende, traded information with the agency, and tried to persuade other US corporations to bring economic pressure to bear against

Chile.[2] A government-corporate assault on the Chilean economy began involving such tactics as asking banks to delay credits, and perhaps it was no coincidence that five US banks – Chase Manhattan, Chemical, First National City, Manufactures Hanover and Morgan Guaranty – did cut off short-term credit to Chile after Allende came to power. This action made it very difficult for the country to afford to pay for essential imports such as food. The Nixon government asked other companies to drag their feet in shipping supplies necessary for Chile's industry. In the words of President Nixon, the intention was to "make the economy scream."[3] The assault succeeded in destabilizing the Chilean economy, preparing the way for the coup of September 11, 1973 and the murder of President Allende.

A brutal and repressive military regime was set up under the leadership of one of the coup's plotters, Augusto Pinochet, who then presided over a reign that can best be described as free market terror.[4] With the aid of the Americans, Chile had been introduced to the horrors of military regimes – executions or massacres, "disappearance" or exile for dissenters, and the systematic torture of prisoners.[5] Pinochet remained in power for 17 years, which he used to introduce a policy of Chicago-school inspired economic neo-liberalism on his country. In Chile it was called *el tratamiento de shock* – "shock treatment" – and was essentially based on freedom for business but repression for labor.[6] The anti-democratic brutalities of Chile's experience serve as an apt precursor of much of the rest of the world's experience with neo-liberalism.

Revelations about ITT's role in this coup and many other multinational abuses shocked the international community represented by the UN to the extent of including corporate crime in its early deliberations over the problem of transnational organized crime. These deliberations considered the complexities of organized crime in ways that ran counter to America's misleadingly simplistic focus on super-criminal organizations. Most significantly, the UN's early thought on the subject emphasized organized criminal *activity* and the involvement of otherwise respectable business institutions or persons in the problem, rather than on the actions of distinct "organized criminal groups" which allegedly "threatened" respectable society.

The Fifth United Nations Congress on the Prevention of Crime in 1975, for example, was concerned about ways to curtail such illegal activities as bribery, price-fixing, smuggling, violation of regulatory laws by private companies, currency offenses such as transfer pricing involving the evasion or avoidance of tax[7] and the behavior of transnational corporations, as much as that of more conventionally understood organized criminal groups. Its focus was to address new forms of criminality including "organized crime as a business" and the monetary costs and wider economic impacts of such crimes. Compiled by the Secretariat, the final summary report of the Congress stated that in the context of organized crime as business, such criminal activities were characterized by, "either the use or misuse of legitimate techniques in business and industry." Furthermore, those involved in committing these crimes "had high social status and/or political power." The Secretariat's concluding paper further elaborated that "such crimes tend to involve a high degree of planning, secrecy and sophistication," enabling them to remain invisible and thus difficult to detect and investigate.[8]

The UN had already showed its commitment to controlling the behavior of powerful transnational business interests by establishing the United Nations Centre for Transnational Corporations (UNCTC) in 1974. The UNCTC began by investigating the activities and economic strength of transnational corporations, concluding in 1985 that the 350 largest transnational organizations, about half of them based in the United States, had combined sales of $2.7 trillion. This figure amounted to one-third of the combined industrial market economies and was far larger than the combined gross national product of all the developing countries, including China. In the wake of revelations about ITT's role in ousting the democratically elected president of Chile, and clearly concerned about other possibilities for the abuse of such concentrated forms of power, the UNCTC also set out elaborate codes of conduct for transnational corporations, most notably codes attempting to check corruption, to ensure respect for human rights and for consumer and environmental protection objectives.

Over the next two decades, however, the UN itself and the UNCTC in particular had come in for intense criticism from the administrations of Presidents Reagan and Bush (Sr.), and pro-business think tanks such as the Heritage Foundation, accompanied by the US refusal to pay UN dues. To remedy what the Americans argued was

UN "waste and inefficiency," Bush's former attorney general, Richard Thornburgh, was appointed under secretary-general of the international organization in 1992. The following year, largely as a result of American pressure, the UNCTC was abolished and UN attempts to establish more effective controls over transnational corporations were largely abandoned.[9]

From the 1990s onwards, discussion of the problem of organized crime under the auspices of the UN narrowed in ways that suited the world view of the American right. It downplayed the criminal involvement of otherwise respectable business institutions or persons in the problem, a position far removed from the concern showed in the 1975 meeting about the involvement of multinational corporations in harmful organized criminal activities. By the 1990s legitimate multinationals were said to be the victims that were threatened by "crime multinationals." "Transnational Organized Crime," according to the new line as presented by UN Secretary-General Boutros Boutros-Ghali and in the background literature to the Convention against Transnational Organized Crime, "poisons," "pollutes" and "infiltrates" legitimate business. This dumbing down of organized crime discourse was no coincidence, since by the 1990s the dominance of neo-liberal ideology was assured, affecting not just the World Bank and the International Monetary Fund but also the UN itself. The term "neo-liberal" now represented the transference of the pro-market, anti-welfare, deregulatory and monetarist Reagan economic program from its American homeland to the global arena. UN Secretary-General Boutros-Ghali and his successors did little to impede neo-liberalism's global advance, since they all wanted and needed big business approval for UN policies and objectives. For these and other reasons, analyses of organized crime that included multinational corporations in particular and misguided laws and policies in general as part of the problem were no longer acceptable. Transnational corporate criminality was therefore off the UN agenda by the new millennium, swept under the carpet, replaced by a global commitment to support American dreams of a global drug prohibition regime, and a hopelessly misleading and inadequate understanding of international organized crime.

2
Building Capacity

Although US drug control policy changed in the 1960s, there was no fundamental break with the essence of past policy, which was based on the irrational moral righteousness of the early twentieth century. Education, treatment and rehabilitation programs were simply added to the policy of bare repression of drug use and sale. Richard Nixon believed in relentless enforcement at home, combined with relentless enforcement abroad. Nixon's position as president of the most powerful nation on earth allowed him to bring the dream of white supremacists like Hamilton Wright and Richmond Hobson closer to reality. Nixon put the bureaucratic infrastructure in place to establish a global drug prohibition regime.

Throughout his time in the White House, Nixon made the war on drugs one of his highest priorities, regularly calling top-level meetings on the issue. These could include his cabinet, top administration officials, ambassadors and even – on June 3, 1971 – the Chairman of the Joint Chiefs of Staff Admiral Thomas H. Moorer, plus General William Westmoreland, commander of US forces in Vietnam and three other top-level military chiefs. The purpose of this meeting, according to the president's background briefing memo, was "To indicate your [Nixon's] determination to attack drug abuse in a comprehensive manner." The memo advised Nixon in his closing remarks to "expect the fullest cooperation and support from all involved departments and agencies," or as a summary of the meeting put it: "President told group that ... Crapping around will not be tolerated." The contribution and reaction of the military chiefs was not recorded.[10] One can speculate, however, that a kind of respectful bemusement and embarrassment was the likely reaction from men whose whole careers had been spent organizing the nation's machinery of war to fight armed adversaries as opposed to the powders and pills that so concerned their commander-in-chief.

* * *

Even before his first year of office was complete, President Nixon showed that he had no intention of confining his war against drugs to American borders. On September 29, 1969 his national security adviser, Henry Kissinger, sent a memo to Secretary of State William Rogers and Attorney General Mitchell containing the essence of the stick-and-carrot approach of American drug control diplomacy as it exists until the present day:

> The President is convinced that the problem of narcotics addiction in the U.S. has reached proportions constituting a threat to our national stability. Most narcotics are grown and processed in foreign countries and smuggled into the U.S.: this is particularly true of heroin. Under these circumstances, the President considers that any country facilitating, or in any way contributing to, international traffic in heroin is committing an act inimical to the United States.

Rogers and Mitchell were then directed "to study this problem on an urgent basis" and:

> Recommend as soon as possible an action program that will make emphatically clear to those countries growing opium poppies that their non-medicinal cultivation must be stopped; and to those countries manufacturing finished heroin that their illicit laboratories must be closed ... In your study you should consider methods of positive persuasion, including financial incentives for cooperation on the control of heroin traffic, as well as those of retaliation, in the event that any country refuses to cooperate in this program.[11]

In brief, from then on efforts to bully or bribe other countries into acceptance of an American-based global drug control regime would be intensified. Bullying involved primarily threatening to withdraw financial aid, and bribing involved offering governing elites in poor countries the means to strengthen their authority by training and equipping their police and military. Plan Colombia and the Merida Initiative would later emerge from this approach.

By the time Kissinger sent his memo, the administration's international effort had already begun. On September 21, 1969 an attempt was made by Customs and Immigration officers to curb the importation of illegal drugs from Mexico by stopping and searching over two million people crossing the United States-Mexico border. Operation Intercept, as it was called, involved "a 100 percent inspection of all persons and vehicles crossing into the United States" with "no exceptions." Officers thoroughly searched the trunk and engine areas, under the seats and behind the cushions and door panels of every car and truck in a process that took far longer than normal customs procedure. To emphasize the military aspects of the operation, planes, boats and radar were also involved in what was accurately acknowledged as the most extensive attempt in United States history to curb the importation of illegal drugs. Although Customs and Immigration officers worked round the clock along the 2,500 miles of the United States-Mexico border, the hopelessness of their task was made clear by the comment of a Texas border scout: "There are areas out there where a small army could cross without detection."[12] After three weeks the operation was called off after complaints by business interests both sides of the border. Operation Intercept resulted in the seizure of a negligible amount of drug contraband, its main effect being the creation of immense traffic jams.[13]

Another expensive international intervention began in 1971, and could be judged a Pyrrhic victory of sorts for the stick-and-carrot policy. Turkey was thought to be the major source of heroin and was vulnerable to diplomatic pressure because of its dependence on massive US economic and military aid. The Turkish government therefore agreed to ban all opium growing for a three-year period in return for a payment of $35 million – intended to assist the development of alternative crops to replace opium. Little of the money reached the tens of thousands of farmers who lost income because of the ban. Most accounts agree, however, that Turkey did cease being a significant source of heroin on American streets. Supply was soon resumed by increased Mexican production (despite Operation Intercept and its successors) and new routes from South East Asia's "golden triangle," as well as Afghanistan, Pakistan and elsewhere. The ending of production in one country could not come close to eliminating the supply. The hopelessness of the Turkish episode was revealed when an economist calculated that the US demand for heroin could be met by the amount of opium poppies grown on between ten and twenty square miles of land.[14] Politicians and drug control officials have never faced up to this kind of logic.

While the Mexican and Turkish interventions were playing out, Nixon was opening up two other fronts in his war on drugs. The first of these involved the use of US diplomatic power through the UN. John E. Ingersoll, director of the Bureau of Narcotics and Dangerous Drugs, was sent to a special session of the UN Commission on Narcotic Drugs in the Autumn of 1970. His brief was to point out the weaknesses of the 1961 UN Single Convention and initiate the first part of a UN plan which, in Ingersoll's words, "could develop into an effective worldwide program."[15] The 1961 Single Convention's primary weakness, according to the American delegation, was the fact that it rested "essentially upon faithful cooperation by all parties in the context of their national decision rather than upon effective international measures." The US decided that the Single Convention had to be amended to "curb and, eventually prevent entirely" the illicit drug traffic. The proposed amendments had two basic objectives: firstly, "to establish enforceable controls and appropriate international machinery to assure compliance, and, secondly, to provide inducements to Parties to perform faithfully all their treaty obligations." Ingersoll's delegation bluntly told the UN's Division of Narcotic Drugs that it "will be expected to pursue their present activities more vigorously but will have to assume new and important responsibilities." These new responsibilities were to include "a capacity for the planning and implementing of technical assistance programs to assist countries ... in the establishment and improvement of national drug control administrations and enforcement machinery, the training of personnel required for these services."[16]

The hubris of these demands was staggering. Although just two years earlier America's premier drug law enforcement agency had been abolished due to endemic corruption, the US was pushing the international community to follow its lead on drug control.[17] In 1968 almost every agent in the New York office of the FBN was fired, forced to resign, transferred or convicted, about one-third of the agency's total manpower. The chief investigator of the affair, Andrew Tartaglino, testified that FBN agents had taken bribes "from all levels of traffickers," had sold "confiscated drugs and firearms," had looted "searched apartments," had provided tip-offs "to suspects and defendants" and had threatened "the lives of fellow agents who dared to expose them."[18] Effectively, federal drug enforcement in New York during these years was a form of organized crime. It helped the American cause that the scandal was barely reported at home, let alone abroad. Despite requests made under the Freedom of Information Act, full details of the investigation will not be released until 2020.

To make sure their proposals for strengthening the global drug prohibition regime stayed high on the UN agenda, the Americans were prepared to pay. They made an initial pledge of $2 million to help establish the United Nations Fund For Drug Abuse Control.[19] Other nations, foundations and private individuals were expected to feed into this fund. From then on the US made sure that, however starved of American contributions the UN might otherwise be, the funding for the international war on drugs would remain flush.

The second of Nixon's new fronts in the war on drugs involved the use of US diplomatic power directly to ensure the compliance of other countries. On June 14, 1971 he called in top State Department officials and ambassadors to South Vietnam, France, Turkey, Thailand and Luxembourg. These five countries were described in the background memo to the meeting as "directly involved in the illicit international drug traffic," and the purpose of the meeting was to stress "the need for a tougher stance abroad." According to the summary of this meeting, the president stated that he considered the "Ambassadors' most important diplomatic mission" to be "discussions with those countries on the drug problem." He then "ordered the Ambassadors to convey to their host governments that the US means business," concluding with the blunt point that "stopping the drug traffic is more important than good temporized relations."[20] From then on the State Department pushed American ambassadors to deliver results on international drug control. If it was considered that they weren't doing this they were replaced.

To complement the high-level work of the ambassadors, US drug control agents were expected to do much more at operational level. As Ethan Nadelmann has explained in *Cops Across Borders*, they also had to act as drug enforcement diplomats and advocates "to push for structural changes in drug enforcement wherever they were stationed, to lobby for tougher laws, to train local police in drug enforcement techniques, to sensitize local officials to US concerns in this area, and so on."[21]

Nixon's administration more than doubled the corps of drug control officers assigned to United States embassies and missions abroad, and their numbers have since continued to expand. By 1976, the DEA's overall budget was $161.1 million, with more than 10 percent of its 2,141 agents stationed overseas, in 68 offices in 43 countries. Today, the agency has more than 5,000 agents and a budget of $2,150.9 million.[22]

The Nixon administration also secured the passage of the Narcotics Control Trade Act of 1974, which would have a damaging international impact in the decades that followed. Essentially the terms of this new law meant that those drug-producing or drug-transit countries that failed to cooperate with the United States' drug prohibition policies would be subject to various sanctions, including the withdrawal of American aid and increases in duties and tariffs. In other words, small countries had to comply with American demands on drugs or be economically squeezed in ways that were not dissimilar to those that helped secure the downfall of Chile's Salvatore Allende.

The United States has played a central role in the treaties and organizations dealing with drugs and drug trafficking since the early twentieth century and, as we have seen, Nixon accelerated the process of establishing global drug prohibition. To institutionalize this process the Bureau of International Narcotic Matters (INM) was created in 1978 in the State Department. The INM existed first and foremost as a "policy shop," representing America in international dealing with drugs, together with the DEA, FBI and other drug enforcement agencies. It also helped organize crop eradication and other anti-drug measures and prepared the annual International Narcotics Control Strategy Report on global drug production, traffic and abuse. This report and the drug control certification process that the INM managed, decided whether other countries were taking measures in line with prohibition policies. Essentially the INM helped manage the effort to persuade or bully other countries into attempting to stop their citizens supplying growing markets, including the richest market in the world. Mainly through the INM, the State Department spent tens of millions of dollars each year on crop eradication or substitution programs. They also used the UN and other international organizations to spread the gospel of US drug control policy, holding it up as a model for other countries to follow.

The INM's original work continues to this day, but in the early 1990s its remit was expanded to include money laundering, arms or other contraband, human trafficking and other forms of transnational crime. Accordingly its name was changed to the Bureau of International Narcotics and Law Enforcement (INL) in 1995. Today, the INL's main task is to work towards the implementation of America's International Crime Control Strategy. It developed this with other agencies in 1998, "as a roadmap for a coordinated, effective, long-term attack on international crime." In the pursuit of this aim American diplomats work incessantly through multilateral and bilateral forums to define what the INL calls "global norms for effective criminal laws," which are in effect American norms. The INL also "actively" encourages "foreign governments to enact and enforce laws based on these norms."[23]

Today, the INL organizes and sponsors law enforcement training to police officers, judges, investigators, prosecutors, court reporters, and customs and border officials in more than 90 countries worldwide.[24] Its website currently describes its mission as working "to keep Americans safe at home by countering international crime, illegal drugs, and instability abroad. INL helps countries deliver justice and fairness by strengthening their police, courts, and corrections systems. These efforts reduce the amount of crime and illegal drugs reaching U.S. shores."[25]

Other countries could thus be bullied and bribed to make futile, often cynical drug control gestures on America's behalf. American consumers continued to pay the top prices and the effort only revealed that plants that could be processed into drugs grow everywhere and that foreign drug enforcers accepted bribes just as enthusiastically as their counterparts in the United States. Under Nixon, drugs as well as organized crime were redefined as national security threats, and were repeatedly said to warrant an approach based mainly on repression at home and the continued export of failed policies abroad. Meanwhile, the sorry story of alcohol and drug prohibition at home became the more tragic and continuing story of drug prohibition globally.

* * *

The most authoritative conclusions about the impact of alcohol prohibition on organized crime in the United States came from a government commission in 1931. The Wickersham Commission's verdict on alcohol prohibition nationally could equally be applied to the more recent international wars on drugs:

> The constant cheapening and simplification of production of alcohol and of alcoholic drinks, the improvement of quality of what may be made by illicit means, the diffusion of knowledge as to how to produce liquor and the perfection of organization of unlawful manufacture and distribution have developed faster than the means of enforcement. But of even more significance is the margin of profit in smuggling liquor, in diversion of alcohol, in illicit distilling and brewing, in bootlegging, and in the manufacture and sale of products of which the bulk goes into illicit or doubtfully lawful making of liquor. This profit makes possible systematic and organized violation of the National Prohibition Act on a large scale and offers rewards on a par with the most important legitimate industries. It makes lavish expenditure in corruption possible. It puts heavy temptation in the way of everyone engaged in enforcement and administration of the law. It affords a financial basis for organized crime.[26]

The story of global drug prohibition since the Nixon era followed a very similar pattern. While enforcement efforts have greatly intensified, the production of prohibited drugs has been simplified, rationalized and considerably cheapened. The diffusion of knowledge as to how to produce, refine, adulterate and distribute these drugs has developed far faster that the means of enforcement. Most significantly, the margin of profit in the production, smuggling and distribution of drugs has made fortunes for a few and boosted the income of many, particularly in countries whose governments are weakened by conflict and corruption. And of course, global drug prohibition provides a financial basis for organized crime across borders. Organized crime that involves routine exchanges of money for illegal goods and services, often accompanied by violence and corruption.

* * *

The INM/INL played and continues to play a key role in the "Americanization" of law enforcement systems of the international community. Ethan Nadelmann chronicled this process most comprehensively in *Cops Across Borders*, writing that:

> The modern era of international law enforcement is one in which US criminal justice priorities and US models of criminalization and criminal investigation have been exported abroad. Foreign governments have responded to US pressures, inducements, and examples by enacting new criminal laws regarding drug trafficking, money laundering, insider trading, and organized crime and by changing financial and corporate secrecy laws as well as their codes of criminal procedure to better accommodate US requests for assistance. Foreign police have adopted US investigative techniques, and foreign courts and legislatures have followed up with the requisite legal authorizations. And foreign governments have devoted substantial police and even military resources to curtailing illicit drug production and trafficking.[27]

"By and large," Nadelmann concluded, "the United States has provided the models, and other governments have done the accommodating."

At the same time as the US was exporting its drug control polices it was clear by the mid-1980s, within America, that US international efforts to stem the flow of drugs from producer countries had failed. A 1984 congressional report, for example, noted that "in most of the major producing countries, illicit narcotic production, manufacture and traffic had dramatically increased."[28] The same year, Congress' GAO concluded that drug availability in the US was on the increase and that seizures only amounted to a small amount of the total supply. City police chiefs were open about failure: "The situation is totally out of hand," claimed Los Angeles Police Chief Daryl Gates, "We're just shovelling sand against the tide."[29]

American government officials needed to distract people, not just in America but throughout the world, from the failure of their anti-drug policies and to distract them from their own domestic failure to control organized crime. Their response involved persuading the international community to accept American-inspired analyses of drug trafficking and organized crime "threats," and at the same time they needed to maintain the false perception that American drug control and organized crime control methods worked. The intention was always to gain an international acceptance of the need for collaboration along the lines prescribed by the US. The successful export of US organized crime control ideology was guaranteed by the mainstream international media. Journalists, as noted earlier, failed to ask about the failure of American policies to control drug crime and organized crime in America. Governments of all nations also took the American interpretation of organized crime as a given, and shied away from setting up independent commissions to understand organized crime in their own contexts and develop alternative organized crime control strategies.

From the 1980s, the Reagan administration and its successors used the INM/INL and other agencies to increase the momentum towards establishing a global prohibition regime. The already muscular American effort was strengthened by the close relationship between Reagan and the UK Prime Minister Margaret Thatcher. This resulted in the addition of British and Commonwealth diplomatic resources to the anti-drug, anti-money laundering cause. Other industrialized nations and the European Union stayed in step. As a result of this intensified, multilateral campaign most governments across the world expanded their drug squads and stiffened their penalties for drug trafficking and related activities. Many governments decided to adopt American-inspired laws permitting the seizure and forfeiture of drug trafficker assets, and international organizations, notably Interpol and the UN's drug control organs, promoted American-inspired model legislation and drug prohibition policies. Most important of all was the successful negotiation of the United Nations Convention Against Illicit Traffic in Narcotics and Psychotropic Substances in 1988. This extended the scope of measures against trafficking, introduced provisions to control money laundering and seize the assets of drug traffickers, allowed for the extradition of major traffickers and improved legal cooperation between countries. It also proposed the criminalization of purchase and possession by users. It was effectively an acknowledgment that America's drug prohibition regime would now be applied in every other country that signed up to the convention. Rather than risk the disapproval of the US and other industrialized nations, and for motives best known to their own governing elites, most countries signed up to the convention and it entered into force in November 1990.[30]

As Amandine Scherrer detailed in *G8 against Transnational Organized Crime*, the internationalization of the fight against drugs was also accompanied by discourses that increasingly advocated mobilization around activities said to be "supportive" to drug trafficking, most notably money laundering, and the effort to establish an anti-money laundering regime preoccupied many institutions at national, regional and international levels. "Seen as the 'motor' which made criminality of all kinds possible," Scherer explained, "money laundering was thus posed as a transnational threat and the fight against it seen to be justified on the grounds that criminal organizations could not operate without access to financial resources and that they were exploiting existing weaknesses in international financial control systems."[31] As we have seen, the fight against money laundering was institutionalized by, in particular, the setting up of the FATF in 1989 whose mission was to draft 40 recommendations to serve as a universal framework in the fight against the new "threat." In 1992 the FATF became a permanent institution based at the offices of the Organization for Economic Co-operation and Development.[32] It encourages countries to build on its initial 40 recommendations and, at the time of writing, has achieved very little given the regular reports of major banks being found to be involved in the laundering of drug profits.

The 1988 convention, among other things, gave another stick to the Americans with which to beat producer countries. Each country that received INM assistance in the previous two years was required to submit a report on the extent to which it had "met the goals and objectives of the United Nations Convention Against Illicit Traffic in Narcotic Drugs and Psychotropic Substances." This included action on such issues as illicit cultivation, production, distribution, sale, transport, financing, money laundering, asset seizure, extradition, mutual legal assistance, law enforcement and transit cooperation, precursor chemical control and demand reduction.

By 1996, 136 countries had ratified the 1988 convention and could no longer simply pay lip-service to American prohibitionist dreams. It was the global equivalent to the Volstead Act being passed to enforce alcohol prohibition in the 1920s, and just as doomed to produce nothing more than violence, corruption and overriding failure. The

UN's own statistics demonstrated continued failure very clearly. In 1986, world opium production was around 2,000 tons. By 1994 this had trebled to over 6,000 tons, and it remains closer to 6,000 than to 2,000 tons. There were an estimated 141 million drug abusers globally in 1994, including eight million heroin addicts, 30 million amphetamine users and 13 million cocaine users.[33] Because of prohibition these were paying inflated prices for drugs that remained cheap to produce. A multitude of growers, smugglers, distributors, corrupt officials and professionals – such as lawyers, accountants and bankers – were sharing the resultant profit. There was a need to explain this failure. This involved dumbing down international discourse on organized crime so that the Americanization of international law enforcement could continue.

First, however, the US needed to enlist overseas allies, most notably the UK, to spread the idea that replicating US drug control methods was the key to eventual success against the drug "epidemic."

3

Americanizing the British Drug Control System

Before the Mafia conspiracy interpretation of organized crime had taken hold, there was an awareness in America that drug prohibition, like alcohol prohibition, handed control of the importation, sale and distribution of drugs to criminals. A report from the Californian Crime Commission in 1950, for example, came to the conclusion that "England and other European countries did not have narcotics problems to compare with those of the United States" despite "the super abundance of the world supply." It therefore recommended further study of drug control policies that could prevent "the development of a narcotics traffic by undercutting the profits of the peddler."[34] In other words, regulating drugs rather than attempting to prohibit them. Harry Anslinger, Head of the FBN, made sure that no such study was undertaken. By the 1970s the UK itself had switched from a relatively successful medicalized approach to drug addiction to a more punitive prohibitive approach.

Three decades later, getting the UK to support global prohibition was particularly significant. It not only had strong influence over the 50 member states of the Commonwealth and a strong voice within the European Union, but its discarded drug control system had once offered an alternative to the brutal and corrupt American version. It helped that its mainstream journalists and politicians believed in the same mythologies about organized crime as their American counterparts.

The earliest evidence that British commentators had been convinced by the idea that American organized crime was a foreign import organized along big business lines can be found in two books published in the early 1960s. These paraphrased the interpretations of Lait, Mortimer, Reid and Sondern. Kenneth Allsop's "true crime" best-seller, *The Bootleggers* (1961), claimed that the Mafia was "a national network of organised, corporation crime, intangibly but intrinsically in control of the industrial, political and social life of most large American cities."[35] Christopher Hibbert, in *The Roots of Evil: A Social History of Crime and Punishment* (1963), summarized the Mafia's history thus: "By the beginning of the twentieth century, the Mafia had become entangled with so much which could be intimidated or corrupted in American society that its entwining grasp on the life of the nation has never been completely broken ... it has ... been profitably involved in every more or less disreputable business and traffic in America."[36]

Once introduced, these kinds of Hearst-Hickman Powell-Anslinger-influenced notions permeated the British establishment. Evidence for this came in a 1967 syndicated article published in *The Oregonian*, based on interviews with British MPs and Scotland Yard sources. Entitled, "England – The New Gambling Paradise," it was about the efforts of a group of American gambling entrepreneurs, including the film star George Raft, to buy into the London casino business. One MP was quoted as saying that:

> We simply cannot afford to let the American gambling interests get a toehold here. They bribe, corrupt, steal, lie, murder. All one has to do is to read the report of President Johnson's Crime Commission. It points out that nine men of Italian extraction supervise 24 Mafia clans in the US, and that these men have become so powerful from gambling profits that they can now manipulate the stock market and rig the price of bread. Like gangrene they spread into everything, ruining whatever they touch.

A Scotland Yard source confirmed that Hickman Powell's founding mythology for organized crime had taken root: "Last year Scotland Yard was tipped off that Meyer Lansky was planning to hold a quiet meeting in a London hotel with other members of the American syndicate ... to divide Great Britain into spheres of interest, just as following the demise of Prohibition in the 1930's they and the Mafia had carved up the US."[37]

Far-fetched American ideas on organized crime became more entrenched in Britain over the following years, as can be seen in a British journalist's television documentary series and book on the

Mafia, *Crime Inc.: The Story of Organized Crime* (1984). Even the title announced that organized crime was to be portrayed as a single corporate entity.

Martin Short began the book thus: "Organized crime is America's biggest business. According to some estimates, its profits are greater than those of *Fortune* magazine's top 500 business and industrial corporations added together."[38] Here and elsewhere in the book and television series, he was reflecting a set of assumptions about the Mafia that had been constantly repeated in most forms of American media communication – newspapers, books, radio, television and movies.

Short, in the same way as many who had preceded him, relied upon the law enforcement community for imaginative claims and estimates. Among the books referenced by Short were several of those discussed earlier as fake histories, including *Ninety Times Guilty* (1939), *Murder Inc.* (1951), *Mafia* (1952), *Lansky* (1971) and Donald Cressey's poorly informed sociological analysis, *Theft of a Nation* (1969).

* * *

The policing of laws against the illegal drug trade in Britain had been a relatively low key and essentially local affair. The overall response to the use of drugs such as heroin, cocaine and cannabis was either to make the use of these drugs a public health issue or, more usually, to turn a blind eye to behavior so long as it did not harm others. There was minimal illegal traffic in heroin before the 1970s primarily because addicts simply had to ask their doctor for a prescription.

Suspicion of drug use had been increasing since the end of the Second World War, when it became linked with the presence of resented minorities. On November 27, 1984, the *Daily Mirror* put itself in the vanguard of a new heroin panic, clearly playing on the fears of parents. The front page of its "Shock Issue" on "Heroin: The Scourge" consisted of a half-page picture of a baby, next to a syringe and a Chinese dragon, with the headline: "Baby Gavin: Heroin Addict." No proof was offered of Baby Gavin's addiction and the baby pictured on the front page looked remarkably healthy. The next day the headline was "Drugs: Fightback!" which included a report that the then prime minister, Margaret Thatcher, had ordered "an instant Government inquiry into drug abuse yesterday after seeing the *Daily Mirror* shock issue on heroin." The Thatcher government and its supporters looked to America for solutions. British parliamentarians made reference to the "sophisticated methods of detection in the United States" in bringing to justice drug-dealing "merchants of death."[39]

In 1985 the House of Commons all-party Home Affairs Committee issued a report based partly on the lessons they said they had learned from a ten-day "fact-finding" trip to the United States, managed by American drug control officials. The rhetoric that accompanied this report was disturbingly close to the rhetoric of American anti-drug crusaders – so close that the British representatives appeared to be reading from a script. There was no acknowledgment that the "British System" of drug control was a feasible alternative to American prohibition-based policy. The committee members declared war on drugs, warning that drug abuse was "the most serious peacetime threat to our national well-being," with the committee's chairman, Sir Edward Gardner, adding that "Every son and daughter of every family in the country is at risk from this terrible epidemic." He was paraphrasing President Richard Nixon. Accounts by MPs recorded in *Hansard* debates make it clear that US officials had taken care to ensure that the British got the intended message by taking them to see evidence of the ravages of addiction followed by evidence of large amounts of seized drug contraband. Thus, gullible British MPs were shown evidence of US drug control failure and returned demanding that the UK must replicate US drug control policies.

The measures the British committee recommended to combat drugs were American-inspired, including bringing in the Royal Navy and Royal Air Force to intercept suspected drug ships and confiscate the proceeds of drug traffickers. In August 1985, Prime Minister Thatcher also closely followed President Reagan's example by visiting the customs area at Heathrow airport accompanied by television and press cameras, and repeating Reagan's warning to traffickers: "We are after you. The pursuit will be relentless. We shall make your life not worth living."[40]

In this emotive atmosphere, as had long been the case in the United States, any efforts to have an informed and open-minded debate on the best way to approach drug control were met with a concerted and negative response. In September 1985, for example, Dr. David Maingot, an experienced treatment center consultant, told medical journalists that as de facto prohibition had failed to control the use of heroin by addicts, there was a need to consider other ways of dealing with the problem. His remarks were roundly criticized as "grotesque and fatheaded."[41]

Britain's pragmatic approach to drugs ended during the 1980s. New types of drug-related stories began to appear in the media, bolstering the familiar, appalled reactions to the sordid devastation of the lives of addicts. Britain now had its own drug "barons," "mafias," "czars" and "Mr. Bigs," seizures were reported not just in weight but in more impressive but fictional "estimated street values," and groups of criminals were now more likely to be described as "armies," "corporations" or national security "threats."

The source given by newspapers for much of the alarmist rhetoric in the late 1980s and early 1990s was the Scotland Yard-based National Drugs Intelligence Unit and its successor, the National Criminal Intelligence Service (NCIS). This was the first of a succession of agencies to be dubbed the "British FBI." Meanwhile, despite the rhetoric and the bureaucratic shell games, illegal substances became as easy to buy as they were in America, suggesting that those who trafficked in drugs at the top end were at worst inconvenienced by the new "tough" responses.

Neil Wood, a former undercover police officer, has related how British drug control came to resemble America's brutal and corrupt version. As undercover police tactics became more successful in achieving arrests and seizures, gangster violence escalated, as in the case of Colin Gunn from Nottingham:

> When a rival dealer was arrested after shooting one of Gunn's crew, the police placed the shooter in solitary confinement so that Gunn couldn't organise a prison murder in revenge. Gunn paid British Telecom engineers to find out where the guy's parents lived, sent his people to the seaside bungalow where they had retired and executed the two pensioners with sawn-off shotguns. When Gunn suspected one of his own lieutenants of disloyalty, he nailed the guy's hands to a bench, doused him in gasoline and flicked matches at him till he confessed. That was how Gunn ran his own crew, and the atmosphere of violence, intimidation and terror filtered down to infect the entire city.[42]

Despite the professionalism displayed by most of the officers involved in locally based drug squads, as well as in the new national policing agencies, the demand for contraband drugs in Britain continued to be met by an assortment of foreign and British drug traffickers. Many of whom, on the American model, had made contact with each other in prison.

4

Dumbing Down the International Response to Drugs and "Organized Crime"

In the 1980s a new generation of journalists and television documentary makers found a way to update and internationalize their organized crime formulas. For example, in *Mafia Wipeout: How the Feds Put Away an Entire Mob Family* (1989), Donald Cox wrote that "A new Oriental Mafia was rising from the ashes of the old Italian-Sicilian Mafia in urban America to rule the underworld."[43] In 1991 the Canadian Yves Lavigne, in *Good Guy, Bad Guy: Drugs and the Changing Face of Organized Crime,* claimed "other organized crime groups had emerged to take their cut" from profits previously monopolized by the La Cosa Nostra. His list included prison gangs, outlaw motorcycle gangs, Chinese Triads, Colombian drug cartels and black drug syndicates. "They have a common goal: money and power through drug trafficking." Lavigne's moral extremism is illustrated in his conclusion where he suggests that "the high cost of investigation, interdiction, law enforcement, prosecution, and incarceration" should be eliminated "by executing drug producers, smugglers, and dealers on sight – on street corners, in parks, in their homes. Blow their planes out of the sky. Torpedo their ships. It would be the ultimate solution. At this stage of the game, it's the only solution."[44] This was the same "solution" proposed by William Randolph Hearst's *Gabriel and the White House* in 1931, and currently proposed and possibly practiced by President Rodigo Duterte of the Philippines.

In 1988, Gerald Posner, in *Warlords of Crime – Chinese Secret Societies: The New Mafia,* went beyond North America to write that as a result of his research he was absolutely convinced "that Chinese Triads are the most powerful criminal syndicates in existence and that they pose the most serious and growing threat confronting law enforcement." He concluded with comments on the seriousness of the Triad "threat" from US law enforcement officers, including a DEA agent: "Chinese criminals have hundreds of years of history and tradition behind them. They are willing to take risks, and they follow their leaders with blind obedience. It's just a matter of time before they take over. What you've seen so far is just the head of the dragon, you can be sure of that."[45]

An earlier book on the Triads written in 1980 by the British writer Fenton Bresler, *The Trail of the Triads*, had already articulated the only serious international solution ever under consideration: "Unless and until the law enforcement agencies of the world come alive to the problem that faces them and expend their time, budget and resources that are required, the 1980s are due to be the decade in which the Triads become as powerful a force for evil as ever the Italian Mafia has been in the past."[46] DEA agents and administrators were the most numerous and prominent of the many members of the international law enforcement community that he acknowledged as sources.

In 1994, James Walsh in an article in *Time* combined the themes of international threat and American past success against organized crime, in an article entitled "Triads Go Global." He quoted an FBI agent as follows: "I think we're at a point right now that is kind of like the formative years of the Cosa Nostra in this country. We're at the stage where we can, perhaps, nip this thing in the bud ... People said we'd never crack them. We did."[47]

Jeffrey Robinson, in his 1998 book *The Laundrymen: Inside the World's Third Largest Business*, and again acknowledging US law enforcement sources, updated the theme of organized crime groups as multinational corporate enterprises. "After all," he concluded, "in order to deal drugs the way they do, the global traffickers have set up huge corporate structures, taken several pages out of the best management books, and constructed their multinational organizations accordingly."[48]

Building on America's favored alien conspiracy and plural revision interpretations, a new understanding of organized crime emerged to explain continued evidence of failure and help sustain the Americanization of international law enforcement.

American officials normally stayed in the background of journalistic accounts, often being thanked for their contribution in the Acknowledgments section. Irving Soloway, a spokesman for the US State Department moved briefly to the foreground in 1993 when he articulated a new "international security threat" in *The Washington Times*. He claimed that American and Sicilian Mafias were "working with their counterparts in Eastern Europe and the former Soviet Union ... to apply strategic planning and market development policies for the new emerging free markets [of eastern Europe] ... and to develop and expand extremely illegal activities." Soloway also claimed that three post-communist "crime summits" had taken place in central and eastern Europe soon after the collapse of the Soviet empire – in Warsaw (1991), Prague (1992) and Berlin (1993) – where he alleged that the leaders of various organized crime groups met to approve alliances, divide territories of interest and organize ways to work together.[49]

Claire Sterling, an American reporter based in Italy, got much more attention elaborating on Soloway's theme. She had originally become known during the 1980s for her claim that the Soviets controlled global terrorism. This was at a time when President Reagan was ratcheting up Cold War tension with "evil empire" rhetoric. There were links between Soviet agents and terrorist groups, just as the CIA often kept similar company, but Sterling's thesis was wildly overstated. However, the support of such notables as Secretary of State Alexandra Haig and CIA Director William Casey helped boost the sales of her 1981 book, *The Terror Network: The Secret War of International Terrorism*.[50]

By the end of the Cold War, Sterling, like her sources in intelligence, was looking for new conspiratorial threats and found them in the world of organized crime. She argued in *Octopus: The Long Reach of the International Sicilian Mafia* (1990) that the Sicilian Mafia controlled the world's supply of heroin in cooperation with terrorists and various other crime organizations such as the Colombian drug "cartels." Four years later she reflected Soloway's ideas in *Thieves' World: The Threat of the New Global Network of Organized Crime* (1994). This claimed that the Sicilian and American Mafias, Colombian drug cartels, Chinese Triads and Japanese Yakusa had joined up with the Russian Mafia. She claimed in essence that the world had experienced its Atlantic City "conference." Her message was that organized crime had gotten its act together worldwide, with various syndicates cooperating and expanding to such an extent that legitimate business, global security and free societies were threatened. She called it a "Pax Mafiosa" – "common strategies, agreements by the crooks to avoid violence and conflict." Her inspiration for this phrase seems to have been Hickman Powell's account in *Ninety Times Guilty* and the claim that "The power of Charlie Lucky had a lot to do with that. Through the underworld he and his allies spread the Pax Siciliano."[51]

Few serious researchers found Sterling's work credible. Unsurprisingly, however, the American intelligence community lauded her. In many ways she was a founder of mainstream transnational organized crime analysis, influencing or reflecting high-level American opinion on the subject. Variations on the Soloway/Sterling line were sold to ill-informed officials from nearly every nation on earth and the UN bureaucracy itself.

The American intelligence community thought highly enough of Sterling to invite her to chair a panel on Russian organized crime at a Washington DC conference of high-level American law enforcement and intelligence community personnel in September 1994. Conference organizer Arnaud de Borchgrave introduced her by praising *Thieves' World* and making the doubtful claim that her previous book, *The Terror Network*, had been "vindicated."[52] He did not substantiate the claim that Sterling had proved that the Soviets had once controlled global terrorism.

Sterling was invited because her theories closely reflected those of the American intelligence community's at the time. The title of the conference – Global Organized Crime: The New Empire of Evil – and the speeches delivered, were classic conspiracy theory, accompanied by unsubstantiated statistical claims. The executive summary of the conference set the tone:

> The dimensions of global organized crime present a greater international security challenge than anything Western democracies had to cope with during the cold war. Worldwide alliances are being forged in every criminal field from money laundering and currency counterfeiting to trafficking in drugs and nuclear materials. Global organized crime is the world's fastest growing business, with profits estimated at $1 trillion.

The keynote speaker at the conference was FBI Director Louis Freeh, who stressed that "the ravages of transnational crime" were the greatest long-term threat to the security of the United States, and warned that the very fabric of democratic society was at risk everywhere. CIA Director R. James Woolsey followed up by noting that "the threats from organized crime transcend traditional law enforcement concerns. They affect critical national security interests ... some governments find their authority besieged at home and their foreign policy interests imperiled abroad."[53]

The message that came from the New Empire of Evil conference, and from a cooperative media, was that this new global threat of organized crime required a tougher and more collaborative international response. More specifically, the threat required more thorough information-sharing between police and intelligence officials in different countries, and improved methods of transcending jurisdictional frontiers in pursuing and prosecuting malefactors.

By the early 1990s American diplomats, and their allies in Britain, Australia, Canada and other Western nations, had already been pushing hard. Two months after the Washington conference, the UN held the World Ministerial Conference on Organized Transnational Crime in Naples. It is clear from studies of the background to this conference that it represented a coincidence of interests between the US, the member states of the European Union and the internal politics of the UN itself.[54] It provided an international forum for the global conspiracy theory of organized crime.

The UN conference was attended by high-level governmental representatives from 138 countries. The rhetoric and analysis was essentially the same as that employed by Freeh, Woolsey and Sterling. According to the UN's press release, participants at the conference recognized the growing threat of organized crime, with its "highly destabilizing and corrupting influence on fundamental social, economic and political institutions." This represented a challenge demanding increased and more effective international cooperation. "The challenge posed by transnational organized crime," the document continued, "can only be met if law enforcement authorities are able to display the same ingenuity and innovation, organizational flexibility and cooperation that characterize the criminal organizations themselves."[55] This was essentially the same analysis as that of American politicians and government officials since the 1960s, informed, as we have seen, by a complete misinterpretation of organized crime history.

UN Secretary-General Boutros-Ghali, as already noted, reflected the new conventional wisdom on organized crime. He opened the conference with the following speech: "Organized crime," he began, "has become a world phenomenon. In Europe, in Asia, in Africa and in America, the forces of darkness are at work and no society is spared." It "scoffs at frontiers," he continued, "and becomes a universal force. Traditional crime organizations have, in a very short time, succeeded in adapting to the new international context to become veritable crime multinationals." Transnational organized crime "undermines the very foundations of the international democratic order. Transnational crime poisons the business climate, corrupts political leaders and undermines human rights. It weakens the effectiveness and credibility of institutions and thus undermines democratic life."[56]

Boutros-Ghali concluded with what was already becoming a familiar call to international action:

> We also know, however, that when the States decide to take effective, voluntary steps to combat Transnational crime, and when they decide to cooperate with each other and harmonize their efforts, legitimate society regains all its power and strength. It is on behalf of this effort to promote the rule of law and to combat transnational crime that we are meeting here in Naples.[57]

Boutros-Ghali was followed by a series of speakers echoing the same themes: the threat posed by organized crime to societies and governmental institutions across the globe and the need for more international cooperation to meet this threat. The seriousness of the perceived threat was emphasized in the language of many of the speeches, which echoed the type of language used by Mussolini in his campaigns against the Mafia. For example, Elias Jassan, Argentina's secretary of justice, described organized crime as "a new monster ... the Anti-State," and Silvio Berlusconi, the Italian prime minister, described crime organizations as "armies of evil" who could be defeated "only by international collaboration."[58] Melchior Wathelet, the Belgian deputy prime minister and minister of justice, claimed that no region of the world "was safe from the large criminal networks" and favored the proposal to elaborate a binding legal instrument along the lines of the precedent set by the 1988 anti-drug treaty.[59] There was no significant dissent from this line at the conference – discussion of organized crime at the highest international level had been frozen by "global conspiracy" images that effectively excluded discussion. Many speakers at Naples implicitly or explicitly emphasized the success of US-approved organized crime control strategies. This deferential consensus was most clearly reflected in a background document which singled out "the 1970 Racketeer Influenced and Corrupt Organizations (RICO) statute" as an example of "dynamic" legislation able to "adapt itself to ... developments." The document then elaborated:

> In the United States, the RICO statute is generally considered to be the starting point of a new process of awareness of organized crime by the United States Government and its criminal justice system. Its effectiveness has been demonstrated in the many indictments and convictions of members of organized crime groups that have resulted since the legislation was passed.[60]

A year after the conference, President Bill Clinton boosted the process of harmonizing the world's efforts against drugs and organized crime. First he gave a speech to the UN on June 26, 1995 that elevated organized crime from a national security threat to an international security threat. "Our enemies," he stated, "are ... international criminals and drug traffickers who threaten the stability of new democracies and the future of our children."[61] On October 21, he added institutional momentum to the process of combating international organized crime by signing Presidential Decision Directive (PDD) 42. This ordered all US government agencies to develop a more aggressive and coordinated attack on international organized crime. PDD42 directed the Departments of Justice, State and the Treasury, and other US agencies, to work towards raising international standards to combat organized crime; to continue to build alliances with like-minded countries; and to put pressure on countries who failed to respond to increase their efforts to meet those standards.[62]

The main result of the Naples conference and the newly coordinated American pressure was to put the elaboration of the UN Convention against Transnational Organized Crime (UNTOC) at the center of discussion. This process culminated in December 2000, when representatives of more than a hundred countries met in Palermo, Sicily to sign up to the convention in principle, and September 23, 2003 when it came into force, having been ratified by the required number of states. The UNTOC defined an "organized crime group" as: "a structured group of three or more persons existing for a period of time and having the aim of committing one or more serious crimes or offences established in accordance with This Convention in order to obtain, directly or indirectly, a financial or other material benefit."[63]

There was little significant objection to this definition from the individual nations. It left it to the authorities of separate nation states to decide who and what was organized crime. The processes by which they do so allow for very little transparency.

Nations that ratified UNTOC commit themselves to the type of American measures deemed to be effective in combating organized crime. Articles 12 to 14, for example, commit states to adopting measures as may be necessary to enable the confiscation and seizure of the proceeds of crime derived from offenses covered by the convention. Article 20 commits each state, if "permitted by the basic principles of its domestic legal system," to "take the necessary measures to allow for the appropriate use of controlled delivery and, where it deems appropriate, for the use of other special investigative techniques such as electronic and other forms of surveillance, and undercover operations, by its competent authorities in its territory for the purpose of effectively combating organized crime." "Controlled delivery" had been defined earlier as meaning the "technique of allowing illicit or suspect consignments to pass out of, through or into the territory of one or more States, with the knowledge and under the supervision of their competent authorities, with a view to the investigation of an offence and the identification of persons involved in the commission of the offence." Most controlled deliveries would consist of illegal drugs. Article 26 on "Measures to enhance cooperation with law enforcement authorities" commits states to take "appropriate measures to encourage persons who participate or who have participated in organized crime groups." Under this article states "shall consider providing for the possibility in appropriate cases, of mitigating punishment of an accused person who provides substantial cooperation in the investigation or prosecution of an offence covered by this Convention." Such witnesses would be covered by protection measures outlined in Article 20.

There are many problems associated with these US-recommended strategies, as we have seen. However, the main problem with them is that they are exclusively concerned with arresting and punishing deviant or harmful people, and obviates the need for a more strategic approach that reduces the opportunities for harmful activity. The American-inspired methods had been in use in the United States, locally and nationally, for decades. They helped secure many important convictions but have not significantly affected the extent of organized crime activity in any measurable way, while other factors, notably neo-liberal economic polices and mass imprisonment, have actually exacerbated American organized crime problems. The diplomats who committed their nations to Americanizing their law enforcement systems demonstrated little or no awareness of the failure within America itself of such approaches.

It was hoped that the convention would finally make global drug prohibition effective. This was implied when an attachment to a draft of the convention put the "illicit traffic in narcotic drugs or psychotropic substances and money-laundering," as defined in the 1988 UN convention, at the top of its list of serious crimes.[64] Had American drug control policies actually worked there may have been some logic to the international community's adoption of these policies, but the evidence suggested otherwise.

The acceptance of the "global pluralist theory"[65] of organized crime, and other assumptions about American crime control superiority, allowed the United States to remain the most prominent nation in setting the international agenda on the analysis and control of drugs, organized crime and transnational organized crime.

There was as little evidence for a merger or Pax Mafiosa of international criminal organizations as there had been for Charles Dawes' super-government of crime, the Atlantic City "conference" or the "Night of the Sicilian Vespers." This time, however, there was no one of the stature of Donald Cressey to emerge from the academic community and add spurious substance to these notions. Perhaps Jeffrey Robinson was the last of the Pax Mafiosa "theorists." The title of his 2000 book spells out his argument – *The Merger: The Conglomeration of International Crime*.[66] It begins: "The anus of the earth is cut into the jungle on the Paraguay side of the Parana River – a home-away-from-home for the South American drug cartels, Chinese Triads, Japanese Yakusa, Italian gangsters, Russian gangsters, Nigerian gangsters, and Hezbollah terrorists – and is called Ciudad del Este."[67] Robinson then repeated the idea that criminal organizations have become multinational corporations. He also acknowledged the help of John McDonnell of the State Department's Bureau of International Narcotics and Law Enforcement, among others from the US law enforcement and intelligence community, which suggests like-mindedness. The US government has since quietly disassociated itself from these notions. The National Security Council's current definition of transnational organized crime, for example, has this inclusive sentence: "There is no single structure under which transnational organized criminals operate; they vary from hierarchies to clans, networks, and cells, and may evolve to other structures."[68] Perhaps there was no longer a need for alarmist rhetoric and simplistic notions, once UNTOC had been ratified in 2003. The "harmonization" of international organized crime control is now securely in the hands of international civil servants who are not paid to learn lessons from the past.

In 2010, the UN, after conducting some serious research on transnational organized crime, announced that notions about super-governments or super-corporations of crime were "a crumbling edifice." The authors of a United Nations Office of Drugs and Crime (UNODC) report, entitled *The Globalization of Crime*, put clearer distance between themselves and the crude "Pax Mafiosa" analyses compared to the US government. These theorists, according to the report, "even suggested that the leadership of the traditional hierarchical groups were coordinating their activities in a vast global conspiracy." "The portrayal of organized crime," the report continued, "provided a kind of local rival army with which to war, and glossed over any structures that did not fit the model." It noted that the media fascination with the image of an underground empire continued to grow and that the fear this generated might have become a source of funding for further law enforcement against these groups. It was only with growing scrutiny over time that this image began to crumble, and "what had appeared to be concerted action was, in many instances, determined to be the activity of a range of actors responding to market forces."[69] *The Globalization of Crime* thus marks an acknowledgment that the UNTOC was built on weak intellectual foundations.

Two years earlier the UNODC's World Drug Report had admitted that the war on drugs itself was built on weak intellectual foundations and had had five devastating unintended consequences:

The *first* unintended consequence is the creation of a criminal black market. There is no shortage of criminals interested in competing in a market in which hundred-fold increases in price from production to retail are not uncommon.

The *second* unintended consequence is what one might call "policy displacement." The expanding criminal black market demands a commensurate law enforcement response, requiring more resources. But resources are finite. Public health, which is the driving concern behind drug control, also needs resources, and may have been forced to take the back seat in the past.

The *third* unintended consequence is geographical displacement. It is often called the balloon effect because squeezing (by tighter controls) in one place produces a swelling (namely, an increase) in another place, though the net effect may be an overall reduction ...

The *fourth* unintended consequence is what one might call substance displacement. If the use of one drug was controlled, by reducing either supply or demand, suppliers and users moved on to another drug with similar psychoactive effects, but less stringent controls. For example, cocaine is easier to control than the amphetamines: with the former, there is a considerable geographical distance between the raw material (the coca bush in the Andean countries) and the consumer (in North America or Europe). The latter can actually be produced in the user's neighbourhood or, literally, in his kitchen. So it is with the retail market: cocaine has to be bought from a street dealer, while various forms of ATS [Amphetamine-type stimulants] can be bought online from an internet pharmacy. The increasing popularity of synthetic drugs over the last few decades can be better understood in this light. Substance displacement can, of course, also move in the opposite direction. In the past couple of years, cocaine has been displacing amphetamine in Europe because of greater availability and higher status. Substance displacement also happens with precursor chemicals, where the same kinds of dynamics apply.

The *fifth* unintended consequence is the way the authorities perceive and deal with the users of illicit drugs. A system appears to have been created in which those who fall into the web of addiction find themselves excluded and marginalized from the social mainstream, tainted with a moral stigma, and often unable to find treatment even when motivated to seek it.[70]

Sadly, however, the UNODC report chose to ignore the logical conclusion from its analysis: that drug prohibition is damaging and counterproductive. Instead it urged the international community to try harder and cooperate more. After almost a decade since the report was issued all five unintended consequences persist.[71] The only change is that the UNODC no longer chooses to draw attention to them. Every country that signed up to UNTOC continues to set up rat traps on the American model at the same time as the neo-liberal and morally hypocritical conditions that breed rats continue to exist.

5

Repression, Profits and Slaughter: The United States in Colombia and Mexico

From the 1980s, guided by the INL, the American government extended the crop eradication programs pioneered in Mexico to such South American nations as Peru, Bolivia and Colombia, but these damaged the Andean nations more than they adequately addressed American drug problems. Eradication, most often by spraying herbicides, always left peasant farmers worse off than before. Although many farmers were encouraged to grow alternative cash crops such as sugar beet, coffee or potatoes, these failed for economic and geographical reasons. Growers were often too far away from markets for legitimate crops and the cash return did not compensate for the effort. Opium, coca and cannabis were worthwhile crops even for the most exploited farmers. Transportation was no problem since it was usually arranged by the traffickers. At best, these campaigns only achieved variations of the already mentioned "balloon effect."

The cocaine traffic became established as an important part of the economies of three Andean countries – Peru, Bolivia and Colombia. The trade in drugs produced billions of dollars annually and employed hundreds and thousands in the cultivation and processing of coca plants. Some top-level drug traffickers, such as Roberto Suárez in Bolivia and Pablo Escobar in Colombia, became multimillionaires and achieved local, regional and even national political influence. They did not, however, head vertically integrated "cartels" that restricted production and set international prices, despite the many claims of American officials and supportive journalists. Michael Kenney's analysis in *Global Crime*, based on interviews with Colombian drug traffickers, found that "even during the respective heydays of the Medellin and Cali 'cartels,' cocaine production and exportation in Colombia was highly competitive as independent trafficking groups in more than a dozen cities smuggled substantial amounts of cocaine to American and European drug markets." There were, of course, prominent and often murderous traffickers, but "their business relations more closely resembled informal producer-export syndicates than public or private cartels that controlled prices and monopolised markets." The cartel myth, he concluded, was "plausible and useful – to those that helped create it: politicians pushing for tougher drug laws, police administrators clamouring for larger budgets, journalists searching for sensational news copy, and citizens fearful of the pernicious effects of drug abuse and addiction."[72]

* * *

The US continued to sell failure as success through two of the most significant American foreign policy initiatives in recent years. These are on the same continuum as Mussolini's recommendation that combating organized crime required mobilizing state power to enable repression, although the Americans have gone further and enlisted the private sector into the effort.

In 2000, the US pledged $1.3 billion in foreign aid and up to 800 US government personnel towards Plan Colombia. The plan was intended as part of the effort against drug trafficking and international organized crime, but the overriding aim was to combat leftist insurgencies. Since 2000, the United States has provided Colombia with over $8 billion in assistance to improve security, fight the drug trade, promote the role of law and achieve development and social objectives. The Colombian state did indeed grow stronger as a result of Washington's generosity with military and police equipment and training in particular.

Plan Colombia also saw the introduction of the private sector in the militarized war on drugs. Most notably the security company Dyncorp took part in eradication missions, training and drug interdiction, as well as in air transport, reconnaissance, search and rescue, airborne medical evacuation and ferrying equipment and personnel from one country to another, as well as aircraft maintenance. DynCorp operated several State Department aircraft, including armed UH-1H Iroquois and Bell-212 Huey-type helicopters and T-65 Thrush crop dusters. The company provided the pilots, technicians and others required to carry out the drug war in Colombia, including administrative personnel.[73]

In 2000, Congresswoman Janice Schakowsky asked questions about the accountability and outsourcing of the war on drugs that still need to be addressed. "Are we outsourcing in order to avoid public scrutiny, controversy or embarrassment? Is it to hide body bags from the media and thus shield them from public opinion?" she asked. "Or is it to provide deniability because these private contractors are not covered by the same rules as active duty U.S. service persons."[74]

A lack of accountability aided government and paramilitary repression. Since the start of Plan Colombia, thousands of trade union leaders have been assassinated and thousands exiled and imprisoned. Húbert "Huber" Ballesteros, a peasant leader, was one of many political prisoners, held in La Picota Prison in Bogotá, Colombia. He was arrested on August 25, 2013 on the day he was in Bogotá approaching the government to negotiate the list of demands presented by agricultural organizations which at the time had been on a national strike. "At that point," he wrote, "several comrades active in the strike in regions all over the country had already been assassinated or imprisoned. From that moment to date, almost 100 members of the Patriotic March have been assassinated and around 300 have been imprisoned." He detailed his case:

> the prosecution accuses me of the crimes of "rebellion" and "financing terrorism," a case based on the paid testimonies of people working for them and using as "evidence" documents planted by the military intelligence services and police on computers supposedly captured from guerilla leaders during military operations ... Everything has been clearly planned and directed from the executive, and the judicial system has been the tool used to punish my trade union activity and public involvement in the political opposition.[75]

On January 13, 2017, after 40 months in jail, he was released from prison and is currently involved in the country's peace process.

"We are facing a legal system which is politicized," he concludes, "and which works to impose the state policy of criminalisation of social protest."[76] The case illuminates the fact that although states can commit themselves to laws and ratify such conventions as UNTOC, these commitments can easily form a smokescreen for quasi-legal repression.

At the same time as Colombia's repressive measures intensified, the *Washington Post* reported that illegal coca cultivation surged.[77]

* * *

Despite the bloody example of Colombia's 1980s drug wars, Mexico remained in line with US prohibitionist goals as indicated by its prompt signing of the 1988 Vienna anti-drug convention and the rhetoric of its leaders, which closely resembled that of US and UN spokespersons. President Miguel de la Madrid Hurtado had already declared drug trafficking to be a national security threat and all his successors followed suit. This, as Peter Andreas has pointed out, was a major departure from the past, given that the language of national security had previously been rare in Mexican political discourse. The change in rhetoric was accompanied by a significant expansion of the state's drug control apparatus, involving a tripling of its drug control budget and personnel in the following decade. Drug control in fact came to dominate the federal criminal justice system and justified increasing the involvement of the Mexican military.[78]

Increased federal and military involvement plus constant pressure from the United States, however, did not come close to controlling Mexican-American drug trafficking. Since the new century it became clear that the drug trade in Mexico represents one of the biggest industries in that country, amounting to billions of dollars collected mainly from American consumers. Money on this scale, as well as enriching entrepreneurs and their employees, goes to pay the salaries of shippers and processors, as well as the bribes that supplement the incomes of officials in both the US and Mexico.

Mexican drug trafficking became, according to Peter H. Smith's description, a good example of the semi-organized nature of international crime. "To put it euphemistically," Smith wrote, "there is a high rate of turnover" in the Mexican drug trade, "especially among the upper echelons of the major syndicates. This is not due to natural causes; leaders usually fade from view either because they are arrested or because they meet an untimely (usually violent) death."[79] Alliances between drug trafficking groups are highly unstable, and there is considerable decentralization and conflict within and between drug trafficking groups. Serious attempts to enforce the law as well as internecine conflict between trafficking groups did not seriously interfere with profitable operations.

The American arms industry has fed the needs of paramilitaries, guerrillas and drug traffickers in South and Central America, as well as armed groups in Africa, Asia and Europe. The curious logic of America's war on drugs has even meant that the United States armed both sides in its Mexican neighbor's own war on drugs. Because of loose gun sale and gun ownership laws, as opposed to strict gun control laws in Mexico, the United States became an open arms bazaar for Mexican drug traffickers and other criminals during the 1990s. These equipped themselves with the latest weaponry north of the border and were often able to outgun Mexican drug agents, killing more than 200 Mexican police in 1996 alone. A 2008 US government report acknowledged the difficulties of interdicting arms which were transported from the United States hidden in "land vehicles, spare tires, seat backs" and "cavities dug out of the car bodies." The most significant arms seizures were made "as a result of searches, discoveries, and shoot-outs between rival gangs." Among the weapons seized were M72 and AT-4 anti-tank rockets, RPG-7 rocket launchers, MGL 37 mm grenade launchers, 39 mm and 40 mm accessories for grenades, fragmentation grenades, Barret 50-caliber rifles and new-generation firearms like submachine guns and the 5.7 × 28 mm FN Herstal pistol.[80]

Instead of taking on the powerful anti-gun control lobby in the United States, successive administrations from the Clinton era onwards decided to step up aid to the Mexican military and provide them with firepower capable of taking on the drug traffickers. Among other forms of aid, for the 1998 fiscal year the administration asked Congress for $9 million in military aid for Mexico for the purchase of new weapons from American arms manufacturers.[81]

There is also every reason to be pessimistic regarding the impact of globalization and free trade on the arms trade. Deregulation and free trade have been a gift to the arms industry. "It is able," Gideon Burrows wrote in *The No-Nonsense Guide to the Arms Trade*, "to reap the benefits of international agreements to break down trade barriers, drawn up by the World Trade Organization and similar bodies, while being subject to few of the restrictions they impose and the standards they demand." Just as companies manufacturing sports equipment, toys and other goods have done, arms manufacturers now locate "their production lines to open up new markets, and wherever labor and tax is cheapest, environmental requirements are non-existent, employment regulations are weakest and regulations for the export of armaments most easily obtained."[82]

Arms companies are no longer state-controlled and -supervised companies. The simple concepts of the arms trade and arms companies have disappeared into a labyrinth of licensed production, joint ventures, conglomerates, strategic partnerships and cooperative armaments programs in the new globalized world. Weapons "systems" may be designed in one country, manufactured piecemeal in several others and sold both to the collaborating states and to others. In a world without borders, arms companies are only nominally subject to the legal, tax and moral obligations of their host countries, yet they are still treasured as national assets by the countries from which they sprang, receiving special treatment and political and financial support.[83]

The arms companies aggressively compete to supply the market for killing and much of the trade in their products is illegal. In theory most major arms-producing countries attempt to regulate the sale of weapons, but in practice smuggling and evasion are easy.[84] Arms are part of a massive global black market economy that consists of a series of arms-length commercial relationships. A modern covert arms deal is likely to take place within a matrix of black market transactions, involving cash or sometimes hostages, specialist middlemen, shell companies situated in offshore havens, ships sailing under flags of convenience, and alliances between groups as varied as career smugglers, legal arms manufacturers, political party bagmen, gangsters, insurgent armies and intelligence service agents.

In the borderlands between Mexico and the United States, as a result of the trade in guns and drugs, the effects of drug prohibition are more catastrophic than anywhere else. In October 2010, approaching 30,000 people had been killed there since 2006, mainly those involved in or caught up in conflict between drug trafficking organizations, but including hundreds of police officers and soldiers. Among these deaths some stand out as representing an almost complete breakdown in law and order. On May 8, 2008, Édgar Eusebio Millán Gómez, one of Mexico's leading police officers with responsibility for drug law enforcement, was shot dead outside his home in Mexico City.[85] On March 14, 2010, gunmen shot dead a pregnant American consulate worker, her husband and another consulate employee as they were leaving a children's party in Ciudad Juárez, the border town most affected by the drug war violence.[86] On May 31, 2010, 55 bodies thought to be the victims of drug gang violence were found in an abandoned silver mine near the city of Taxco in Guerrero state, which is situated in the south, well away from the northern border areas where most of the violence has taken place.[87] Slaughter had become so routine that in 2014 the *Global Post* put up a list of "The worst massacres and mass graves in Mexico's drug war."[88]

The US government's foreign aid/organized crime control policy in Mexico has been conducted under the banner of the Merida Initiative since 2008. This is described on the Department of State's (DOS) website as "an unprecedented partnership between the United States and Mexico to fight organized crime and associated violence while furthering respect for human rights and the rule of law." Under the heading "Programs and Activities," the DOS noted that "the U.S. Congress has appropriated $2.3 billion since the Merida Initiative began in Fiscal Year 2008." It then listed the benefits coming from the initiative. These amounted to an Americanization of the Mexican law enforcement, criminal justice and prison systems. "Mexico's implementation of comprehensive justice sector reforms," it noted, "has been supported through the training of justice sector personnel ... and support to Mexican law schools – all in preparation for Mexico's transition to a new accusatory criminal justice system."

It was clearly intended that this new system will provide more inmates for Mexican prisons, which the DOS notes approvingly "are working to receive independent accreditation from the American Correctional Association (ACA)."[89] The assumptions throughout the State Department document are that American organized crime control and prison policy work. The Mexican government chose not to challenge these assumptions, subordinating a more rational approach and acquiescing to its northern neighbor's carrot-and-stick tactics.

As in Colombia, private security companies are getting their share of Merida funds. After surveying this privatization of the war on drugs, Christopher Hobson argued that it further entrenches a costly and unsuccessful way of dealing with drugs. The use of private security companies "creates another strong vested interest in maintaining an increasingly problematic and costly status quo."[90]

Increasing federal and military involvement, supported by Merida Initiative funds, has not come close to controlling Mexican-American drug trafficking. The drug trade in Mexico represents one of the biggest industries in that country, amounting to billions of dollars collected mainly from American consumers. Money on this scale, as well as enriching entrepreneurs and their employees, goes to pay the salaries of shippers and processors, as well as the bribes that supplement the incomes of officials in both the US and Mexico.

6

The Atlantic Alliance as
a Money Laundry

The brutal futility and duplicity behind Plan Colombia and the
Merida Initiative has been demonstrated many times, most recently in
2016 when a US congressional report revealed the following about the
anti-money laundering (AML) regime:

> According to court documents, from 2006 to 2010, HSBC Bank
> USA severely understaffed its AML compliance function and
> failed to implement an anti-money laundering program capable of
> adequately monitoring suspicious transactions and activities from
> HSBC Group Affiliates, particularly HSBC Mexico, one of HSBC
> Bank USA's largest Mexican customers. This included a failure to
> monitor billions of dollars in purchases of physical U.S. dollars,
> or "banknotes," from these affiliates. Despite evidence of serious
> money laundering risks associated with doing business in Mexico,
> from at least 2006 to 2009, HSBC Bank USA rated Mexico as
> "standard" risk, its lowest AML risk category. As a result, HSBC
> Bank USA failed to monitor over $670 billion in wire transfers and
> over $9.4 billion in purchases of physical U.S. dollars from HSBC
> Mexico during this period, when HSBC Mexico's own lax AML
> controls caused it to be the preferred financial institution for drug
> cartels and money launderers.[91]

As a result of HSBC Bank USA's AML failures," the report continued:

> at least $881 million in drug trafficking proceeds – including
> proceeds of drug trafficking by the Sinaloa Cartel in Mexico and
> the Norte del Valle Cartel in Colombia – were laundered through
> HSBC Bank USA. HSBC Group admitted it did not inform HSBC
> Bank USA of significant AML deficiencies at HSBC Mexico,

despite knowing of these problems and their effect on the potential flow of illicit funds through HSBC Bank USA.

The report was prepared by Republican party staff of the House of Representatives Committee on Financial Services and released on July 16, 2016. Entitled, *Too Big to Jail: Inside the Obama Justice Department's Decision not to Hold Wall Street Accountable*, it detailed how the AML system could apparently be fixed at the highest level. It added detail on the ways regulators and prosecutors could turn potential criminal prosecutions of powerful institutions into weak settlements that insulated executives.

Part of this process involved a letter from George Osborne, the UK's chancellor of the exchequer to Federal Reserve Chairman Ben Bernanke (with a copy transmitted to Treasury Secretary Timothy Geithner) on September 10, 2012, to express the UK's concerns regarding US enforcement actions against British banks. Chancellor Osborne warned Chairman Bernanke and Secretary Geithner that prosecuting a "systemically important financial institution" such as HSBC "could lead to [financial] contagion" and pose "very serious implications for financial and economic stability, particularly in Europe and Asia." This view may have influenced top-level administration officials, and the eventual terms of the agreement between the US government and HSBC appear to be very lenient.

There have been other large cases. In 2010, Wachovia, for example, was sanctioned for failing to apply adequate money laundering controls on $378.4 billion in transfers originating from Mexico. Jeffery Sloman, the federal prosecutor who handled the case, commented that "Wachovia's blatant disregard for our banking laws gave international cocaine cartels a virtual carte blanche to finance their operations."[92] However, under the kind of deferred prosecution agreement that has become familiar, Wachovia only had to pay a $160 million fine for its role in laundering hundreds of billions of dollars.

Kevin Edmonds, writing for the North American Congress on Latin America, details another scandal involving the Bank of America, and made the following point about the type of settlements in these cases:

It has become very clear that banks such as HSBC, Wachovia, and the Bank of America are integral components of the drug trade, which operate with impunity ... What does the settlement do to fight the cartels? Nothing. It encourages the cartels and anyone who wants to make money by laundering their blood dollars. While pushing further on the topic of direct, multifaceted US involvement in the international drug trade is a taboo subject, to ignore its role as a key source of profit for banks, prisons and the military is even more dangerous and costly.[93]

Edmunds also put the career of the world's current most notorious gangster in context. Commenting on the arrest of Joaquín "El Chapo" Guzmán, he wrote that El Chapo did not rise up the ranks of the cartel and into *Forbes* magazine's list of the world's 100 most powerful people just through being incredibly shrewd or ruthless. He was a semi-illiterate peasant who "would not have got far without the collusion of businessmen, politicians, and policemen, and all those who exercise everyday power from behind a false halo of legality. We see their faces all the time, not in the mug shots of most wanted felons ... but in the front-page stories, business sections, and society columns of the main papers."[94]

There are large numbers of participants in the drug trade who make spectacular profits and remain able to launder these through some of the world's most respectable financial institutions, using exactly the same mechanisms and subterfuges – shell banks, trusts, dummy corporations – that corporations have been using for decades to avoid or evade taxation.[95] Requiring financial institutions to file "suspicious activity reports" and making bankers "sheriffs" in organized crime control efforts has not come close to addressing the practice of money laundering and therefore has failed as an organized crime control tactic.

"Western banks," Raymond Baker reported in *Capitalism's Achilles Heel*,

solicit, transfer, accumulate and manage dirty money in the trillions of dollars, raking in hundreds of billions every year. The tension between anti-money compliance and bringing in business is no contest. New bank deposits, private accounts, and fee services win nearly every time. When knowledgeable experts on these matters get together, they often talk about how anti-money laundering regimes are designed, first to offer financial institutions "plausible deniability" when caught with laundered money and only secondarily to avoid actually receiving dirty money.[96]

Charles Goredema, a money laundering expert at the Institute for Security Studies at Cape Town, has also captured many of the reasons why the AML regime, and therefore the organized crime control regime, has failed. Speaking to the anthropologist Carolyn Nordstrom, he explained that:

> There is no agreed-upon definition of what "money" we consider in money laundering. It certainly isn't all the money in the world that is laundered. Generally the experts focus on the high-profile criminal profits: drugs, illegal arms, mafia enterprises, that sort of thing. But even here, experts don't agree. Do we include (unreliable) estimates on small-scale low-impact drugs or stick with the large criminal networks? Consider unrecorded arms transfers by governments or only non-state? What about the sex industry? – something, curiously, many don't include.[97]

"What about white-collar crime?" Nordstrom asked. "Those who define laundering by focusing on the heavily criminal don't tend to even recognize white-collar profits," Goredema answered, "it is not generally included in figures on yearly global laundering." He also noted that no one ever tries to figure in all the unrecorded trade in the basics: food, petrol, medicines; or the high-tech goods like computers, software and industrial equipment.[98] It is all very selective and it all benefits financial institutions that are too big to charge or check.

The AML regime was thus always going to fail. In 2014 a major study confirmed this. Entitled, Global Surveillance of Dirty Money: Assessing Assessments of Regimes to Control Money Laundering and Combat the Financing of Terrorism, it cast doubt on the credibility of the entire AML and Combat the Financing of Terrorism (CFT) regime. The authors, Terrence C. Halliday, Michael Levi and Peter Reuter, concluded that: "Several of the world's most prominent international banks have been caught in flagrant and enormous repeat violations of AML/CFT regimes in countries where those regimes might have been thought to be most effective (ie. US/UK)." This revelation alone, the authors conclude, undermines the credibility of the entire AML/CFT system.[99]

Much of the world's dirty money therefore gets washed in the financial institutions of two of the leaders in the global campaign against organized crime and dirty money – the US and the UK. Few of the inconvenient realities about the illegal activities collectively known as organized crime and transnational organized crime are allowed to inform the public or their representatives in government. All are trapped in discourses of national and international security that do not permit informed discussion. The world's regulatory regimes remain too weak to check organized business crime. The world's borders remain too porous to check smuggling in legal or illegal goods. And the world's bankers remain as keen on money as they always have been, whether or not it is "clean" or "dirty." Whistleblowing on any of the above is not encouraged. The incentives to turn a blind eye are much higher.

* * *

As we have seen, the British approach to organized crime developed from Thatcher's war on drugs. Her government set up the Scotland Yard-based National Drugs Intelligence Unit. This evolved into the National Criminal Intelligence Service (NCIS), established in 1992 and labeled the British FBI by the media. It was disbanded in 2006. The NCIS evolved into the Serious Organised Crime Agency (SOCA), again labeled the British FBI. SOCA was disbanded in October 2013 and replaced by the National Crime Agency (NCA) – Britain's current FBI. Although this evolution began with drug prohibition, illegal substances have become easier to buy in Britain.[100] Good policing continues to result in the arrest and conviction of drug traffickers, but market forces ensure that any demand is met. The majority of drug traffickers were at worst inconvenienced by the alphabet soup of agencies.

Good policing has also resulted in the arrest and conviction of large numbers of other organized criminals such as human traffickers, cyber-criminals and various types of fraudster and extortionist, but on the UK government's own admission there is a damning contradiction in UK organized crime control policy. Its 2015 *National Security Strategy and Strategic Defence and Security Review* admitted that "substantial funds from crime conducted around the world are laundered through London, including in the UK's foreign exchange turnover which is reported as $2.7 trillion in London daily."[101] Although the review failed to highlight the pivotal role of the UK's other financial secrecy jurisdictions such as the Cayman Islands in facilitating organized crime, its estimates confirmed an insight articulated by the Italian journalist Roberto Saviano. Saviano stated that the City of London's financial services industry facilitates a system that makes the UK the most corrupt nation in the world. Speaking at the Hay literary festival in May 2016, Saviano stated that "[n]inety per cent of the owners of capital in London have their headquarters offshore," and that "Jersey and the Caymans are the access gates to criminal capital in Europe and the UK is the country that allows it."[102]

It is also worth noting that the UK government remains reluctant to specify that tax evasion is organized crime. Tax evasion is excluded from the range of illicit activities listed by the government's National Security Strategy Review. In many ways therefore, the attitude towards tax evasion in Britain resembles that of corporate actors engaged in violations of the law. Tax evasion is illegal but not really criminal. Evasion, however, should clearly be seen as organized crime involving a range of legitimate world actors such as lawyers, bankers, accountants and estate agents who, to use the favored jargon, act as "enablers."

High-end property prices in London and other financial centers have been driven by dirty money flows. The money laundering expert Diane Francis has also noted the phenomenon in New York, Miami, Toronto, Vancouver, Sydney, Melbourne and Hong Kong. "The latest attraction in London," she wrote in 2016, "is the Kleptocracy Tour, organized by anti-corruption groups. They drive customers through neighborhoods that have become the world's most expensive square footage, thanks to the flood of dirty money bidding up real estate values."[103] Governments are considering addressing this by requiring secrecy havens to disclose beneficial ownership, but progress is slow and is thus allowing criminal money managers to adapt. The point that the UK government continues to avoid facing is that organized crime thus benefits – rather than threatens – many professionals in its financial services industry.

The financial systems of Japan, Australia, Canada and Hong Kong, as well as those in the US and the European Union, are as accommodating to dirty money from abroad as those of the UK. Dirty money, Baker explained in *Capitalism's Achilles Heel*, is money that is illegally earned, illegally transferred or illegally utilized. All forms of dirty money – criminal, corrupt and commercial – use basically the same subterfuges to roll through international channels: false documentation, dummy corporations, shell banks, tax havens, offshore secrecy jurisdiction, mispricing, collusion, kickbacks, numbered accounts, transfers that disguise transactions and so on. Western business and banking sectors have developed and promoted the mechanisms for bringing in dirty money from other countries for more than a century: gangsters and corrupt dictators lagged behind corporations in taking advantage of these mechanisms.[104]

Baker was particularly revealing about the practice of transfer pricing within multinational corporations and the setting up of offshore dummy companies. The first is the use of trade to shift money at will among parent organizations, subsidiaries and affiliates operating in dozens of countries to minimize taxes and maximize profits. Exaggerated transfer pricing has been standard procedure for many corporations for decades. Needless to say, the UN warnings about it in 1975 had been ignored (see Part IV, Chapter 1).

Baker then explained the links between these techniques and mechanisms and the looting of countries in Africa, Asia and South America and the plundering of Russia after the fall of communism. Using credible sources, he estimated the flow of global cross-border dirty money at roughly $500 billion annually, mainly flowing from poor countries to rich countries.[105] If this amount of money had not been stolen, he argued, it would have done more to alleviate and prevent poverty than all the West's economic aid, export promotion, foreign investment and free trade policies put together. But that of course did not happen, and the means to hide and legitimate stolen money are as available as ever. "Holes intentionally left in anti-money laundering laws," wrote Baker, "provide a road map to foreigners showing them how to re-label their money in order to get it into the western financial system."[106]

Financial professionals have thus succeeded in making a nonsense of all efforts to control international organized crime. Gangsters, drug traffickers, human traffickers, gun traffickers and anyone involved in significant illegal activity know that Western financial institutions usually either miss or turn a blind eye to dirty money.[107] Only the careless get caught out – the business of organized crime continues.

Epilogue

In the 1920s, in the pursuit of political power, the banker Charles Dawes put the weight of his opinion behind an idea that there was a foreign super-government of crime in America. We now know that not only was he wrong, but he was also the leading financial criminal of his time. In the early 1930s Benito Mussolini put the weight of his opinion behind the idea that the way to defeat super-governments of crime was to mobilize state power in order to enable repression. We now know his reputation as an anti-Mafia crusader was not justified. We also know that fascist repression was not the answer to organized crime in Italy and that Mussolini himself was one of the leading state-organized criminals of his time. In the late 1930s, Hickman Powell was the first to claim that Lucky Luciano centralized organized crime in America – in other words, Luciano, he claimed, created a super-government of crime – and Powell used his imagination to support this claim. Although other imaginative writers built on Powell's foundation, we now know that the stories were inventions. In the early 1950s Powell retired with a New York State pension courtesy of the politician whose career he advanced with these stories. In the early 1950s, Harry Anslinger put the weight of the FBN behind the claim that Luciano and the Mafia ran the international drug traffic – in other words ran a super-government of crime. We now know that Luciano and the Mafia did not run the international drug traffic and the FBN was a particularly dishonest and corrupt agency. It had to be abolished in 1968 because of the extent of corruption in its ranks. In the late 1950s, FBI Director J. Edgar Hoover directed that the "Mafia Monograph" be compiled as the "bible" to inform FBI officials charged with investigating organized crime. We now know that the Monograph's "research" derived ultimately from Powell's and the FBN's. We also know that suppressing dissent and supporting order rather than law was Hoover's overriding priority.

Dawes, Mussolini, Powell, Anslinger, Hoover and many others were part of a process that gave the phrase "organized crime" a meaning that excluded or at least de-emphasized the part played by representatives of business, criminal justice, law enforcement or any of the "respectable" classes in the problem. Professionals and business people were clearly and often shown to be involved in systematic and organized violation of laws, but discourse was dumbed down to such a point that their activities were not thought to be organized crime. The US government got to choose what organized crime was and then exported its ill-informed and contradictory organized crime control methods to the rest of the world.

* * *

In 1969, Richard Nixon was told by a group of experts that "Organized crime will continue to thrive so long as the community relies primarily on criminal sanctions to discourage gambling and the use of drugs."[1] He ignored this advice and instead, in 1970, added the prestige of the presidency to the claim that there was an Italian American super-government of crime. He did this to push through the Organized Crime Control Act and the Comprehensive Drug Abuse Control Act. These laws increased the use of criminal sanctions to discourage gambling and the use of drugs. We now know that Nixon was dishonest – prepared to pursue and attempt to cover up his own criminal behavior if it served his political ambition. The potential for repression from the anti-drug and anti-organized crime laws motivated Nixon more than any real concern about gambling, drug use and illegal profit-making opportunities. As we have seen, the laws have taken rights and assets away from innocent Americans without affecting opportunities for organized criminals. Most organized criminals active today in the US are born in the US, despite the FBI website's indications that this is not the case.

During Nixon's administration, a flawed and, to date, unsuccessful organized crime control policy template was set in stone by the 1970 laws. This was built on by the Reagan administration and exported first to Britain during the Thatcher years and, with British support, to the rest of the international community through UN conventions and other mechanisms in the years that followed. Most of the representatives who signed up to these conventions had little or no background in law enforcement and no real idea what organized crime actually was. Despite this, they committed their countries to ape the law enforcement and criminal justice systems of the United States. The significant criminals from these poorer parts of the world, meanwhile, chose to safeguard their fortunes in British, American and other financial secrecy havens, far away from institutions in their own countries that might have aided development.

Double Crossed has made the case that national and international efforts to control organized crime have failed and will continue to fail so long as the path chosen by opportunist politicians and careerist bureaucrats in the US and elsewhere is followed. This path consists of over-policing the poor and under-policing the rich and better-off. The mass incarceration of recent decades has increased the number of criminal networks who are likely to be ready, willing and able to resort to violence in order to run their rackets and prevent detection. The deregulation of recent decades was a major contributing factor in the financial meltdown of 2007/8 since it allowed much organized criminal activity to go unpunished and thus undeterred.

At the time of writing Donald Trump has been sworn in as president of the US for the next four years, and his words and cabinet appointments indicate an approach modeled on Presidents Nixon and Reagan – "tough on crime," "get the cartels" rhetoric while turning a blind eye to increasing opportunities for organized business and financial crime. We may be about to get a better idea of what would have happened had Franklin Roosevelt not won the 1932 presidential election.

The US will remain the world's dominant power, ideologically as well as militarily and economically, during the Trump era and the understanding of organized crime and its control is unlikely to change. Governing elites in most other countries, including Russia and China, can see the attraction of organized crime control policies based on the American model. Like Mussolini and his American supporters in the 1920s and 1930s, authoritarians know that suppressing organized crime is a popular state policy. They also know that they choose which organized criminals to identify or not.

Between 1929 and 1931 the US Wickersham Commission undertook the first and last scientific and objective government-sponsored inquiry into organized crime, broadly defined, in any country. The commission concluded that "[i]ntelligent action," on organized crime, "requires knowledge – not, as in too many cases, a mere redoubling of effort in the absence of adequate information and a definite plan." Its primary recommendation was, "for immediate, comprehensive, and scientific, nation-wide inquiry into organized crime" to "make possible the development of an intelligent plan for its control." Sadly no such inquiry took place and the concept of organized crime was captured by the succession of politicians, bureaucrats and media outlets detailed in these pages.

The Wickersham inquiry looked first at *events* called organized crime rather than *people* called organized crime before making their recommendations for its control. Dwight C. Smith, in a neglected but important journal article on the evolution of an "official" definition for organized crime, argued that the distinction between looking first at *events* rather than *people* is critical. "The observer who looks first at events and then at the persons associated with them," he concluded "is more likely to adopt a scientific, value-free and causal analytical style." In contrast the observer who defined a universe by the people it contained, was "more prone to bias and to nontestable assumptions – in short, to conclusions that are based more on ideology than on logic."[2]

Police officers involved in organized crime control efforts around the world are far better trained and more professional than they have ever been. But policymakers have given them a task that can only be compared to that of the mythological Sisyphus, who was condemned to repeat forever the task of pushing a rock up a mountain – only to see it roll down again.

The authoritarian and xenophobic tendencies already characterizing Trump's presidency are a motivation for national and international inquiries that look first at events called organized crime. These inquiries might make possible an intelligent plan for its control to emerge. In the meantime, organized crime control will continue to do nothing to prevent a proliferation of entrepreneurial gangster networks, including many formed in prisons, and a virtual carte blanche for organized criminality within business and financial systems.

Notes

Preface

1. Misha Glenny, *McMafia: Crime Without Frontiers* (London: The Bodley Head, 2008); William F. Wechsler, "Combating Transnational Organized Crime," Deputy Assistant Secretary of Defence for Counternarcotics and Global Threats, remarks prepared for delivery at the Washington Institute, April 26, 2012.
2. See Richard Hofstadter, *The Paranoid Style in American Politics* (New York: Vintage, 1967), for one of the best descriptions of the construction of conspiracy theories.

Part I Dumbing Down: Constructing an Acceptable Understanding of "Organized Crime"

1. For an account of European and American antecedents of organized crime, see Michael Woodiwiss, *Organized Crime and American Power: A History* (Toronto: University of Toronto Press, 2001), pp. 1–105.
2. R. Jeffrey Lustig, *Corporate Liberalism: The Origins of Modern American Political Theory, 1890–1920* (Berkeley: University of California Press, 1982), p. 304.
3. Henry Demerest Lloyd, *Wealth Against Commonwealth* (Westport, Connecticut: Greenwood Press, 1976. First published in 1894), pp. 169–70.
4. Ida M. Tarbell, "John D Rockefeller: A Character Study, Part Two," *McClure's Magazine* 25:4, August 1905, p. 399.
5. Gustavus Myers, *History of Great American Fortunes* (New York: The Modern Library, 1936), pp. 380–4.
6. Myers, *History of Great American Fortunes*, pp. 368–9.
7. David Rosner and Gerald Markowitz (eds.), *Dying for Work: Workers' Safety and Health in Twentieth Century America* (Bloomington: Indiana University Press, 1989), p. xi.
8. Lincoln Steffens, *The Shame of the Cities* (New York: Hill and Wang, 1963), pp. 1–21.
9. Ibid., p. 26.
10. Ibid., p. 123.
11. Louis Filler, *Crusaders for American Liberalism: The Story of the Muckrakers* (New York: Collier Books, 1961), p. 337.

12. Ibid., pp. 337–8.

13. Samuel Walker, *Popular Justice: A History of American Criminal Justice* (New York: Oxford University Press, 1980), pp. 169–70.

14. Henry Barrett Chamberlin, "The Chicago Crime Commission – How the Businessmen of Chicago are Fighting Crime," *Journal of Criminal Law and Criminology*, November, 1920, p. 397.

15. New York Society for the Prevention of Crime, Annual Report, 1896 quoted in Paul W. Rishell and Albert E. Roraback, *A History of the Society for the Prevention of Crime*, p. 29 (unpublished and undated document held in Box 9, SPC Collection, Rare Books and Manuscript Library, Columbia University, New York).

16. Jerome S. Auerbach, *Labor and Liberty: The La Follette Committee and the New Deal* (New York: Bobbs-Merrill, 1966), pp. 17–18.

17. Samuel Walker, *Popular Justice: A History of American Criminal Justice* (New York: Oxford University Press, 1980), p. 171.

18. Timothy Gilfoyle, *City of Eros: New York City, Prostitution and the Commercialization of Vice* (New York: W.W. Norton, 1992), pp. 256–7.

19. Andrew Sinclair, *Prohibition: The Era of Excess* (London: Faber and Faber, 1962), p. 49.

20. David F. Musto, *The American Disease: Origins of Narcotic Control* (New York: Oxford University Press, 1987), p. 305; and John John Rumbarger, *Power, Profits and Prohibition* (Albany: State University of New York Press, 1989), pp. 177–8.

21. John Helmer, *Drugs and Minority Oppression* (New York: The Seabury Press, 1975), p. 12.

22. Francisco E. Thoumi, *Illegal Drugs, Economy and Society in the Andes* (London: Johns Hopkins University Press, 2003), p. 20.

23. Alan A. Block and William Chambliss, *Organizing Crime* (New York: Elsevier, 1981), p. 53.

24. Rufus King, *The Drug Hang-Up: America's Fifty Year Folly* (New York: W.W. Norton, 1972), p. 25.

25. David Bewley-Taylor, *The United States and International Drug Control, 1909–1997* (London: Pinter, 1999), p. 36.

26. E.R. Hawkings and Willard Waller, "Critical Notes on the Cost of Crime," *Journal of Criminal Law and Criminology*, 26, 1936, pp. 679–94.

27. *Report of the Select Committee Appointed to Examine Tenement Houses in New York and Brooklyn*, 185, quoted in Gus Tyler, *Organized Crime in America: A Book of Readings* (Ann Arbor: University of Michigan Press, 1962), p. 57.

28. For the development of Mafia mythology see Dwight Smith, *The Mafia Mystique* (New York: Basic Books, 1975).

29. Humbert S. Nelli, *The Business of Crime: Italians and Syndicate Crime in the United States* (New York: Oxford University Press, 1976), p. 50.

30. Ibid., p. 51.

31. Ibid., p. 62.

32. Ed Reid, *Mafia* (New York: Signet, 1954), p. 149.

33. Salvatore J. LaGumina, *Wop! Anti-Italian Discrimination in the United States* (San Francisco: Straight Arrow Books, 1973), pp. 74–83.

34. Some blackmailers used a black hand symbol to panic their victims in early twentieth-century America. There was no separate "Black Hand" society or "black hand warfare". See Robert M. Lombardo, "The Black Hand: A Study in Moral Panic," *Global Crime*, 6:3–4, August–November 2004, pp. 267–84.

35. Dennis E. Hoffman, *Scarface Al and the Crime Crusaders: Chicago's Private War against Capone* (Carbondale and Edwardsville: Southern Illinois University Press, 1991), p. 11.

36. Edward Alsworth Ross. *Sin and Society: An Analysis of Latter-Day Iniquity* (Boston: Houghton Mifflin Company, 1907), pp. 45–71 at https://brocku.ca/MeadProject/Ross/Ross_1907/Ross_1907_03.html.

37. "Charles G. Dawes – Biographical". Nobelprize.org. Nobel Media AB 2014.

38. "General Raps Lawlessness; Hits Unions" in *Morning Star* (Rockford, IL), August 17, 1923.

39. Editorial, "Dawes Minute Men on Guard," *St Louis Post-Dispatch* reprinted in *Omaha World Telegram* (Omaha, NE), May 10, 1923.

40. National Democratic Magazine, "Dawes 'Cussed' Way Into Vice-Presidency Nomination," *Greensboro Record* (Greensboro, NC), August 25, 1924.

41. Raymond B. Vickers, *Panic in the Loop: Chicago's Banking Crisis of 1932* (New York: Lexington Books, 2013), pp. 24–5; "Connects Dawes in Bank Failure," Dallas *Morning News*, September 21, 1924.

42. John Kobler, *The Life and World of Al Capone* (London: Coronet, 1971), pp. 158–9; "Federal Aid Asked in Chicago Clean-Up," *Trenton Evening Times* (Trenton, NJ), February 28, 1926.

43. "Urge Dawes to Lead Campaign Against Crime," *Daily Register Gazette*, July 28, 1928; "Red Meat," *Plain Dealer* (Cleveland, OH), June 17, 1930.

44. "Dawes Quits Presidency of Finance Corp.," *Tampa Tribune* (Tampa, Florida), June 7, 1932.

45. Vickers, *Panic in the Loop*, p. 194.

46. Ibid., p. 195.

47. Ibid., p. 233.

48. Bascom N. Timmons, *Portrait of an American: Charles G. Dawes* (New York: Henry Holt, 1953); Wayne Gard, "Canny Charles Dawes In His Financial Era," *Dallas Morning News*, May 31, 1953.

49. Charles A. Beard, "The Myth of Rugged American Individualism," in Howard Zinn (ed.), *New Deal Thought* (Indianapolis: Bobbs-Merrill, 1967), p. 10.

50. Walter Lippmann, "The Underworld as Servant," in Tyler, *Crime in America*, p. 61.

51. Murray Gurfein, "The Racket Defined," in Tyler, *Crime in America*, pp. 181–8.
52. "Al 'Scarface' Capone Wants to See End of Chicago Gang Murders," *Augusta Chronicle* (Augusta GA), October 14, 1926.
53. Hoffman, *Scarface Al and the Crime Crusaders*, pp. 32–3.
54. Ibid., p. 51; Gus Russo, *The Outfit: The Role of Chicago's Underworld in the Shaping of Modern America* (London: Bloomsbury, 2001), p. 495.
55. Andrew Wender Cohen, *The Racketeers' Progress: Chicago and the Struggle for the Modern American Economy, 1940–1940* (New York: Cambridge University Press, 2004), p. 269.
56. Russo, *The Outfit*, p. 45.
57. Laurence Bergreen, *Capone: The Man and the Era* (New York: Simon & Schuster, 1996), pp. 365–6.
58. "Tapped Wires Closed Net on Scarface Al – Eliot Ness, Graduate of Chicago University, Wins Credit for Long Effort," *San Francisco Chronicle*, June 13, 1931.
59. Bergreen, *Capone*, p. 154.
60. Russo, *The Outfit*, p. 45.
61. Elmer Irey, *The Tax Dodgers: The Inside Story of the T Mens' War with America's Political and Underworld Hoodlums* (New York: The Greenberg Press, 1948), p. 19.
62. Kobler, *Capone: The Life and World of Al Capone* (London: Coronet, 1971), pp. 312–30.
63. "Says Capone Seeks Liberty by Politics," *Omaha World-Herald* (Omaha, NE), March 25, 1932; Cohen, *The Racketeer's Progress*, p. 269.
64. Kenneth Allsop, *The Bootleggers* (London: Arrow, 1970), p. 338.
65. Mark H. Haller, "Illegal Enterprise: A Theoretical and Historical Interpretation," in Nikos Passas (ed.) *Organized Crime* (Aldershot: Dartmouth, 1995), pp. 225–53.
66. Robert Lacey, *Little Man: Meyer Lansky and the Gangster Life* (London: Arrow, 1991), p. 61.
67. Donald Henderson Clarke, *In the Reign of Rothstein* (New York: Vangard Press, 1929), p. 9.
68. Russo, *The Outfit*, p. 45.
69. Fred D. Pasley, *Al Capone* (London: Faber & Faber, 1966. First published 1931), p. 9.
70. Kobler, *Capone*, p. 10.
71. Martin Short, *Crime Inc.: The Story of Organized Crime* (London: Thames, 1984), p. 84.
72. Jonathan Eig, *Get Capone: The Secret Plot that Captured America's Most Wanted Gangster* (New York: Simon & Schuster, 2010), p. 38.
73. Hergé, *Tin Tin in America* (London: Egmost, 2011).
74. Laurence Bergreen, *Capone: The Man and the Era* (New York: Simon & Schuster, 1994), pp. 44–6, 548–605.
75. *Pittsburg Sun Telegraph*, February 12, 1936.

76. Kobler, *Capone*, p. 362.

77. "Scarface Al," *Morning Star* (Rockford, Illinois), September 20, 1926.

78. Kobler, *Capone*, p. 128.

79. Ibid., pp. 199–202; Robert J. Schoenberg, *Mr Capone* (New York: Quill, 1992), pp. 188–92; Associated Press, "Prisoner in His Own Home," *Daily Register Gazette* (Rockford, IL), December 18, 1927.

80. Schoenberg, *Mr Capone*, p. 195.

81. Bergreen, *Capone: The Man and the Era*, pp. 594–6.

82. Ibid., pp. 597–601.

83. Ibid., pp. 611–12.

84. Allsop, *The Bootleggers*, pp. 368–9.

85. John Diggins, *Mussolini and Fascism: The View from America* (Princeton: Princeton University Press, 1972), p. 72.

86. Ibid., p.279.

87. Ibid., p. 173.

88. R.J.B. Bosworth, *Mussolini* (London: Bloomsbury, 2010), pp. 223–4.

89. Diggins, *Mussolini and Fascism*, pp. 28–9.

90. Ibid., p. 30.

91. Christopher Duggan, *Fascism and the Mafia* (Newhaven: Yale University Press, 1989), p. 12.

92. Ibid., p. 232.

93. "Mussolini Gives Mafia Death Blow: Many Brigands Convicted of Various Crime in Italy," *Repository* (Canton, OH), January 11, 1928.

94. Duggan, *Fascism and the Mafia*, p. 233.

95. Richard Washburn Child, "How Mussolini Smashed the Mafia – Chapter I," *San Diego Union*, April 22, 1928.

96. Richard Washburn Child, "How Mussolini Smashed the Mafia – Chapter II," *San Diego Union*, April 29, 1928.

97. Richard Washburn Child, "How Mussolini Smashed the Mafia – Chapter VII" *San Diego Union*, June 3, 1928.

98. Duggan, *Fascism and the Mafia*, p. 188.

99. Michele Pantaleone, *The Mafia and Politics* (London: Chatto & Windus, 1966), p. 49.

100. Salvatore Lupo, *History of the Mafia* (New York: Columbia Press, 2011), p. 175.

101. Anton Blok, *The Mafia of a Sicilian Village, 1860–1960* (New York: Harper & Row, 1975), p. 144; Gaia Servadio, *Mafioso: A History of the Mafia from its Origins to the Present Day* (London: Secker & Warberg, 1976), pp. 74–5.

102. Pantaleone, *The Mafia and Politics*, p. 49.

103. Duggan, *Fascism and the Mafia*, p. 240.

104. Ibid., p. 231.

105. Panatleone, *The Mafia and Politics*, p. 50.

106. Duggan, pp. 237–8, 295 n.81; Richard Washburn Child, "How Mussolini Smashed the Mafia – Chapter III," *San Diego Union*, May 6, 1928.

107. Duggan, *Fascism and the Mafia*, p. 247.

108. Vittorio Coco, "The *Pentiti* of the Sicilian Mafia in the 1930s," *Modern Italy*, 18:3, 2013, p. 247.

109. Ibid, p. 252.

110. R.J.B. Bosworth, "Everyday Mussolinism: Friends, Family, Locality and Violence in Fascist Italy," *Contemporary European History*, 14:1, 2005.

111. Michael R. Ebner, *Ordinary Violence in Mussolini's Italy* (Cambridge: Cambridge University Press, 2010), pp. 4–5.

112. Paul Corner, *The Fascist Party and Popular Opinion in Mussolini's Italy* (Oxford: Oxford University Press, 2012), pp. 174–5.

113. W.A. Swanberg, *Citizen Hearst* (New York: Bantam, 1971), p. 556.

114. Benito Mussolini, "Insists Governments Suppress Organized Crime," *Plain Dealer* (Cleveland, OH), October 23, 1932.

115. Benito Mussolini, "Highest-Placed Criminals Must Be Mercilessly Suppressed, Says Mussolini," *Sentinel* (Milwaukee, WI), October 23, 1932.

116. Ibid.

117. Carlos Clarens, *Crime Movies: An Illustrated History* (London: W.W. Norton, 1979), pp. 106–7.

118. Ben Urwand, *The Collaboration: Hollywood's Pact with Hitler* (Cambridge, MA: Harvard University Press, 2013), pp. 106–12.

119. Richard E. Hays, "Gabriel Over the White House is Stirring Play," *Seattle Daily Times*, March 31, 1933; *Morning Olympian* (Olympia, Washington State), April 16, 1933; Fred M. White, "Gabriel Over the White House Stars Huston," *The Oregonian*, April 15, 1933; W.R. Wilkinson cited in "Notes on the Passing Show – Gabriel over the White House," *Dallas Morning News*, March 9, 1933.

120. Ira Katznelson, *Fear Itself: The New Deal and the Origins of Our Time* (New York: W.W. Norton and Company, 2013), p. 13.

121. Richard Gid Powers, *G-Men: Hoover's FBI in American Popular Culture* (Carbondale and Edwardsville: Southern Illinois University Press, 1983), p. 9.

122. L.M. Harris, "What is Mussolini Method? – Suppression of Mafia Ought to Show Us How to Suppress Gangs," *Oregonian* (Portland, OR), March 15, 1932.

123. Ibid., pp. 39–40.

124. Kobler, *Capone*, p. 337.

125. Powers, *G-Men*, p. 298.

126. Cummings quoted in Kenneth O'Reilly, "A New Deal for the FBI: The Roosevelt Administration, Crime Control and National Security," *Journal of American History*, 69:3, December 1982, p. 643.

127. Frederick Lewis Allen, *Since Yesterday: The 1930s in America* (New York: Harper & Row, 1972), pp. 146–7.

128. Andrew Bergman, *We're in the Money: Depression America and its Films* (London: Harper & Row, 1972), p. 13.

129. Hank Messick and Burt Goldblatt, *Gangs and Gangsters: The Illustrated History of Gangs* (New York: Ballantine Books, 1974), pp. 160–4.

130. Sherrill, *The Saturday Night Special*, pp. 48–9.

131. "TIME's 20 most influential 'Builders & Titans'" at www.everything 2000.com/news/news/buildertitan.asp.

132. Benjamin Strolberg, "Thomas E. Dewey: Self-Made Myth," *American Mercury*, June 1940, pp. 140–7.

133. Clarens, *Crime Movies*, p. 154.

134. "Organized Crime Took the Rap – Right Down Line in 1930 – 40 Decade," *Trenton Evening Times*, December 31, 1939.

135. Burton Turkus and Sid Feder, *Murder Inc.: The Story of "The Syndicate"* (London: Victor Gollancz, 1952), p. 19.

136. Alan A. Block, *Perspectives on Organizing Crime: Essays in Opposition* (London: Elsevier, 1991), pp. 9–10.

Part II   Lies about Criminals: Constructing an Acceptable "History" of Organized Crime

1. David Critchley, *The Origin of Organized Crime in America: The New York City Mafia, 1891–1931* (New York: Routledge, 2009), p. 283. Dr. Critchley was the first to cast doubt on the standard accounts of the "conference" and I am grateful to him for sharing his insights on "histories" of organized crime; *The Post Crescent* (Appleton, WI), May 18, 1929.

2. Critchley, *The Origin of Organized Crime in America*, n. 49, p. 283.

3. Ibid., n. 49, p. 142.

4. Damon Runyon, *Guys and Dolls and Other Stories* (London: Penguin, 1997), pp. 245–60; Marc Mappen, *Prohibition Gangsters: The Rise and Fall of a Bad Generation* (London: Rutgers University Press, 2013), pp. 97–104.

5. Hickman Powell, *Ninety Times Guilty* (London: Robert Hale, 1940), p. 68.

6. Ibid, pp. 82–3.

7. Ibid, p. 68.

8. Michael Woodiwiss, *Crime, Crusades and Corruption: Prohibitions in the United States, 1900–1987* (London: Pinter, 1988), p. 50.

9. Powell, *Ninety Times Guilty*, p. 80.

10. "The Underworld: Crime Described in 'Ninety Times Guilty'," *Springfield Republican* (Springfield, MA), June 12, 1939.

11. "Nice Propaganda for Brother Dewey," *Evening Standard* (Uniontown, PA), August 25, 1939.

12. J. Richard "Dixie" Davis, "Things I Couldn't Tell Till Now," *Colliers*, July 22, July 29, August 5, August 12, August 19, August 26, 1939.

13. *The Daily Independent* (Murphysboro, IL), August 12, 1939.

14. Jack Lait, "Broadway and Elsewhere," *Morning Herald* (Hagerstown, MD), December 10, 1940: Jack Lait, "Broadway and Elsewhere," *Logansport Pharos Tribune* (Logansport, IN), July 22, 1949.

15. William Moore, *The Kefauver Committee and the Politics of Crime* (Columbia: University of Missouri Press, 1974), p. 85.

16. Frederic Sondern, *Brotherhood of Evil: The Mafia* (London: Panther, 1961), pp. 62–3.

17. Walter Winchell, "Walter Winchell in New York," *The High Point Enterprise* (High Point, NC), November 1, 1965.

18. President's Commission on Law Enforcement and the Administration of Justice, *The Challenge of Crime in a Free Society* (Washington, DC: Government Printing Office, 1967), p. 192.

19. Michael Woodiwiss, "Enterprise not Ethnicity: An Interview with Dwight C. Smith," *Trends in Organized Crime*, 18:1–2, June 2015, pp. 46–7.

20. Ralph Salerno and John S. Tompkins, *The Crime Confederation*, (New York: Popular Library, 1969), p. 275.

21. Hank Messick, *Lansky* (London: Robert Hale, 1971), p. 38.

22. Tony Scaduto, *Lucky Luciano* (London, Sphere Books, 1976), p. 197.

23. Martin Gosch and Richard Hammer, *The Last Testament of Lucky Luciano* (Boston: Little, Brown and Company, 1975), p. viii.

24. Scaduto, *Lucky Luciano*, p. 207.

25. Nicholas Gage, "Luciano Story Called 'Fiction'," *Dallas Morning News*, December 19, 1974.

26. Nelson Johnson, *Boardwalk Empire* (London: Embury Press, 2010), pp. 100, 260.

27. Powell, *Ninety Times Guilty*, pp. 79–83.

28. Burton B. Turkus and Sid Feder *Murder Inc.: The Story of the Syndicate* (London: Purnell and Sons, 1952), pp. 73–4.

29. FBI Records: The Vault, *Mafia Monograph* (1958) available at https://vault.fbi.gov/Mafia%20Monograph.

30. President's Commission, *The Challenge of Crime in a Free Society*, pp. 448–9.

31. Cosa Nostra was the preferred FBI terminology, popular writers continued the use the term "Mafia" to describe what they considered to be a united, centralized organization.

32. Alan A. Block, "History and the Study of Organized Crime," *Urban Life*, 6:4, January 1978, p. 457.

33. Peter Maas, *The Valachi Papers* (New York: G.P. Putnams Sons, 1968), p. 111.

34. Block, "History and the Study of Organized Crime," p. 460.
35. United States Congress, Senate, Committee on Governmental Affairs, Permanent Subcommittee on Investigations, *Organized Crime: 25 Years after Valachi: Hearings before the Permanent Subcommittee on Investigations of the Committee on Governmental Affairs*, United States Senate, One Hundredth Congress, second session, April 11, 15, 21, 22, 29, 1988, pp. 300–1.
36. Claire Sterling, *The Mafia* (London: Harper Collins, 1991), p. 63.
37. FBI, "What We Investigate – Organized Crime – History of La Cosa Nostra," at www.fbi.gov/investigate/organized-crime/history-of-la-cosa-nostra.
38. Moore, *The Politics of Crime*, p. 21.
39. The Luciano letter is held in the Thomas E. Dewey papers, Rare Books and Special Collections, University of Rochester Library.
40. Matthew R. Pembleton, "The Voice of the Bureau: How Frederic Sondern and the Bureau of Narcotics Crafted a Drug War and Shaped Popular Understanding of Drug Addiction," *The Journal of American Culture*, 38:2, June 2015, pp. 113–29.
41. Robert Ruark, "Dispelling the Luciano Myth – Did Nothing For Sicily Invasion," *The Decatur Herald* (Decatur, IL), March 1, 1947.
42. *The Bismarck Tribune* (Bismarck), February 28, 1951.
43. *Valley Morning Star* (Harlingen, TX), March 10, 1952.
44. Frank Adams, "He Leads by Stupidity: *The Luciano Story*. By Sid Feder and Joachim Joesten," *Richmond Times Dispatch*, February 12, 1955.
45. Woodiwiss, *Crime, Crusades and Corruption*, p. 110.
46. Ibid, p. 111.
47. Drew Pearson, "Mafia Crime Group Controls Most U.S. Rackets," *Lubbock Evening Journal* (Lubbock, TX) October 10, 1950.
48. Tim Newark, *Lucky Luciano: The Real and Fake Gangster* (New York: St. Martin's Press: 2010), p. 245.
49. Earl Wilson, "Luciano Blames Boyhood for His Predicament," *Washington Post*, August 14, 1951.
50. Jeffrey Scott McIllwain, "Organized Crime: A Social Network Approach," *Crime, Law and Social Change*, 32, 1999, pp. 318–19.

Part III   Covering up Failure: Constructing an Acceptable Response to "Organized Crime"

1. US Congress, Senate Special Committee to Investigate Crime in Interstate Commerce (hereafter called the Kefauver Committee), 82nd Congress, *Third Interim Report*, Washington, DC, 1951, pp. 147–50.
2. Lester Velie, "Rudolph Halley: How He Nailed America's Racketeers" *Colliers Magazine*, May 19, 1951.
3. Kefauver Committee Hearings, *Moretti Testimony*, part 7, pp. 334, 348.

4. Moore, *The Politics of Crime*, p. 113.
5. Estes Kefauver, *Crime in America* (London: Victor Gollancz, 1952), p. 249.
6. "Dope Seller Gets Life in Prison," *Greensboro Record* (Greensboro, NC), May 18, 1957.
7. Rufus King, *The Drug Hang Up: America's Fifty Year Folly* (New York: Norton, 1972).
8. See Michael Woodiwiss, *Organized Crime and American Power: A History* (Toronto: University of Toronto Press, 2001), pp. 227–65.
9. *New York Times*, January 30, 1960. See Lee Bernstein, *The Greatest Menace: Organized Crime in Cold War America* (Boston: University of Massachusetts Press, 2002), p. 5.
10. President's Commission, *The Challenge of Crime in a Free Society*, pp. 448–9.
11. Donald R. Cressey, *Theft of the Nation: The Structure and Operations of Organized Crime in America* (New York: Harper and Row, 1969), pp. 323–4.
12. Woodiwiss, *Crime, Crusades and Corruption*, p. 144.
13. Ed Reid, *The Grim Reapers* (Chicago: Regnery, 1969), p. 1.
14. Ed Reid, *Mafia* (New York: Random House, 1952), p. 41.
15. Murray Kempton, "Crime Does Not Pay," *The New York Review of Books*, September 11, 1969.
16. "The Mafia vs. America," August 22, 1969.
17. See Woodiwiss, *Organized Crime and American Power: A History*, chapter 5.
18. Woodiwiss, *Organized Crime and American Power*, pp. 269–71.
19. All quotes taken from Executive Office of the President, President's Advisory Council on Executive Organization, *Organized Crime Strike Force Report*, Washington, DC, November 19, 1969, folder: Sourcebook, Organized Crime, Egil Krogh Files: Box 50, WHCF (PACEO), Nixon Presidential Materials Staff, National Archives.
20. *Wall Street Journal*, March 16, 1982.
21. Robert Lacey, *Little Man*, p. 301.
22. Joseph Albini, *The American Mafia: Genesis of a Legend* (New York: Appleton-Century-Crofts, 1971), p. 288.
23. Joseph Albini, "Reactions to the Questioning of the Mafia Myth," in Israel. L. Barak-Glantz and C. Ronald Huff (eds.), *The Mad, the Bad, and the Different: Essays in Honor of Simon Dinitz* (Lexington: Lexington Books, 1981), p. 126.
24. Jeffrey Scott McIllwain, "On the History, Theory, and Practice of Organized Crime: The Life and Work of Criminology's Revisionist 'Godfather,' Joseph L. Albini (1930–2013)," *Trends in Organized Crime*, 18:1–2, June 2015, p. 23.
25. Joseph Albini, "Reactions to the Questioning of the Mafia Myth," p. 131.

26. Francis and Elizabeth Ianni, *A Family Business: Kinship and Social Control in Organized Crime* (New York: Russell Sage Foundation, 1972), p. 153.
27. Ibid.
28. Dwight C. Smith, *The Mafia Mystique* (New York: Basic Books, 1975); Dwight C. Smith "Organized Crime and Entrepreneurship," *International Journal of Criminology and Penology*, 6, May 1978, pp. 161–77; Dwight C. Smith "Paragons, Pariahs, and Pirates: A Spectrum-Based Theory of Enterprise," *Crime and Delinquency*, 26:3, July, 1980, pp. 358–86.
29. Smith, "Organized Crime and Entrepreneurship," p. 164.
30. Gay Talese, *Honor Thy Father* (New York: Fawcett Books, 1972), p. xv.
31. Ibid., p. 391.
32. Ibid.
33. Jack Newfield, "The Myth of Godfather Journalism," *The Village Voice*, July 23, 1979.
34. Ovid Demaris, *The Last Mafioso* (London: Corgi, 1981), pp. 452–3.
35. Ibid.
36. Ronald A. Farrell and Carole Case, *The Black Book and the Mob: The Untold Story of the Control of Nevada's Casinos* (Madison: University of Wisconsin Press, 1995), pp. 60–78.
37. Reuter, *Disorganized Crime*, pp. xi–7.
38. For reasons of space the issue of organized crime and the American labor movement is not discussed in this book. David Witwer's *Shadow of the Racketeer* (Urbana-Champaign: University of Illinois Press, 2009) is recommended.
39. James B. Jacobs, Christopher Panarella and Jay Worthington, *Busting the Mob: United States v. Cosa Nostra* (New York: New York University Press, 1994), p. 80.
40. "Mafia Defeat," *Evansville Chronicle and Press*, January 21, 1987.
41. "3 top Mafia bosses get 100 years each," *Springfield Union* (Springfield, MA), January 14, 1987.
42. *New York Daily News*, November 20, 1986.
43. "Eight Convicted as Mob Kingpins," *Springfield Union*, November 20, 1986.
44. Michael White, "Mafia May Have Sanctioned Big Paul's Killing," *The Guardian*, December 19, 1985.
45. Janet Daley, "Predictable Escape from a US Epidemic," *The Independent*, August 29, 1990.
46. Block, *The Business of Crime*, p. 258.
47. James Goode, *Wiretap: Listening in on the American Mafia* (New York: Simon & Schuster, 1988), pp. 64–5.
48. Jocelyn Targett, "Boss of the USA," *The Guardian*, August 10–11, 1991.

49. Mark Tran, "Mafia Families Feel the Heat as the Teflon Don Comes to a Sticky End," *The Guardian*, April 3, 1992, p. 5; Rod Nordland, "Goodbye, Don," *Newsweek*, April 13, 1992, pp. 28–33.
50. *The Gotti Tapes* (London: Arrow, 1992), p. 118.
51. Rod Nordland, "Goodbye, Don," *Newsweek*, April 13, 1992, p. 33.
52. Stephen Fox, *Blood and Power: Organized Crime in Twentieth Century America* (New York: Penguin, 1989), pp. 357–405.
53. Peter Reuter, *The Organization of Illegal Markets* (Washington, DC: National Institute of Justice, 1985).
54. James B. Jacobs, *Gotham Unbound: How New York City was Liberated from the Grip of Organized Crime* (New York: NYU Press, 1999), p. 9.
55. Sidney Raab, "Omerta May Be Dead but the Mafia Isn't," *New York Times*, January 23, 2011.
56. Reagan's speech is printed in full in *Drug Enforcement*, Spring 1983, *New York Times*, October 15, 1982.
57. Kaufman Commission, *Hearing 1, Organized Crime: Federal Law Enforcement Perspective*, November 29, 1983.
58. Kaufman Commission, *Hearing III, Organized Crime of Asian Origin*, 23–25 October 1984, pp. 27–9. Ko-Lin Chin's research contradicts Harmon's assertions. See *The Golden Triangle: Inside Southeast Asia's Drug Trade* (Ithaca, NY: Cornell University Press, 2009).
59. Jane Rosen, "Gangs Set to Usurp Mafia," *The Guardian*, November 31, 1986.
60. *Narcotics Control Digest*, March 19, 1986.
61. Gary W. Potter, *Criminal Organizations: Vice, Racketeering, and Politics in an American City* (Prospect Heights, IL: Waveland Press, 1994), p. 7.
62. Gustavus Myers, *History of the Great American Fortunes* (New York: The Modern Library, 1936).
63. Kaufman Commission, *The Cash Connection: Organized Crime, Financial Institutions and Money Laundering* (Washington, DC: Government Printing Office, 1984), p. 27.
64. Ibid., p. iv.
65. Ibid., p. 62.
66. Ibid., p. x.
67. Ibid, p. 63.
68. Raymond Baker, *Capitalism's Achilles Heel: Dirty Money and How to Renew the Free-Market System* (Hoboken, NJ: John Wiley & Sons, 2007), p. 175.
69. Stephen Platt, *Criminal Capital* (Basingstoke: Palgrave, 2015), p. 22.
70. Jeffrey Robinson, *The Laundrymen: Inside the World's Third Largest Business* (London: Simon & Schuster, 1998), p. 136.
71. Jeffrey Robinson, *The Sink: How Banks, Lawyers and Accountants Finance Terrorism and Crime – and Why Governments Can't Stop Them* (Toronto: McClelland & Stewart, 2003).
72. "The Conglomerate of Crime," *Time*, April 2, 1969.

73. Hank Messick, "Lansky Rules Crime Cartel from Florida," *Miami Herald*, December 12, 1965.

74. Nicholas Gage, *The Mafia is Not an Equal Opportunity Employer* (New York: McGraw-Hill, 1971).

75. Ronald Lacey, *Little Man: Meyer Lansky and the Gangster Life* (London: Arrow, 1992), pp. 284–5.

76. Ibid., pp. 304–5.

77. David May, "Godfather of the Godfathers," *Sunday Times*, January 16, 1983.

78. Ibid., pp. 311–12.

79. Ibid., pp. 436–9.

80. Melanie Nayer, "FBI Documents Acknowledge Barboza's Guilt and Association with Deegan Murder," *New Bedford Standard-Times*, March 2002; Gato quote from Hearings before the Committee on Government Reform, House of Representatives, One Hundred Seventh Congress, First Session, May 3, 2001, Serial No. 107-25, *The FBI's Controversial Handling of Organized Crime Investigations in Boston: The Case of Joseph Salvati* (Washington, DC: US Government Printing Office, 2001), pp. 29–30.

81. Pete Earley and Gerald Shur, *WITSEC: Inside the Federal Witness Protection Program* (New York: Bantam Books, 2002), pp. 153–5.

82. Thomas Powers, "Secrets of September 11," *New York Review of Books*, October 10, 2002, pp. 47–8.

83. Sean Patrick Griffin, *Philadelphia's Black Mafia: A Social and Political History* (Dordrecht: Kluwer, 2003), pp. 103–4.

84. The Associated Press, "Ex-Agents: FBI Enlist Violent Informants," *New York Times*, March 2, 2003.

85. Michael Woodiwiss, "'Britain's FBI' Must Learn Hard Lessons from US Law Enforcement," *The Conversation*, August 19, 2013.

86. Personal communication.

87. Ibid.

88. R.T. Naylor, *The Wages of Crime: Black Markets, Illegal Finance, and the Underworld Economy* (Ithaca, NY: Cornell University Press, 2002), p. 263.

89. Richard Grant, "Drugs in America: Zero Tolerance," *Independent on Sunday*, June 20, 1993, pp. 14–16; Terence G. Reed, "American Forfeiture Law: Property Owners Meet the Prosecutor," *Policy Analysis*, September 29, 1992.

90. Christopher Ingraham, "How the DEA Took a Young Man's Life Savings Without Ever Charging Him With a Crime," *Washington Post*, May 10, 2015.

91. John Yoder and Brad Cates, "Government Self-Interest Corrupted a Crime-Fighting Tool into an Evil" *Washington Post*, September 18, 2014. John Yoder was director of the Justice Department's Asset Forfeiture

Office from 1983 to 1985. Brad Coates was the director of the office from 1985 to 1989.

92. Ibid.

93. "An Asset for your Asset Forfeiture Efforts!" Advert in *National Fraternal Order of Police Journal*, Fall/Winter 1992, p. 47; Robert O'Harrow Jr., "Asset Seizures Fuel Police Spending," *Washington Post*, October 11, 2014.

94. *Pittsburg Press*, August 11, 1991.

95. Ingraham, "How the DEA Took a Young Man's Life Savings."

96. Radley Balko, "Tennessee Asset Forfeiture Bill Seeks to Abolish Abusive Police Practice," *Huffington Post*, March 22, 2013.

97. Sarah Stillman, "Taken: Under Civil Forfeiture, Americans who Haven't Been Charged with Wrongdoing Can Be Stripped of Their Cash, Cars, and Even Homes," *New Yorker*, August 12 and 19, 2013.

98. Ibid.

99. *Pittsburg Press*, August 14, 1991.

100. Office of the Inspector General US Department of Justice, *Audit of the Drug Enforcement Administration's Management and Oversight of its Confidential Source Program*, September 2016 at https://oig.justice.gov/reports/2016/a1633.pdf.

101. Ibid.

102. H.R. Haldeman, *Haldeman Diaries* (New York: G.P. Putnam's Sons, 1994), p. 52.

103. Dan Baum, "Legalize It All – How to Win the War on Drugs," *Harper's*, April 2016.

104. Kenneth B. Nunn, "The Drug War as Race War," *Race, Racism and the Law* at http://racism.org/index.php?option=com_content&view=article&id=820:crime09-1&catid=142&Itemid=155.

105. Daniel Robelo, "Eight Ways Drug War Hurts Latino and Latin American Communities – and What We're Doing About It," *Drug War Alliance*, 9 June 2015.

106. Jonathan Simon, "Governing Through Crime," in Lawrence M. Friedman and George Fisher (eds.), *The Crime Conundrum: Essays on Criminal Justice* (Boulder, CO: Westview Press, 1996), pp. 173–4.

107. Figures reproduced in *Drug War Facts*, http://drugwarfacts.org/cms/node/2365#sthash.algvfI1j.dpbs.

108. Nicole Flatow, "Police Made More Arrests for Drug Violations than Anything Else in 2012," *Think Progress*, September 17, 2013.

109. Steven R. Doninger (ed.), *The Real War on Crime: The Report of the National Criminal Justice Commission* (New York: Harper Perennial, 1996), p. 15.

110. Roy Walmsley, *World Prison Population List*, 9th edition (London: Institute for Criminal Policy Research, 2011) at www.prisonstudies.org/resources/world-prison-population-list-9th-edition.

111. Francis A. J. Ianni, *Black Mafia: Ethnic Succession in Organized Crime* (London: New English Library, 1976), pp. 157–98.

112. Geoffrey Hunt et al., "Changes in Prison Culture: Prison Gangs and the Case of the Pepsi Generation," *Social Problems*, 40:3, August 1993, p. 404.

113. James C. Howell, *The History of Street Gangs in the United States: Their Origins and Transformations* (New York: Lexington Books, 2015), pp. 71–2.

114. Ibid., p. 96.

115. Ibid., pp. 50–2.

116. Ibid., p. 209.

117. Michael E. Miller, "Meth, Torture and the Grip of the Aryan Brotherhood," *Washington Post*, June 10, 2015.

118. Marguerite Cawley, "Mexican Cartel – US Gang Ties Deepening as Criminal Landscape Fragments," *InsightCrime*, April 18, 2014.

119. Seth Ferranti, "Mexican Cartels Tap US Prisons to Expand Operations and Draft New Talent," *The Daily Beast*, September 6, 2013.

120. See note 108.

121. Angela Williams, "Bribery Sentencing Delayed Indefinitely for Ebbs, McCrory," *16 WAPT News*, June 8, 2015; Alan Blinder, "2 Former Mississippi Officials Plead Guilty in a Graft Case Involving Private Prisons," *New York Times*, February 25, 2015.

122. Samuel Walker, *Popular Justice: A History of American Criminal Justice* (Oxford: Oxford University Press, 1980), p. 42.

123. Alan Dawley, *Struggles for Justice: Social Responsibility and the Liberal State* (London: Belknap Press, 1991), p. 348.

124. David Kennedy, *Freedom from Fear: The American People in Depression and War, 1929–45* (Oxford: Oxford University Press, 1999), pp. 366–7.

125. Ronald Edsforth, *The New Deal* (London: John Wiley & Sons, 2000), p. 194; Arthur M. Schlesinger, *Age of Roosevelt: The Coming of the New Deal* (Boston: Houghton Mifflin, 1959), p. 426.

126. See Susan P. Shapiro, *Wayward Capitalists: Targets of the Securities and Exchange Commission* (New Haven: Yale University Press, 1987) for a history of the SEC's enforcement policies.

127. Roosevelt quoted in Joel Bakan, *The Corporation: The Pathological Pursuit of Profit and Power* (London: Constable-Robinson, 2004), p. 86.

128. Edwin H. Sutherland, *White Collar Crime: The Uncut Version* (New Haven: Yale University Press, 1983), pp. 7, 8, 79–152.

129. Joseph A. Page and Mary-Win O'Brien, *Bitter Wages* (New York: Grossman, 1973).

130. Gilbert Geis and Colin Goff, "Introduction" to Sutherland, *White Collar Crime*, p. x.

131. Russell Mokhiber, *Corporate Crime and Violence: Big Business Power and the Abuse of the Public Trust* (San Francisco: Sierra Club Books, 1988), pp. 214–15.

132. Gilbert Geis, "The Heavy Electrical Equipment Antitrust Cases of 1961," in Gilbert Geis, *White-Collar Criminal: The Offender in Business and the Professions* (New York: Atherton Press, 1968), p. 105.

133. Ibid., pp. 107–8.

134. Steven Box, *Power, Crime, and Mystification* (London: Tavistock, 1983), p. 31.

135. Geis, "The Heavy Electrical Equipment Antitrust Cases of 1961," p. 106.

136. James W. Coleman, *The Criminal Elite: The Sociology of White Collar Crime* (New York: St Martin's Press, 1989), p. 39.

137. Donald J. Rebovich, *Dangerous Ground: The World of Hazardous Waste Crime* (New Brunswick: Transaction, 1992), p. xiv–xv.

138. Gary W. Potter and Karen S. Miller, "Thinking about White Collar Crime," in Gary W. Potter, *Controversies in White Collar Crime* (Conklin, NY: Matthew Bender, 2002), pp. 18–20.

139. David Burnham, *Above the Law: Secret Deals, Political Fixes and Other Misadventures in the Department of Justice* (New York: Scribner, 1996), p. 220.

140. Stephen M. Rosoff, Henry N. Pontell and Robert H. Tillman, *Profit Without Honor: White Collar Crime and the Looting of America* (New York: Prentice-Hall, 2003).

141. Tricia Cruciotti and Rick A. Matthews, "The Exxon Valdez Oil Spill," in Raymond J. Michalowski and Ronald C. Kramer (eds.), *State Corporate Crime: Wrongdoing at the Intersection of Business and Government* (New Brunswick: Rutgers University Press, 2006), pp. 157–9; Elizabeth A. Bradshaw, "Deepwater, Deep Ties, Deep Trouble: A State-Corporate Environmental Crime Analysis of the 2010 Gulf of Mexico Oil Spill" (2012), Dissertations, Paper 53, Western Michigan University. Bradshaw's study is indispensible for all students of Deepwater.

142. Bradshaw, "Deepwater, Deep Ties, Deep Trouble," pp. 162–9.

143. Ibid., pp. 218–19.

144. "BP gets record US criminal fine over Deepwater disaster," *BBC News*, November 15, 2012.

145. Jayne O'Donnell, "Wal-Mart Pleads Guilty to Dumping Hazardous Waste," *USA Today*, May 28, 2013.

146. Clinard, *The Criminal Elite*, pp. 14–15.

147. Burnham, *Above the Law*, p. 246.

148. Mokhiber, *Corporate Crime and Violence*, p. 206.

149. Coleman, *The Criminal Elite*, p. 15.

150. Frank Pearce, *Crimes of the Powerful* (London: Pluto Press, 1976), p. 78.

151. M. J. Heale, *Twentieth Century America: Politics and Power in the United States, 1900–2000* (London: Arnold, 2004), p. 292.

152. Quoted in Mary Beth Norton et al., *A People and a Nation: A History of the United States* (Boston: Houghton Mifflin, 1994), p. 1034.

153. Kitty Calavita and Henry Pontell, "'Other People's Money' Revisited: Collective Embezzlement in the Savings and Loan and Insurance Industries," *Social Problems*, 38:1, February 1991, p. 99.

154. Quoted in James Ring Adams, *The Big Fix: Inside the S&L Scandal* (New York: John Wiley, 1990), p. 274.

155. John Hagan, *Who are the Criminals: The Politics of Crime Policy from the Age of Roosevelt to the Age of Reagan* (Princeton: Princeton University Press, 2010), p. 181.

156. Calavita and Pontell, "'Other People's Money' Revisited," p. 94; John Kenneth Galbraith, *The Culture of Contentment* (Harmondsworth: Penguin, 1992), p. 61.

157. Frank Partnoy, *Infectious Greed: How Deceit and Risk Corrupted the Financial Markets* (London: Profile, 2004), p. 143.

158. Ibid., p. 145.

159. PBS Homepage, *Frontline*, "The Long Demise of Glass-Steagall," May 8, 2003 at www.pbs.org/wgbh/pages/frontline/shows/wallstreet/weill/demise.html.

160. Partnoy, *Infectious Greed*, p. 402.

161. Ibid., p. 348.

162. Steven Weiss, "The Fall of a Giant: Enron's Campaign Contributions and Lobbying," *Money in Politics Alert*, November 9, 2001, 6:31.

163. "Tapes: Enron Traders Discussed Manipulation," *USA Today*, June 3, 2004.

164. Lowenstein, *Origins of the Crash*, p. 143.

165. Jeff Madrick, "Enron: Seduction and Betrayal," *The New York Review of Books*, March 14, 2002, p. 21.

166. Partnoy, *Infectious Greed*, pp. 350–1.

167. Robert Bremner, "Towards the Precipice," *London Review of Books*, February 6, 2003, p. 20.

168. Ibid., p. 22.

169. "It's Time to Punish WorldCom/MCI," June 17, 2003, on the US Labor against the War website.

170. Justin O'Brien, "Conflicts of Interest on Wall Street: Corrupted Actors or System?" Paper presented at the XI International Anti-Corruption conference in Seoul, 2003.

171. The Financial Crisis Inquiry Commission, *Final Report of the National Commission on the Causes of the Financial and Economic Crisis in the United States* (2011), at http://fcic-static.law.stanford.edu/cdn_media/fcic-reports/fcic_final_report_full.pdf, pp. 12–13.

172. Ibid., p. 160.

173. Federal Bureau of Investigation, *Financial Crimes Report to the Public 2005*, at www.fbi.gov/stats-services/publications/fcs_report2005.

174. The Financial Crisis Inquiry Commission, *Final Report*, written statement of William K. Black, September 21, 2010.

175. The Financial Crisis Inquiry Commission, *Final Report*, p. xvi.

176. Ibid., p. 354.
177. Ibid., p. 390.
178. Ibid., p. 408.
179. Lynn Parramore, "When Giant Banks Pay Fines, Where Does the Money Go? Does It Stop Crime?" *Alternet*, October 8, 2013.
180. Charles Ferguson in *Inside Job: The Financiers who Pulled Off the Heist of the Century* (Oxford: Oneworld, 2012), p. 202.
181. Laureen Snider, "The Technological Advantages of Stock Market Traders," in Susan Will, Stephen Handelmann and David C. Brotherton (eds.), *How They Got Away With It: White Collar Criminals and the Financial Meltdown* (New York: Columbia University Press, 2013), p. 153.
182. Ibid.
183. A list of GAO reports can be found on the agency's website.
184. Kaufman Commission, *The Impact: Organized Crime Today* (Washington, DC: Government Printing Office), pp. 171–9.
185. Joel Brinkley, "Meese Supports Drug Testing for US Employees," *New York Times*, March 5, 1986.
186. Jules Bonavolonta and Brian Duffy, *The Good Guys: How We Turned the FBI Round and Finally Broke the Mob* (New York: Pocket Books, 1997); Ernest Volkman, *Gangbusters: The Destruction of America's Last Great Mafia Dynasty* (New York: Avon books, 1999); Joe Griffin and Don Denevi, *Mob Nemesis: How the FBI Crippled Organized Crime* (Amherst: Prometheus Books, 2002).
187. Jeffrey Ian Ross, "Grants-R-Us: Inside a Federal Grant-Making Agency," *American Behavioral Scientist*, 10:10, pp. 1704–23. See also Sean Patrick Griffin, *Philadelphia's "Black Mafia"* (Dordrecht: Kluwer, 2003), pp. 173–82 for an informed discussion on the current state of organized crime research.
188. Rensselaer W. Lee III, "Transnational Organized Crime: An Overview," in Tom Farer (ed.), *Transnational Crime in the Americas*, (London: Routledge, 1999), p. 11.
189. www.fbi.gov/investigate/organized-crime.
190. Ibid.
191. Frank Donner, *The Age of Surveillance* (New York: Knopf, 1980), p. 358.
192. US Senate Subcommittee on Terrorism, Narcotics and International Operations of the Committee on Foreign Relations, *Drugs, Law Enforcement and Foreign Policy* (Washington, DC: Government Printing Office, 1989), p. 36.
193. Steven Shapiro, "Nailing Sanctuary Givers," *Los Angeles Daily Journal*, March 12, 1984.
194. Partnership for Civil Justice Fund, "FBI Documents Reveal Secret Nationwide Occupy Monitoring," posted on December 21, 2012 at www.justiceonline.org/fbi_files_ows.

195. Jed S. Rakoff, "Why Innocent People Plead Guilty," *New York Review of Books*, November 20, 2014.

196. Spencer Ackerman, "Homan Square Revealed: How Chicago Police 'Disappeared' 7,000 People," *Guardian*, October 19, 2015.

Part IV Selling Failure: Setting the Global Agenda on Drugs, Organized Crime and Money Laundering

1. Burnham, *Above the Law*, p. 222.

2. Coleman, *The Criminal Elite*, p. 71.

3. "'Make the Economy Scream': Secret Documents Show Nixon, Kissinger Role Backing 1973 Chile Coup," *Democracy Now*, September 10, 2013.

4. Morton Halperin, Jerry Berman, Robert Borosage and Christine Marwick, *The Lawless State: The Crimes of the U.S. Intelligence Agencies* (Harmondsworth: Penguin, 1976), pp. 15–29; Anthony Sampson, *The Sovereign State: The Secret History of ITT* (London: Coronet, 1974), pp. 242–56; Coleman, *The Criminal Elite*, pp. 70–2.

5. Eric Hobsbaum, *Age of Extremes: The Short Twentieth Century, 1914–1991* (London: Abacus, 1995), p. 442.

6. Susan George, "How to Win the War of Ideas: Lessons from the Gramscian Right," *Dissent*, 44:3, Summer 1997.

7. Transfer pricing can be described as "the over-invoicing and under-invoicing of international trade transactions" which creates economic activity that is neither taxed nor recorded in the official statistics. It has now been effectively decriminalized but, as we shall see, remains at the heart of the organized crime problem. On transfer pricing, see Ingo Walter in *Secret Money* (London: Unwin, 1988), p. 16.

8. United Nations, *Fifth United Nations Congress on the Prevention of Crime and the Treatment of Offenders*, report prepared by the Secretariat (Geneva, 1–2 September, 1975), pp. 10–11; Mary Alice Young, "Western Hypocrisy and the Never Changing Face of Financial Secrecy Jurisdictions: Burying the 1975 UN Agenda," *The European Law Review*, January–February 2017, p. 10.

9. Information on UNCTC from Human Rights Sub-Commission 2000, *Relations between the United Nations and Transnational Corporations*, at www.cetim.ch/20000/00FS04W4.htm; Gerald Piel, "Globalopolies," *The Nation*, May 18, 1992; Friends of the Earth – International Forum of Globalization, *Towards a Progressive International Economy: A History of Attempts to Control the Activities of Transnational Corporations: What Lessons Can Be Learned?*, at www.foe.org/progressive-economy/history.html.

10. Egil Krogh, "Meeting on Drugs with Top Administration Officials and Military Chiefs," memo for the president, June 2, 1971; "Summary,

Narcotic Meeting, State Dining Room, 3 June 1971," Egil Krogh Files: Box 4, WHCF, 1971, Nixon Presidential Materials Staff, National Archives.

11. Henry Kissinger, "Study of Means to Stop International Traffic in Heroin," memo for the secretary of state, the attorney general, September 29, 1969, Egil Krogh Files: Box 30, WHCF, Folder: Heroin/Turkey – 1969, Nixon Presidential Materials Staff, National Archives.

12. Quotes from contemporary newspapers and magazines in Lawrence A. Gooberman, *Operation Intercept: The Multiple Consequences of Public Policy* (New York: Pergamon Press, 1974), available on the website of the Schaffer Library of Drug Policy at www.druglibrary.org/schaffer/history/e1960/intercept/chapter1.htm.

13. Albert Goldman, *Grass Roots* (New York: Harper and Row, 1979), p. 100; Richard C. Schroeder, *The Politics of Drugs* (Washington, DC: Congressional Quarterly Inc., 1980), p. 123.

14. The Drug Abuse Council, *The Facts about "Drug Abuse"* (New York: The Free Press, 1980), p. 38; Richard Schroeder, *The Politics of Drugs*, p. 130; David Musto, *The American Disease: Origins of Narcotic Control* (New York: Oxford University Press, 1987), pp. 256–7.

15. John E. Ingersoll, "Delegation Report of the Second Special Session of the U.N. Commission on Narcotic Drugs," Memo to Egil Krogh, November 2, 1970, Egil Krogh Files, Box 31, Folder: International Trafficking – UN Commission, Box 31, WHCF, 1970, Nixon Presidential Materials Staff, National Archives.

16. Commission on Narcotic Drugs, Special Session, Geneva, September 25 to October 3, 1970, *Preliminary US Proposals*, Talking Paper, Egil Krogh Files, Box 31, Folder: International Trafficking – UN Commission, Box 31, WHCF, 1970, Nixon Presidential Materials Staff, National Archives.

17. For an account of the scandal that led to the abolition of the Federal Bureau of Narcotics, see Woodiwiss, *Organized Crime and American Power*, pp. 256–7; see also Douglas Valentine, *The Strength of the Wolf: The Secret History of America's War on Drugs* (London: Verso, 2004).

18. Tartaglino testimony from US Senate hearings before the Permanent Subcommittee on Investigations of the Committee on Government Operations, *Federal Drug Enforcement*, 94th Congress, 1st Session, June 9, 10 and 11, 1975, Part 1, pp. 134–44.

19. David Bewley-Taylor, *The United States and International Drug Control* (London: Pinter, 1999), p. 167.

20. Egil Krogh, "Meeting on Drugs with Top State Department Officials, Top Administration officials, CIA Officials and Ambassadors to South Vietnam, France, Turkey, Thailand and Luxembourg, 14 June 1971," memo for the president, June 11, 1971; "Meeting with Ambassadors and State department Officials on International Narcotics Trafficking, 14 June 1971," memo for the president's file, July 26, 1971, Egil Krogh

Files: Box 4, WHCF, 1971, Nixon Presidential Materials Staff, National Archives.

21. Ethan A. Nadelmann, *Cops Across Borders: The Internationalization of U.S. Criminal Law Enforcement* (University Park: Pennsylvania State University Press, 1993), p. 141.

22. Ibid, p. 14. For DEA staffing and budget figures see the DEA website at www.usdoj.gov/dea/agency/staffing.htm.

23. Information on the Bureau for International and Law Enforcement Affairs taken from the State Department's website at www.state.gov/www/publications/statemag_dec99/bom.htmlt, accessed November 15, 2003.

24. Sherman Hinson, "Bureau of the Month: On the Front Lines: International Narcotics and Law Enforcement Affairs," *State Magazine: Bureau of the Month*, May 1997, at www.state.gov/www/publications/statemag_may/bom.html.

25. Information on the Bureau for International and Law Enforcement Affairs taken from the State Department's website at https://www.state.gov/j/inl/, accessed January 7, 2017.

26. National Commission on Law Observance and Enforcement, *Final Report* (Washington, DC: Government Printing Office, 1931), p. 51.

27. Nadelmann, *Cops Across Borders*, p. 470.

28. Michael Woodiwiss, *Crime, Crusades and Corruption*, p. 216.

29. *U.S. News and World Report*, February 8, 1984.

30. Richard Hartnoll in Coomber, *The Control of Drugs and Drug Users: Reason or Reaction?*, pp. 235–6.

31. Amandine Scherrer, *G8 against Transnational Organized Crime* (Farnham: Ashgate, 2009), p. 19.

32. Ibid., pp. 14–15.

33. UN statistics available from www.undcp.org.

34. State of California, Special Study Commission on Organized Crime, *Third Progress Report*, Sacramento, January 31, 1950, p. 100.

35. Kenneth Allsop, *The Bootleggers* (London: Hutchinson, 1961), p. 355.

36. Christopher Hibbert, *The Roots of Evil: A Social History of Crime and Punishment*. (Harmondsworth: Penguin, 1963), p. 362.

37. "England – The Gambling Paradise," *The Oregonian*, April 9, 1967.

38. Martin Short, *Crime Inc.: The Story of Organized Crime* (London: Thames Methuen, 1984), pp. x, xiii.

39. Hansard, Controlled Drugs (Penalties) Bill, April 19, 1985, Vol. 77 cc 562–82.

40. Woodiwiss, *Crime, Crusades and Corruption*, p. 222.

41. H.B. Spear, *Heroin Addiction Care and Control: The British System, 1916–1984* (London: Drugscope, 2002), pp. 304–5.

42. Neil Wood, *Good Cop, Bad War: My Undercover Life Inside Britain's Biggest Drug Gangs* (London: Ebury Press, 2016), p. 194.

43. Donald Cox, *Mafia Wipeout: How the Feds Put Away an Entire Mob Family* (New York: Shapolsky Publishers, 1989), p. 387.
44. Yves Lavigne, *Good Guy, Bad Guy: Drugs and the Changing Face of Organized Crime* (Toronto: Ballantine Books, 1991), pp. 7, 499.
45. Gerald Posner, *Warlords of Crime – Chinese Secret Societies: The New Mafia* (London: Macdonald, 1988), pp. xiv, 260–1.
46. Fenton Bresler, *The Trail of the Triads* (London: Weidenfeld and Nicolson, 1980) 217–18.
47. James Walsh, "Triads Go Global," *Time*, February 1, 1994.
48. Robinson, *The Laundrymen*, p. 401.
49. "Crime Syndicates Form East-West International Link," *The Washington Times*, November 22, 1993.
50. John Ranelagh, *The Agency*, 697–8.
51. Powell, *Ninety Times Guilty*, p. 80.
52. Linnea P. Raine and Frank J. Cilluffo, *Global Organized Crime: The New Empire of Evil* (Washington, DC: Center for Strategic and International Studies, 1994), p. 106.
53. Ibid., ix.
54. Adam Edwards and Peter Gill (eds.), *Transnational Organised Crime: Perspectives on Global Security* (London: Routledge, 2003), pp. 8–9.
55. United Nations, Background Release, *World Ministerial Conference on Organised Transnational Crime to be Held in Naples, Italy, From 21 to 23 November*, November 17, 1994.
56. United Nations Background Release, *Statement by the Secretary-General on the Occasion of the World Ministerial Conference on Organised Transnational Crime*, Naples, November 21, 1994.
57. Ibid.
58. All quotes taken from United Nations Background Release, *Proposed Formulation of Global Convention Against Organised Crime Discussed at World Ministerial Conference*, November 22, 1994.
59. All quotes taken from United Nations Background Release, *Proposed Formulation of Global Convention Against Organised Crime Discussed at World Ministerial Conference*, November 22, 1994.
60. United Nations Economic and Social Council, *Appropriate Modalities and Guidelines for the Prevention and Control of Organised Transnational Crime at the Regional and International Levels, Background Document*, E/CONF.88/5, September 19, 1994.
61. William J. Clinton, *Public Papers of the Presidents*, volume 1, "Remarks on the 50th Anniversary of the United Nations Charter," in San Francisco, California, June 26, 1995.
62. Jonathan M. Winer, "The U.S. New International Crime Control Strategy," *Trends in Organized Crime*, 4:1, 1998, pp. 63–70.
63. The UN Convention against Transnational Organized Crime (Document A/55/383) is available at www.odccp.org/palermo/the convention.html.

64. United Nations General Assembly, Ad Hoc Committee on the Elaboration of a Convention against Transnational Organized Crime, *Revised Draft United Nations Convention against Transnational Organized Crime*, July 19, 1999.

65. Woodiwiss, *Organized Crime and American Power*, p. 386.

66. Jeffrey Robinson, *The Merger: The Conglomeration of International Crime* (New York: Simon & Schuster, 1999).

67. Ibid., p. 13.

68. "Strategy to Combat Transnational Organized Crime: Definition" available on the National Security Council's website at www.whitehouse. gov/administration/eop/nsc/transnational-crime/definition.

69. United Nations Office of Drugs and Crime, *The Globalization of Crime*, 28.

70. United Nations Office of Drugs and Crime, *2008 World Drug Report*, at www.unodc.org/documents/wdr/WDR_2008/WDR_2008_eng_web. pdf, p. 212.

71. Transform Drug Policy Foundation, *Count the Costs of the War on Drugs* at www.countthecosts.org/sites/default/files/War%20on%20Drugs%20 -%20Count%20othe%20Costs%207%20cost%20summary.pdf.

72. Michael Kenney, "The Architecture of Drug Trafficking: Network Forms of Organization in the Colombian Cocaine Trade," *Global Crime*, August 2007, pp. 233–5.

73. Jeremy Bigwood, "DynCorp in Colombia," *CorpWatch*, May 23, 2001.

74. Ibid.

75. Húbert Ballesteros, "Phoney Charges – A Tool of Repression in Colombia," *Workers World*, September 23, 2015.

76. Ibid.

77. Nick Miroff, "Colombia is Again the World's Top Coca Producer," *Washington Post*, November 10, 2015.

78. Peter Andreas, "When Policies Collide: Market Reform, Market Prohibition, and the Narcotization of the Mexican Economy," in Richard Friman and Peter Andreas (eds.), *The Illicit Global Economy and State Power* (Lanham, MD: Rowman & Littlefield, 1999), pp. 135–6.

79. Peter H. Smith, "Semiorganized International Crime: Drug Trafficking in Mexico," in Tom Farer (ed.), *Transnational Crime in the Americas* (New York: Routledge, 1999), pp. 198–9.

80. Phil Williams, "Illicit Markets, Weak States, and Violence: Iraq and Mexico," *Crime, Law and Social Change*, 52:3, September 2009, p. 329.

81. Lora Lumpe, "The US Arms Both Sides of Mexico's Drug War," *Covert Action Quarterly*, 61, Summer 1997, pp. 39–46.

82. Gideon Burrows, *The No-Nonsense Guide to the Arms Trade* (London: Verso, 2002), p. 72.

83. Ibid., pp. 13–22.

84. R.T. Naylor, "The Rise of the Modern Arms Black Market and the Fall of Supply-Side Control," in Phil Williams and Dimitri Vlasssis

(eds.), *Combatting Transnational Crime* (London: Frank Cass, 2001), pp. 218–21.

85. Manuel Roig-Franzia, "Mexico's Police Chief is Killed in Brazen Attack by Gunmen," *Washington Post*, May 9, 2008.

86. Marc Lacey and Ginger Thompson, "Two Drug Slayings Rock US Consulate," *New York Times*, March 15, 2010.

87. BBC News, "Mexican Mass Grave in Abandoned Mine has 55 Bodies," June 7, 2010.

88. "The Worst Massacres and Mass Graves in Mexico's Drug War," *Global Post*, July 2, 2014.

89. US Department of State, *Merida Initiative*, www.state.gov/j/inl/merida/.

90. Christopher Hobson, "Privatising the War on Drugs," *Third World Quarterly*, 35:8, 2014, p. 1441.

91. US Government, House of Representatives, *Too Big to Jail: Inside the Obama Justice Department's Decision not to Hold Wall Street Accountable*, report prepared by the Republican Staff of the Committee on Financial Services, July 11, 2016, at http://financialservices.house.gov/uploadedfiles/07072016_oi_tbtj_sr.pdf.

92. Kevin Edmonds, "El Chapo's Arrest: Money Laundering and Mexico's Drug War," *Nacla*, April 25, 2014.

93. Ibid.

94. Ibid.

95. Raymond Baker, *Capitalism's Achilles Heel: Dirty Money and How to Renew the Free-Market System* (Hoboken, NJ: John Wiley & Sons, 2007).

96. Ibid., p. 190.

97. Carolyn Nordstrom, *Global Outlaws: Crime, Money, and Power in the Contemporary World* (London: University of California Press, 2007), p. 169.

98. Ibid.

99. Terence C. Halliday, Michael Levi and Peter Reuter, *Global Surveillance of Dirty Money: Assessing Assessments of Regimes to Control Money Laundering and Combat the Financing of Terrorism*, Center on Law and Globalization, January 27, 2014.

100. *United Kingdom Drug Situation: Annual Report to the European Monitoring Centre for Drugs and Drug Addiction (EMCDDA)* (London: Department of Health, 2015), at www.nta.nhs.uk/uploads/2015-focal-point-annual-report.pdf.

101. National Security Strategy and Strategic Defence and Security Review 2015, *A Secure and Prosperous United Kingdom*, at www.gov.uk/government/publications.

102. "Roberto Saviano: London is Heart of Global Financial Corruption," *Guardian*, May 29, 2016.

103. Diane Francis, "All Canadians are Paying the Price for 'Conceal' Estate in Toronto and Vancouver," *Financial Post*, February 26, 2016.

104. Baker, *Capitalism's Achilles Heel*, pp. 24–47.

105. Ibid., pp. 165–209.

106. Ibid., p. 190.

107. "Kleptocracies" can be described as regimes whose principal purpose is to enrich the rulers. For an account of American complicity with state-organized criminals, such as Mohammed Suharto of Indonesia, Ferdinand Marcos of the Philippines, and Mobuto Sese Soko of Zaire, see Michael Woodiwiss, *Gangster Capitalism: The United States and the Global Rise of Organized Crime* (London: Constable & Robinson, 2005), pp. 169–78.

Epilogue

1. See Part III, note 19.

2. Dwight C. Smith, "Wickersham to Sutherland to Katzenbach: Evolving an 'Official' Definition for Organized Crime," *Crime, Law and Social Change*, 16:2, 1991, pp. 135–54.

Index

Potter, Gary, *Criminal Organizations* (1994)
133
Pound, Roscoe 14–15
Powell, Hickman, publicist 65, 76, 85, 103
and 1931 Mafia "purge" 86
and Dixie Davis 77–9
and Luciano 185, 247
Ninety Times Guilty (1939) 75–9, 221
Presser, Nancy 65
prison gangs, rise of 153–9
prison sentences, mandatory minimum (for
drug offenses) 107, 138, 190
prisons and imprisonment 38, 61, 153, 156
and increase in crime 157–9
mass incarceration 152, 153–4, 189–90,
249
private sector in 158
unintended consequences 158–9, 190
Progressive reform (early 20th century)
10–11
Prohibition 15–17, 206
effect on organized crime 207, 212
property, and money laundering 243
Protestant values 13
public opinion 144–5
"purge", 1931 Mafia 73, 86–8
Puzo, Mario, *The Godfather* (1969) 112

racism
and alcohol prohibition 16–17
and crime 3
and drug prohibition 151–2
racketeering 30–1
Racketeering Influenced and Corrupt
Organizations Act (RICO) (1970) 114,
180–1, 224
Raft, George 213
Rakoff, Jed S., on criminal justice system
190
Reagan, Ronald, US President 102, 198
Commission on Organized Crime (1983)
131–3, 136
and deregulation 171–2
and drug war 151–2, 153, 187–8, 209
and revision of view of organized crime
131–4
Rebovich, Donald J. 166
Reconstruction Finance Corporation
(RFC) 28–9
Reed, David, Senator 59
regulation
of business 3–4, 30–1, 160
see also deregulation
Reid, Ed
Mafia (1952) 111
The Grim Reaper (1969) 110–12
Reles, Abe "Kid Twist" 68–9

religious groups, US government
surveillance 188
*Report on the International Opium
Commission* (1910) 17
Reuter, Peter, *Disorganized Crime* (1983)
122–3
Rhinehart-Dennis Construction Company
163
Rivers, Joseph 148
Roaring Twenties (film) 67
Robinson, Edward G. 62, 67
Robinson, Jeffrey 138–9
The Laundrymen (1998) 219
The Merger (2000) 226–7
Rockefeller, John D. 5–6
Rockefeller, Nelson 190
Rogers, William, Secretary of State 201
Roosevelt, Franklin Delano, US President
58, 160
and banking reform 160, 161–2
and Mussolini 44, 59
Roosevelt, Theodore, US President 8, 9
Rosner, David, and Markowitz, Gerald,
Dying for Work (1989) 7
Ross, Edward A. 170, 181
Sin and Society (1907) 7–9
Ross, Jeffrey Ian, NIJ 184
Rothstein, Arnold 33–4, 36–7, 95–6
Runyon, Damon xiv–xv, 75
Russia, post-communist 244
Russians, as Mafiosi 185, 220
Russo, Gus 35
Russo, Louis 88
Ryan, Thomas F. 6

St. Louis, corruption 7
St. Valentine's Day massacre (1929) 33, 37
Salerno, Anthony "Fat Tony" 124, 126–7
Salerno, Sergeant Ralph, New York Police
82–3, 87
Saltis, Joe 74
Salvati, Joseph 142
Saviano, Roberto 243
Savings and Loans (S&L) institutions 172
Savitt, Marc S. 177
Scaduto, Tony, *Luciano* (1975) 84–5
Schakowsky, Janice, Congresswoman 232
Scherrer, Amandine, *G8 against
Transnational Organized Crime* (2009)
210
Second World War 55, 162
"Secret Six" (businessmen) 34–5
Securities Act (1933) 161
Securities and Exchange Act (1934) 31,
161
Securities and Exchange Commission
(SEC) 31, 161, 173
security *see* national security threat